W9-BUZ-476

Taking Charge of Anger

LINCOLN LIBRARY

August 2012   152.4

Taking Charge of Anger

SECOND EDITION

*Six Steps to Asserting Yourself
without Losing Control*

W. Robert Nay, PhD

THE GUILFORD PRESS
New York   London

© 2012 The Guilford Press
A Division of Guilford Publications, Inc.
72 Spring Street, New York, NY 10012
www.guilford.com

All rights reserved

The information in this volume is not intended as a substitute for
consultation with healthcare professionals. Each individual's health
concerns should be evaluated by a qualified professional.

Except as indicated, no part of this book may be reproduced, translated,
stored in a retrieval system, or transmitted, in any form or by any means,
electronic, mechanical, photocopying, microfilming, recording, or
otherwise, without written permission from the publisher.

Printed in the United States of America

This book is printed on acid-free paper.

Last digit is print number: 9 8 7 6 5 4 3 2 1

Library of Congress Cataloging-in-Publication Data

Nay, W. Robert.
  Taking charge of anger : six steps to asserting yourself without losing
control / W. Robert Nay. — 2nd ed.
      p.   cm.
  Includes bibliographical references and index.
  ISBN 978-1-4625-0242-4 (pbk.) — ISBN 978-1-4625-0380-3
(hardcover) 1. Anger.   2. Interpersonal conflict.   3. Self-
control.   I. Title.
    BF575.A5N39 2012
    152.4′7—dc23
                                                    2011042317

To my wife, Joyce

And again, to my parents, Bill and Jane

If you can keep your head when all about you
Are losing theirs and blaming it on you;
If you can trust yourself when all men doubt you,
But make allowance for their doubting too;
If you can wait and not be tired by waiting,
Or, being lied about, don't deal in lies,
Or being hated don't give way to hating,
And yet don't look too good, nor talk too wise . . .
—RUDYARD KIPLING, "If"

Acknowledgments

For the past 20 years I have been working with good and caring people who sometimes do just the opposite of their nature: They let their anger control them, to the detriment of their most important relationships. I wrote two graduate textbooks some years ago, but I knew I wanted to write a book that would appeal to a broad audience who, as fallible humans, sometimes let their anger get the best of them. The question was how. How to make it readable and filled with useful information that might have an impact on the reader's thinking and subsequent approach to anger?

I have many people to thank for this second edition of *Taking Charge of Anger*, the outcome of my yearning to reach the most critical audience for any book: those people who can use the information to immediately begin to transform their lives. First, I would like to thank the many clients who shared their experiences with anger as I tried to steer them on a different life course. I have learned much from their candor and vulnerability in sharing painful information with me. It's not easy to admit that you've acted in socially undesirable ways, that you have an "anger problem." But they were brave enough to come into treatment and get some help. I am grateful to all of them.

I also have learned a lot from my colleagues. I have offered training in anger management to more than 4,000 mental health, substance abuse, and educational professionals internationally. I have been enriched by the clinical thinking and experiences my colleagues have shared with me. I rarely give a seminar where I don't learn something new.

I have appreciated the opportunity to work with clients and to teach medical students and residents at Georgetown Medical School. I also must express appreciation to my graduate students and colleagues at Virginia Commonwealth University and the University of Illinois, who over the years have greatly influenced my thinking about anger and cognitive-behavioral therapy. I particularly want to thank Jim McCullough and Ric Ostrander for being dear friends and colleagues who have influenced my career.

My editors at The Guilford Press have had one goal in mind: of the many books on anger, this will be among the best. Kitty Moore is a truly dedicated and loyal executive editor. She has an unyielding focus on quality and is always able to provide reassurance when she knows I need it. She had the idea for this project, and I will be forever grateful. Christine Benton, my developmental editor, guided me through the revisions that made the first edition successful and has all the great qualities of an editor: high standards, great writing talent, an eye toward the audience for the book at all times, and compassion. If this second edition succeeds, it is in no small measure due to her efforts.

Finally, I wish to thank my family—Don, Greg, Jack, Christopher, Alan, Michael, and Jamea, my mother, Jane, as well as my siblings, Tom, Rich, Pamela, and Alex—who were so supportive and encouraging during the writing process. My wife, Joyce, has been with me across academic and clinical adventures. She has unfailingly supported me in my writing and often added editorial comments to my drafts that I felt were much better than what I wrote. Her guiding presence keeps me on course.

Contents

Taking Charge of Anger

Introduction

Marilyn was clearly angry when she arrived at my office, and she wanted me to know in no uncertain terms that counseling was likely to be a waste of her time. "I can't count on anybody to do what they agree to do," she said about her job. "It's always more on my plate—and now I have to see you, putting me further behind."

I knew Marilyn had been referred to me by her employer because she "needed to get a grip on her temper" with coworkers. What I learned a little later was that this bright, dedicated employee would lose her job if she couldn't learn to manage her anger and intensity. As valuable as she was to her firm, others could not tolerate her blowups and constant expressions of dissatisfaction.

I'm happy to report that Marilyn is still employed today. With a little time and dedicated effort, she has learned to calm herself at the first signs of rising temper and can now defuse troublesome situations before her anger escalates beyond control. Perhaps even more important, she has also learned to identify and alter a lot of unrealistic expectations that, when unmet—as they were bound to be—infuriated her over and over throughout the day.

Austin's fiancée "made" him come to see me. When I clarified that he had made the appointment and had come of his own volition, he allowed that he wanted to save this relationship but questioned his ability to change. "I just can't take any more conflict with Laura. She is constantly trying to discuss her feelings about this and that, and it usually ends in an argument, with me walking out. She says that I'm 'passive-aggressive' and take my anger out on her by refusing to talk and 'for-

1

getting' to do things she asks me to do. Now she won't go through with the wedding until I get help in being direct and honest with my anger. This is how I am. How can she expect me to change my personality?"

Austin felt he was just doing what came naturally in his interactions with Laura. But he too learned a different way to act on his feelings of anger and indignation, and today the couple is married and happily getting to know each other—over paths rocky and smooth.

Marilyn and Austin are clearly two very different people in how they express intense feelings, but they have one thing in common. The ways that they were expressing their anger were impacting others so negatively that both were in danger of losing what they valued most.

They are not alone. You have only to pick up a newspaper or magazine or listen to the news to learn about the many ways that poorly handled anger damages lives—in public settings, at the workplace, in schools and universities, and in our most human relationships. While these big explosions are always in the headlines, there are also many smaller, daily blowups and smolderings that cause less visible damage but greatly affect people's lives. Marilyn and Austin are prime examples. They may never make the six o'clock news, but the quality of their lives and relationships is being eroded by the wear and tear of poorly expressed anger.

Every week in my practice I see good and caring individuals who tell me they "can't" control their anger. While it is hard for them to admit this, perhaps because being angry feels like a flaw or losing control seems "weak," their lives are being affected in significant ways. I often meet men and women like Marilyn and Austin who have acted out their anger in ways that hurt the people they care about the most. Many experience health problems and physical discomfort, and their ability to work effectively is compromised by troubling anger-evoking thoughts and intense feelings that distract and disrupt. Some hold long-term resentments that create rifts in important relationships and find their ability to communicate disrupted by conflict unwittingly created by the ways they express anger.

I could see, early in my career, that helping my clients manage their anger would have a huge impact on their lives and pay extra dividends. Research shows, for example, that children are much less likely to become aggressive when their parents and the other adults around them effectively handle conflict with civility.

On a more personal level, I became interested in studying and treating anger because of my own journey with this powerful emotion.

Early in my marriage I found myself losing my temper to the extent that my wife and I became concerned and she suggested counseling for both of us. At first, I resisted. After all, I was an expert, right? I didn't need help from others, or so I thought. Once I was able to put aside my false pride, we met with a delightful and competent therapist who helped us see the real issues in our relationship and helped me focus on managing my anger. To this day, I am thankful for the lessons learned. I can also appreciate how hard it is for my clients to overcome their own reservations in seeking outside help.

In 2004 the first edition of *Taking Charge of Anger* was published, and I was very pleased with its reception by readers like you and by counselors who recommended it to their clients, as well as how helpful it has seemed to be to my own clients. This six-step program of anger management was developed over the past 25 years based on three resources. First, each separate step of this program has been well researched, or a clear foundation exists in the human learning literature in psychology. Most programs of anger management include one or more of the strategies I will present to you. Second, the sequence of steps, the examples, and the ideas for applying them are my own, based on the hundreds of people who have been willing to work with me to understand and alter their approach to anger in their lives. Since the first edition eight years ago I am even more convinced that anger and sometimes aggression are a part of the lives of all of us. Some of us cope with the stresses of too little time, too many things to do, and the impact of stressors like the economic downturn since 2008 better than others. Sometimes good people say and do "bad" things when their temper gets the best of them, and this book has been written for them. Third, I have trained more than 4,000 mental health, medical, social work, substance abuse, and school counselors from around the country in this program over the past 10 years. The dialogues we've had, the written feedback I've received on the program, and our discussions of real-world problems in implementing anger management have helped me further revise the six-step program you will read about in this book.

So, how did this book come about? First of all, the handouts I was giving therapists who attended my workshops were getting thicker and thicker: a great compendium of ideas from which a practitioner could choose, but a little unwieldy. Second, other therapists and I wished more and more that we had something to pass on to the individuals we were counseling. But nothing in print seemed to reflect the approach

I was taking. Most of the published books and training materials on "anger management" continue to focus on the intense, outward expressions of temper, like arguing, shouting, or physical aggression. Yet I've found that anger is often expressed in other, indirect ways, that it has "faces" that, while less extreme, can be equally problematic. I'm talking about cold anger, refusing to talk or withdrawing from others when angry; passive–aggression, withholding something others want as a way of punishing them; and sarcasm, putting others down with innuendo, hostile joking, and a caustic tone. Many of us express anger in one or more of these ways, and even though it seems less radical and "in your face," it can be just as destructive to lives and relationships. Therefore this book, unlike most others, focuses on the full range of anger expression, each of five "faces" of anger that you will learn to identify in yourself and others and to manage in yourself. In the following chapters, I'm confident that you'll find case stories that you can identify with. Each case I present is a composite of the many different and challenging clients I have worked with, disguised to protect confidentiality.

When I reviewed the books on anger management available to laypeople, I also found that they generally fit into two categories, neither of which was wholly effective in the way that my program seemed to be. Most offering practical help were workbooks, lacking depth and conceptual discussion, while those concentrating on theory gave abstract presentations that were hard to transfer to real life. In this book, therefore, I've attempted to offer an in-depth presentation of anger and its "anatomy" while also giving many step-by-step suggestions for practice and application of anger management skills in the real world. It's difficult to practice a skill without comprehending why it works, and it's impossible to develop a practical skill when all you have are abstract ideas.

The program in this book is based on my conviction that you need to fully understand and address each component part of an anger episode for a truly successful anger management outcome. Giving you techniques without a complete explanation of why and how they address each component of your developing anger is like trying to build a house without plans. You may have the lumber and bricks, but without a set of plans you don't see the big picture of what you're trying to accomplish. Therefore, this book will address each major component of your anger as you learn to:

1. Spot the unrealistic expectations you have for yourself, other people, and things that, when unmet, trigger your anger. You will understand the nature of expectations, how you learned them, and how and why it is so important to examine and alter some of them.

2. Dampen your rising anger before its flame becomes too intense to control. You will learn about the physiology of anger: how your body reacts and how you can learn to read each of these physical changes, early on, so you can exert control before the surge of your anger washes you along with it.

3. Identify how the thoughts that pop into your head once your anger is triggered can direct you toward or away from an unwanted face of anger. Using the ideas and techniques of cognitive-behavioral therapy (CBT), you will gain a conceptual understanding of the kinds of thinking that directly affect anger and how to alter your own unhelpful thinking.

4. Communicate your thoughts and feelings clearly, using a powerful face of anger I call "assertive problem solving." You will learn common pitfalls that disrupt your efforts to be understood by another person, often eliciting anger in response. You'll learn to defuse conflict and to derail others whose anger and tactics may have triggered your own anger in the past.

As you gain an understanding of the anatomy of your own anger, you will learn the most important key to transforming your current approach to anger: *self-awareness*. You'll learn to be fully aware as your anger is triggered, as anger-producing thoughts arise, as your body begins to react emotionally. You'll also see clearly how you express your anger to others. This self-awareness will allow you to replace your old automatic responses at any point in an anger episode: how to dampen physical arousal before it reaches the point of no return, how to catch and challenge automatic thoughts that fuel anger, how to look unflinchingly at how you're really feeling and behaving once you get angry so that you have the option of changing anything that isn't serving you well. You'll also see how entrenched resentments of others, anger that was never resolved and continues to "fester" just beneath the surface of everyday life, can give you a hair-trigger temper and how various elements of your lifestyle can counter your efforts to stay in control, whether it's the amount and quality of sleep you get or how much coffee or alcohol you consume. You will learn how to alter those stressors and to identify and confront your resentments in a new way that may lead to a final resolution of this hidden ire. You will also read about the benefits and issues of deciding to forgive someone who is important to you, but for whom you harbor resentment that does not seem to be lessening with time and may be affecting not only you but other loved ones who bear the brunt of it.

If this all sounds like a lot to learn and a lot to do, rest assured that that's the point of the six steps. I've broken it all down into skills that are eminently manageable for learning but also readily accessible once they're acquired, so you can grab a single simple skill when needed to head off a surge of anger. One of the biggest difficulties with controlling anger, after all, is that it seems to take hold so quickly. You've blown up before you were ever conscious that the fuse had been lit. With a collection of skills that can be put into play at various points in a single incidence of anger, you can halt the juggernaut and react to any stimulus with calm, assertive problem solving.

So even if you're not sure you want to work through this whole program, you might want to read through the book to get a sense of how manageable the six steps can be. And if you're not convinced that your anger is such a big problem in the first place, take an open-minded look at the following list and see if any of these descriptions rings true for you.

> ➤ You always have an indignant "Who, me?" response, but others in your life are starting to complain that your anger is a problem.

> ➤ Your wife (or husband, or children, or partner, or boss …) has told you several times that your blowup was the last straw. You have to do something about "your problem—or else."

> ➤ You've been feeling exhausted and irritable a lot lately and often snap at others, then regret it.

> ➤ When you get angry, you find yourself holding it inside, punishing the object of your anger by not doing what he or she asks or by responding minimally when asked if something is wrong: "No—nothing. I'm fine."

➤ You sometimes minimally respond or avoid speaking entirely with your spouse (or best friend, or colleague at work ...) for days at a time when angry. You kind of enjoy others working hard to find out what's wrong with some version of "Why are you not talking? Is it something I did? Please talk to me."

➤ You can be downright sarcastic when someone irritates you. For example, you tell a personal and embarrassing story on the person or kind of make fun at her expense. When she reacts, you make her feel like she is overreacting: "What do you mean? ... I was just having some fun with you. Why are you so sensitive?" The real issue is you're angry and don't come out and say it.

➤ You have frequent aches and pains (e.g., a throbbing headache or backache) when your work gets too aggravating. You often feel exhausted and out of sorts by the time you get home and sometimes take it out on your family.

➤ You've just "had it" lately and sometimes blow up at anyone who annoys you. You often lose it with "rude" drivers, clerks in stores, and anybody else who fails to meet your high standards for how people should act (e.g., competent, courteous, and mannerly).

➤ If you see yourself in the mirror I just held up, you can change things without making a major sacrifice in altering your personality or disrupting your life. It is not your worth or personality that is the problem. It is what you do when angry that must be changed, and the anger management steps beginning in Chapter 1 will provide you with all you need to get on this new track. Read this book to evaluate further (in Step One) exactly which faces of anger are negatively impacting your life and then read on to do something to change it.

How to Use This Book

I recommend that you read the book from beginning to end without skipping around, because each chapter provides a foundation for the next. Once you've finished, you can go back for a refresher to the chapters that best meet your needs. Be sure to do the "Just for Practice" exercises suggested at the end of certain chapters since they will greatly help you make these new "habits" automatic when you're in the middle of an aggravating situation.

If someone you care about is often involved when your unhelpful faces of anger show up, I suggest that you refer this person to my book *Overcoming Anger in Your Relationship: How to Break the Cycle of Arguments, Put-Downs, and Stony Silences*, also published by The Guilford Press (see Suggested Resources). Also, you might try reading and discussing the chapters of *Taking Charge of Anger* together. For example, couples often attend anger management workshops together so both can learn to identify and alter triggers that might inflame a discussion. The calmer party can also learn how to be most helpful when the other's anger emerges, to avoid inflaming it further and to set the stage for assertive problem solving, the face of anger recommended in this book. It often feels good and motivates the "angrier" partner to know the other is willing to take responsibility for helping in the solution, not just blame and point a finger. Seek the help of a therapist if your anger is getting out of control too often or in ways that are potentially damaging to another person or to a relationship (more on when to get professional help in Chapter 2).

Here is the way the book is organized around the six steps I've been referring to.

> *Is anger a problem for you?* Step One, Chapters 1 and 2, will help you decide whether your expression of anger is a problem. Maybe someone has suggested you need some help with your anger and you're not sure. Guidelines for diagnosing whether you have an anger problem will be followed by a brief questionnaire that helps you decide once and for all if you need to address your anger and which faces of anger are the culprits. You will also learn the components of an anger episode: why certain events trigger your anger, how your anger is escalated by how you think, and ideas for what you can do to resolve problems.

> *What triggers your anger?* Step Two, included in Chapter 3, will help you identify the kinds of situations that trip your anger, called *triggers*. Childhood experiences caused you to expect certain things from yourself, family, friends, and others and to have clear standards for how things should go in the world around you. Your anger is triggered when these expectations are not realized. But sometimes we expect too much or something that is very unlikely to happen. Learning how to

recognize and to alter your unrealistic expectations will be the focus for the remainder of this chapter.

> *How can you manage the intensity of your anger?* Step Three, comprised of Chapters 4 and 5, teaches you to be aware of your anger as it is first developing. At a lower level it is easier to contain and redirect your ire. You will learn to identify the physical changes (e.g., shoulders tight, face hot, breathing shallow) that signal your anger is escalating. Once you learn these anger signals, you will learn to dampen your anger by using one or more relaxation strategies that derail your body's anger response.

> *How can you use your thoughts to get at the root of your anger?* In Chapters 6 and 7, Step Four of anger management, you will learn that your thinking in the form of inner ideas or self-talk and the pictures or images you see on your mind's screen determine how you feel. Hundreds of research studies have attested to the power of your thinking to affect important emotions like depression, anxiety, and anger. You will learn to combat and replace cognitive distortions—self-talk that almost always fuels unhelpful anger—thus curtailing your anger before it can escalate.

> *How can you communicate calmly when conflict arises—staying the course even when provoked?* Step Five, Chapters 8 and 9, helps you identify ways of communicating that inflame conflict and make it difficult to remain calm when a difficult issue arises in your important relationships. Then ideas for communicating effectively will highlight assertive problem solving, the method I recommend for staying calm so you can resolve differences and come up with a mutually agreeable solution. You will then learn to manage difficult people and provocative situations while staying the course, defusing conflict as it arises.

> *How can you make what you've learned automatic?* Finally, in Step Six, you will learn to build up these new anger skills as the habits that guide your everyday behavior quite naturally. How can you change longstanding ways in which you've reacted? In Chapter 10 you will learn to make your new anger skills stick, to have them there when you need them as you let go of your old faces of anger. The new Chapter 11 will help you cope with unresolved resentments of others and to decide when and how to forgive in a way that sets you free of anger that may be affecting your own health and wellness. You've learned how to

express your anger over many years, however, so you just can't expect
to change overnight. In Chapter 12 you will learn the common reasons
for a setback and how to get back on track.

    None of this means, of course, that you will no longer get angry.
Anger is a most human and powerful emotion, imbued with passion
and conviction that can have positive results as well as the negative
ones we've been discussing. Anger can provide the energy for us to
right a wrong, fight a righteous battle, and address important issues in
our most personal relationships. It's what we *do* when angry that determines whether it is a helpful energy source or merely the fuel to create
tension and conflict in our lives. The important question for you is:
What is the role of anger in your life? Is it mostly helpful or more often
than not a hindrance in realizing your hopes and dreams?

    If you answer that your anger is mostly a problem, don't be too
hard on yourself. The vast majority of people who act out anger in
ways that are uncomfortable or even frightening to others are good
and caring individuals who are reading from a lousy script. They've
learned these negative faces of anger by trial and error or through the
actions of powerful models (parents, aggressive peers, even teachers
and coaches), not because they enjoy being mean-spirited, but as a way
they've learned to get their immediate needs met. In my experience,
once they learn that there are calm and effective alternatives like assertive problem solving, change comes quickly. After all, constant anger
and argument, upset and uproar, are not fun and are inherently painful for all parties involved. The six steps of anger management are your
new script, and the chapters ahead will help direct your efforts at playing a new role, one with less wear and tear for all concerned.

    If you still have doubts, the first two chapters will make very clear
just how significantly anger may be impacting the quality of your
life, health, work, and most critical relationships. The material in the
remaining chapters will arm you to approach any annoying or downright angering situation with new confidence that you can stay the
course in controlling your emotions and take leadership in resolving
conflicts.

    Even if you end up concluding that anger is only a minimal prob-
lem for you personally, this book should be of immense value in preparing you to deal with the slings and arrows that others send your
way. We live in what Dr. Deborah Tannen, a communication expert,
calls an "Argument Culture" and must surmount the aggressive words

and actions of others all too often, even if we try to remain civil in our own demeanor. This book will provide you with new tools to quickly assess the angry expressions of others so you can cut off conflict before it takes root and defuse the most threatening situation or know when to make a graceful exit. Thus anyone who lives or works with others who display unhelpful faces of anger can benefit from this book.

The first step, Chapters 1 and 2, should immediately clarify where you stand and what you may need to focus on as you read the remaining chapters. Beginning that first step requires only turning a page or two. Good luck!

Step One

Understanding and Recognizing Anger

CHAPTERS 1 AND 2 WILL HELP YOU UNDERSTAND HOW YOU experience anger and when it becomes a problem. You will be challenged to observe yourself better when confronted with aggravating situations. How will you respond emotionally? What will you do when provoked? You must recognize your anger before you can decide how you wish to react in the future.

1

The Faces of Anger
Whom Do You See in the Mirror?

Marcy is hard to figure. Well liked by friends and colleagues at work and in a long-term relationship with her husband, Frank, Marcy seems to have an evil twin. Things are "right with the world" when her two children get off to school without a fuss, when the traffic is smooth, and when others do what they have agreed, quickly and "competently." The problem is that people often fall short of Marcy's expectations, and she gets "aggravated" and so verbally intense that others often avoid her. Lately, with more responsibilities at work, Marcy's anger is creating problems with the very people who are usually her greatest fans. When confronted by her most recent outbursts, Marcy becomes defensive: "Why can't you realize I'm under a lot of stress lately? Get over it."

Samuel gets angry as often as Marcy but expresses it differently. Rather than becoming intense or loud, he withdraws when angry, often for hours and even days at a time. He is described by a coworker as "passive–aggressive" when he fails to follow company policy he disagrees with, yet denies his omission is intentional. His fiancée knows when Samuel is angry because he goes to bed early, as if punishing her, and vents through sarcastic remarks, protesting "You're too sensitive" when she complains. Samuel's more passive and indirect approach to his anger frustrates others, not because he "loses" his temper. In fact, Samuel denies his anger is a problem. Those who have to interact with him would disagree.

What do Marcy and Samuel have in common? Anger has become a daily visitor in their lives, even if expressed in very different ways, and others are beginning to complain. Yet both would prefer to evade the whole issue. Either it's not a problem or it's someone else's problem.

Why is it so hard for these two bright and otherwise insightful people to see that their anger has become a problem? I guess none of us likes to admit to a loss of control, even if only occasionally. Depending on how we were raised, getting angry might feel like a character flaw. I have found that most of us are uncomfortable admitting we are angry when it starts to create problems.

In actuality, anger is a valuable emotion that tells us we need to address an issue. For some of us, it's heard as a soft tone in the background, signaling that all is not right. Others don't hear this signal that change is needed until it becomes a loud alarm bell. Either way, when recognized and understood, anger can be the first step toward problem resolution, providing us with the energy to right a wrong, stand up for an issue we believe in, or stay the course of managing conflict. Unfortunately, many of us, like Marcy and Samuel, don't use our anger for problem resolution. We simply don't—or won't—see that we're angry or that the way we are expressing this feeling has become a problem in itself.

How can you know when your anger is no longer a valuable prelude to change but is becoming a problem that needs to be addressed in its own right?

How Is Anger a Problem?

Anger becomes a problem when it has certain effects on you and your life. The questions that follow will help you identify the ways in which anger may be a problem for you.

"Does My Anger Negatively Impact Others?"

While Marcy felt her anger was "just occasional, no big problem," this was far from the view of her family and coworkers. Her husband resented having to take over all parental responsibilities in the morning to protect the children from Marcy's frequent outbursts, triggered when her son "dawdled" in getting dressed for school. At work, her secretary asked to be transferred to another position, knowing Marcy was not approachable about her temper and intensity. Similarly, Samuel's withholding of affection and withdrawal into himself was beginning to wear down his fiancée's patience. Increasingly, she was not seeking him out to offer the apology he seemed to demand and they were becoming more distant as they often slept and ate apart.

Neither Marcy nor Samuel saw this problem building, perhaps because they both had found their anger useful in dealing with others in the past. You may have had the same experience. Maybe it worked when you withdrew from the situation to underscore a point. Or perhaps you got in someone's face to make him or her see your position, even if the other person was a little intimidated by you. It worked. Your anger may have made you feel on top of things. You could rely on its energy to push you into asserting your opinions and righting a wrong. But now your anger may be a problem, perhaps because times have changed. Your current supervisor, your present spouse or friends, or the culture of your current job does not seem to react positively to what worked before.

Have you experienced any of these telltale signs that others are having a problem with the way you express anger?

1. Others comment on your reaction to a stressful situation or criticize your behavior. Remember, most people will not readily discuss their feelings about your actions, so when they do it usually means the problem is relatively serious.

2. You feel embarrassed following an anger outburst. Don't ignore your inner feelings that you may have stepped over the line. They may be valid.

3. A relationship you value is strained or lost. Another person may seek you out less or even cut off a friendship or family tie. Have you explored why the relationship is cooling?

If you know or suspect that your anger is a problem for significant others, it's a problem you will eventually have to deal with. To get an idea of how your anger may be affecting a loved one, have this person fill out the Relationship Anger Profile (RAP) in Appendix 5 of this book, score it, and then review the results together. If you and your partner or others you care about agree that your relationship is being compromised, you both will probably want to go on to read my book *Overcoming Anger in Your Relationship* (see Suggested Resources), where the RAP first appeared.

"Is Anger Affecting My Efficiency and Performance?"

Marcy found it hard to concentrate on work when she was irritated, causing her to fall behind. Her team's performance was set back when two key employees decided they could not work with her due to her outbursts. At home, her increasing aggravation with her "poor playing" caused her to give up the tennis lessons that used to be relaxing. Samuel found that his withdrawal from his coworkers made it hard for him to keep up with new developments at work. As others felt distant from him, they were less likely to open up or invite him to be a part of team meetings.

Research shows that when your stress rises beyond a moderate level, performance deteriorates rapidly. Think about times when stress might have negatively affected an exam in college, a presentation at work, or a physical activity like golf or tennis. Unresolved anger is a silent brake on your efforts, taking a toll you may not even be aware of.

"Is My Health or Quality of Life Suffering Because of My Anger?"

As will be illustrated further in Chapter 2, anger is associated with a variety of physical symptoms we experience when under stress. Marcy's daily tension headaches, fueled by tight shoulder and neck muscles, made it hard to concentrate. Ruminating about her aggravating day, she often found it hard to fall asleep, making her even more irritable in the morning. For Samuel, the quality of his life suffered as he held on to his resentments and withdrew from the people who really mattered. Unhappy and disillusioned, he was not sure how to break out of this pattern.

Do you notice any of the following signs that anger may be affecting your health or level of comfort?

1. Your energy level, physical comfort, or sense of satisfaction is not what it used to be.

2. A health problem has been aggravated lately or flares up when you feel particularly "stressed" or irritated.

3. You find it harder to relax, let your hair down, and have fun. Others have commented on your being too serious or preoccupied. Everything seems like a chore.

4. You avoid activities with people, hobbies, or sports because they now seem too much of a hassle or aggravate you.

Before the quality of your life and health deteriorates further, it's time to stand back and examine how anger is robbing you of enjoyment, the rewards of your work.

When Is Anger a Problem?

Each of us has no doubt apologized and been forgiven for an occasional temper outburst or loss of decorum. Our work and play may have suffered, or we may have consumed a few more antacids than usual after a fruitless day at work or an aggravating afternoon of holiday shopping. Such is life.

But when these episodes of anger begin occurring more often and taking up more time, we may not be able to view them as forgivable flukes anymore. Anger as a frequent intruder can be exhausting and may cause you enough discomfort to consider the possibility that you need to make a change. Ask yourself the following questions.

"How Often Do I Experience Anger?"

When Marcy first came to work, her quick wit and clear ability won everyone over. So what if she was intense and occasionally lost her cool? But for some reason, unknown to them and baffling to her husband, Marcy's anger evolved into a daily event to be avoided at all costs. At that point, it was not only less forgivable but also a source of stress for those who caught her wrath. Noticing more of these outbursts, her husband tried to talk with Marcy, but she deflected all discussion with the vague "I'm just stressed out lately."

Any behavior that serves a normal function in life, including anger, is likely to have a negative impact on you and others when its frequency becomes too high or too low. Whether it's eating, sleeping, working, or playing, too much or too little threatens your physical, emotional, and mental balance. Anger is no exception. Imagine your concern if a friend couldn't get angry, even when directly provoked or abused. In contrast, there is someone like Marcy, who was angry so often that others could no longer tolerate it, even though they liked her and wished things could be different.

"How Intense Is My Anger and How Long Does It Last?"

Marcy's upset at her son's slow progress in the morning did not blow away easily. She often left the house so irritated that her drive to work was an ordeal of cursing and gesticulating at "hopelessly slow and out-to-lunch" drivers, which set the stage for her first encounter at the office. Her secretary dreaded the forceful barrage of questions and obvious frustration that pervaded Marcy's mood. Once triggered, her anger was very intense, long-lasting, and difficult to quell.

Similarly, Samuel's withdrawal from his fiancée was hard to turn off. He would avoid speaking to her for long periods and seemed unable to move quickly beyond whatever had angered him in the first place. In evaluating your own anger, consider how intense it becomes and how long it lasts. Others likely will be noticing.

Is Anger a Problem for You?

Keeping in mind what you have just learned about anger, do you think you have a problem with your own anger expression? I have developed a brief assessment that should help you decide and also reveal how you tend to express your anger. For example, when you think of "anger," do you associate it with loud, intense talk or some outward act of aggression? Many people do. Maybe that's why we're so uncomfortable admitting to it. In fact, anger is expressed in a variety of ways we will call "faces of anger" that include not only these intense and highly visible actions but also more passive and indirect behaviors. Recall how Samuel expressed his anger by withholding what others wanted or by using a sarcastic tone of voice, actions that can create problems to the same degree as their more intense cousins. By better understanding your mode of anger expression, you can answer the questions about how anger is affecting your life with more precision.

I encourage you to take a few minutes to complete the following questionnaire, which will help you assess your own anger.

What Does Your Anger Look Like?
Self-Assessment of Anger Questionnaire (SAQ)

First, check the box in front of any of the following descriptions that apply to you.

HOW BIG A PART DOES ANGER PLAY IN YOUR LIFE?

Reflect on the past six months: what you recall about your own experiences and what others have said to you about your anger. Add up the scores of the items you checked off.

❑ You handled an aggravating situation poorly. (score 1)

❑ You feel/felt embarrassed or guilty about the way you handled your anger. (score 2)

❑ Another person has told you that your way of expressing anger was a problem. (score 2)

❑ An important relationship at home, at work, or among friends or family has been strained by your expression of anger. (score 3)

❑ Someone you care about has urged you to get help for managing your anger. (score 3)

❑ You have gotten into serious trouble because of the way you expressed your anger. Examples might include a reprimand at work, a legal problem or arrest for "road rage" or assault, being hurt or hurting another, a separation or divorce. (score 4)

Scoring. Add up your scores. If you scored *3 or more*, you likely have a problem with anger that should be addressed. A score of *6 or more* indicates you may have a serious problem with the way you express your anger. Don't put this book down. *If you checked off the last item, you should consider seeking the help of a mental health professional who specializes in treating anger issues.*

HOW DO YOU EXPRESS YOUR ANGER?

Next, consider the following 10 challenging situations. As you read each of them, think how you might react if this or a similar situation occurred in your own life now or in the recent past (within the last 30 days). Because you may express your anger in various ways, perhaps depending on how you felt at a given time, be sure to circle as many of the possible reactions as apply to you for each item. For each situation described, circle one or more of the reactions you could see yourself having to this or a similar situation. If none of the specific descriptions applies, circle "Other."

1. Your partner does something you've repeatedly said you dislike. Your reactions might include:

   ➤ Withdrawing from your partner, just wanting to be alone and not to discuss it. [C]
   ➤ Thinking of something to say that will make your partner squirm or feel uncomfortable. [B]
   ➤ Acting very forceful in getting your point across. It's important that your partner hear how upset you are whether he/she wants to hear it or not. [E]
   ➤ Feeling very intense and irritable, which could lead you to do things like talk louder, slam a door, or drive faster. [D]
   ➤ Thinking to yourself, "Just wait until he/she wants something from me." [A]
   ➤ Other. It's unlikely I would react in any of these ways.

2. On your way to work in the morning with some friends, another driver suddenly pulls in front of you, forcing you to slam on your brakes. The reactions you might have include:

   ➤ Feeling so intense and angry it's hard to shake it off as you begin your day at work. [D]
   ➤ Trying to pull next to the other driver to tell him/her off or make a rude gesture. [E]
   ➤ Trying to pull ahead of the other driver, then slowing down, holding him/her up as a payback. [A]
   ➤ Trying to think of put-downs or cutting remarks that describe his/her lousy driving skills. [B]
   ➤ Getting so upset you stop talking with others in the car with you, holding in your anger. [C]
   ➤ Other. It's unlikely I would react in any of these ways.

3. A close friend keeps you waiting at a restaurant for 30 minutes. When he/she arrives unapologetic, acting as if nothing happened, your reactions might include:

   ➤ Immediately accusing him/her of acting inconsiderately, raising your voice to let him/her know just how irritated you are with this rude behavior. [E]
   ➤ Feeling so upset that you eat fast, get impatient with the waiter, and in general feel tense and grumpy during the entire meal. Hard to shake it off. [D]
   ➤ Minimally responding to his/her comments. Making him/her do most of the talking because you just can't act like everything is fine—it isn't. [A]
   ➤ Telling the other person you cannot remain any longer and leave him/her sitting there. Now maybe the other person will realize just how rude he/she was. [C]
   ➤ Making a biting remark like "I'm really glad you value our friendship so much that it's at the top of your priorities." [B]
   ➤ Other. It's unlikely I would react in any of these ways.

4. You are waiting in a long line in a convenience store. The checkout clerk is "gabbing" with a coworker and not paying attention to her job. Your reactions might include:

   ➤ Muttering under your breath and to other customers something like "This person is clearly incompetent" and/or "The store should never have hired him/her." [D]
   ➤ Getting so upset you end up leaving your items in the store and walking out and/or deciding never to do business there again. [C]
   ➤ When you finally get to the counter, acting like you are praising the clerk with a remark like "Keep up the good work. You have a real future here." [B]
   ➤ Deciding to tell the clerk just how angry you are and how incompetent and inconsiderate the store is for hiring him/her with a remark like "If you can't do this job properly, you should care enough about the customers to quit." [E]
   ➤ Slowly placing your items on the counter with the computer

codes turned away so the clerk has to work harder to scan them. [A]

> Other. It's unlikely I would react in any of these ways.

5. You are furious with your spouse/partner for making plans for you both to go out with friends without asking you. As he/she is telling a story to these friends at the restaurant, you might react by:

> Walking away on some pretext (e.g., going to the rest room) as soon as he/she begins telling the story. You are not going to sit there and be an audience. [C]

> Making a wry remark to your friends that kind of puts down his/her story with humor, like "What an interesting story. Are you plumbing the depths of *Reader's Digest* again, dear?" [B]

> Avoiding eye contact with your spouse/partner, not reacting in any way to his/her story and quickly changing the topic. [A]

> Putting down what he/she says by forcefully questioning his/her facts or criticizing. You are angry and he/she needs to know it. [E]

> Feeling impatient for him/her to finish the story. After a brief time, interrupting him/her to ask someone else a question. [D]

> Other. It's unlikely I would react in any of these ways.

6. You feel hurt and angry because your partner seems to be neglecting you/is not affectionate enough and won't talk about it. You might react by:

> Deciding that the next time he/she wants something from you, "Forget it." You will show him/her how it feels. [A]

> Giving the other a dose of his/her own medicine by withdrawing from conversation and going to bed early. [C]

> Making a remark with an edge, like "It's really great that you're so loving—I can always count on you to be there for me." [B]

> Letting your anger out by forcefully telling the other that he/she is cold and acting like a [fill in an uncomplimentary name]. You are not standing for this. [E]

> Feeling so upset and tense about his/her letting you down you find yourself irritated with others (e.g., your children, a friend, your fellow drivers). [D]

> Other. It's unlikely I would react in any of these ways.

7. You have just been told that your supervisor is giving another employee a perk or position you think you should have been given and never even discussed it with you. Ways you might handle this include:

   ➤ Going to your supervisor and letting him/her have it. You are not going to take this unfair mistreatment, and he/she is going to know it. [E]

   ➤ Running thoughts through your mind about just quitting and getting out of there. If they don't appreciate you, why stick around? [C]

   ➤ Deciding you will be too busy to help your supervisor out by staying late or taking on additional work. [A]

   ➤ The next time you see your supervisor, making a remark like "I really appreciate the fair way you treat your employees. It's great working for you." [B]

   ➤ Noticing more muscle tension and inner tightness and more impatience with others and things (e.g., slow elevators, busy signals). [D]

   ➤ Other. It's unlikely I would react in any of these ways.

8. You are ready to leave for an important occasion, and your partner is already 20 minutes late after you have specifically told him/her how important this is to you. Your reactions might include:

   ➤ Finding yourself increasingly tense, pacing and/or muttering under your breath, "I can't believe how long this is taking." It is hard to relax and accept this lateness. [D]

   ➤ When he/she is finally ready to leave, telling him/her off by saying something like "I can't believe anyone could be so rude [or hopeless or just plain irresponsible]." [E]

   ➤ Making a remark like "I can see you really listened to my feelings about getting there on time. You are a wizard of efficiency and organization." [B]

   ➤ Not speaking as you usher him/her to the car. You avoid him/her for a long time. [C]

   ➤ Even though the other did something special or well, refusing to compliment him/her for the rest of the day. Why should you? [A]

   ➤ Other. It's unlikely I would react in any of these ways.

9. After putting in a lot of effort on a community project, the committee chairperson acknowledges everyone else but you at an awards banquet. You feel angry at the slight, and your reactions might include:

 ➤ Refusing to speak or responding minimally to the chairperson later in the evening when he/she tries to talk with you. [C]
 ➤ When the chairperson acknowledges the omission, not acknowledging his/her statement and changing the topic. You will not let him/her off the hook that easily. [A]
 ➤ Finding yourself telling an embarrassing story about the chairperson to other committee members and kind of enjoying seeing his/her discomfort when others laugh. [B]
 ➤ Telling him/her off for being so inconsiderate of your feelings and noticing that he/she is kind of intimidated by your intense voice. This feels good given what he/she put you through. [E]
 ➤ Being so upset that on your way home you find yourself driving faster and being more likely to yell at other drivers' behavior. Feeling tense and noticing that you are easily irritated for the rest of the evening. [D]
 ➤ Other. It's unlikely I would react in any of these ways.

10. Your neighbor fails to return something he/she borrowed from you even though you've mentioned it numerous times. You see this neighbor using your item in the yard and might handle your irritation by:

 ➤ Ignoring the person when he/she tries to start up a friendly conversation. How can you talk to so inconsiderate a person? [C]
 ➤ Deciding to park your minivan in front of the neighbor's house when you know it infuriates him/her. [A]
 ➤ Telling your neighbor you really appreciate living next door to someone who is so considerate. [B]
 ➤ Deciding to do yard work later and going inside because just looking at your neighbor causes you stress. You find it difficult to "let go" of your tension quickly. [D]
 ➤ Forcefully demanding your item back, telling him/her to forget borrowing in the future and to stay away from you. Why be around someone with no morals? [E]
 ➤ Other. It's unlikely I would react in any of these ways.

SCORING THE SAQ

How you express your anger is indicated by your score on each of five scales. As will be illustrated in more detail in Chapter 2, each scale represents a mode of expression, a "face" of anger that is unhelpful and likely to lead to further problems for you or others who interact with you.

To obtain your scores, add up how many A, B, C, D, and E items you circled. Now fill in your totals on the corresponding scales below.

SCALE A: PASSIVE–AGGRESSION _____. You tend to withhold from others when you are angry by failing to do what they want, being late, or otherwise holding back. You minimize or deny that you are angry when others express frustration or question your actions.

SCALE B: SARCASM _____. You use sarcasm, biting wit, or "humorous" put-downs as a way of expressing your anger indirectly. Your facial expression/tone of voice may convey disgust or criticism, which you deny. When others find your comments or actions hurtful or complain, you may accuse them of being too sensitive or minimize their feedback.

SCALE C: COLD ANGER _____. When angry you refuse to talk things out and may withdraw from others, with minimal or no contact for hours or days at a time. You may secretly enjoy punishing others by making them work hard to get you to respond but would not admit it.

SCALE D: HOSTILITY _____. You handle stress poorly, often feeling very intense and acting it out with a loud, forceful voice and disgust and disapproval when others or situations do not meet your expectations. You may sigh, roll your eyes, and in general make nasty comments that others often find stressful and intrusive. You hate to wait and suffer "fools" poorly.

SCALE E: AGGRESSION _____. You act in a manner that may intimidate or harm another person, either emotionally or physically, whether you intend to or not. Yelling, name calling, and put-downs may threaten or intimidate your spouse, friend, or coworker. While not directly assessed by the SAQ, physical aggression includes physically blocking, holding, pushing, hitting, or restraining another person without express permission to touch. This face of anger is the most serious and often requires professional help, especially when levels of verbal and/or physical abuse are harming others.

Did you score highest on one particular scale? This mode of anger expression should be a focus for your efforts at making changes as you apply what you learn about anger management in the chapters ahead. Are you surprised at scoring highest on this scale?

Did you score on multiple scales? If so, you need to reflect on the "mix" of behaviors you reveal to others and decide which to target for change first as you set priorities.

How does someone who knows you well see your anger? If you're reading this book because someone else has said you need help, but you don't see that reflected in your scores on the questionnaire, get another opinion. In addition to the person who urged you to do something about your anger, give the SAQ to another person who is significant in your life and knows you well— spouse, partner, close friend, or colleague (or give it to two or three to get a broad representation of how people see you)—and ask him or her to fill out the questionnaire too. A copy of the SAQ suitable for reproducing is included in Appendix 1. If several others agree with you, the problem may lie with the perceptions of the person who said you need help. But if not, take a close look at what your friends or relatives have said about you. Not only might they give you a different view of how big a role anger plays in your life, but they may also help you see ways that you express your anger that you're not wholly conscious of but that you need to address. In addition, consider having your partner fill out the Relationship Anger Profile in Appendix 5 for insights into how he or she reacts to you anger episodes.

"Where Do I Stand in My Relationship with Anger?"

So, what do you think? After reviewing the SAQ and thinking about how anger has impacted your life, what have you concluded about your relationship with anger?

> Can you identify with one or more of the dysfunctional faces of anger? Which one(s)?

> How is your anger expression affecting others who are important to you, even if you are okay with it?

> Is it affecting your enjoyment or performance at work, at home, or at play?

> Is your health, sense of wellness, or the quality of your life suffering as a result of your anger?

> How often do you get angry in the ways you've identified through the questionnaire?

> How intense is your anger, and how long does it last?

Still have doubts that your anger is a problem for you? You're not alone. Anger by nature usually comes with a sense of righteousness; we're angry because we've been wronged, and expressing that anger is a vehicle for getting the wrong righted. What would we do without it?

I'm not suggesting that you do without it. But if, like many of the people I have worked with over the years, you have opened this book at the urging of someone who cares about you, you're apparently willing to entertain the possibility that anger is standing in your way. So, rather than answering the question "Is anger a problem for me?" with a strict yes or no, think of the possible answers as ranging from "not at all" to "yes, definitely." If you are somewhere in between, this book can help you improve the quality of your life and relationships.

Charting a New Course

My job is not to eliminate anger from your emotional repertoire but to guide you on a journey that will change your relationship with anger. If

I am successful, your anger will retain its role as a valuable signal that you need to change something and provide you with the energy to stay the course. Your anger will be expressed in a way that does not make problems worse but leads to calm resolution. Your relationships as well as your ability to get things done and to feel more in control of your life will be enhanced.

Afraid you can't change entrenched habits? Ask yourself this: Are you the same person you were even 10 years ago? Some of us are moving from the self-focused behaviors of early adulthood to the committed "settling" into a marriage or a first significant relationship. Others are having children and learning how to be parents, while still others are transitioning from the world of work to retirement. It doesn't matter what age you are or what your background is. You have faced choices throughout your life, and you have made changes. The critical issue is your personal motivation to change.

If you decide to read on, the next chapter will help you recognize your anger, what triggers it, sustains it, and directs how you express it to others. Once you are able to understand and recognize the "anatomy" of your anger, later chapters will help you direct your anger in ways that better meet your needs.

2

Behind the Mask
Understanding Anger and Its Expression

Lately Jonathan has noticed tightness in his shoulders and neck and now feels another headache coming on. Reaching for the Tylenol, he shakes his head over the amount of stress his sales management job is causing. His secretary informs him that one of his best accounts has been calling for the last two days. "Can't you see I'm completely swamped?" he yells. "Tell them I'll call when I have time. That's it. There's nothing I can do about it right now. Can't you see that?"

Feeling angry and guilty at the same time, Jonathan sits staring at the pile of work and unanswered pink telephone slips on his desk. Unsure whether he wants to cry, shove everything off his desk, or just walk out of the building, he wonders why he took it out on his secretary, who has been so loyal to him. Jonathan's life seems overwhelming and out of his control.

When he arrives home, his wife, Sean, immediately senses his mood when Jonathan yells at her to keep their two preschool sons quiet so he can "unwind" in peace. Sean appreciates his stress at work but can't help being irritated that he loses his temper so often at home. Uncomfortable confronting him, she finds herself withdrawing more each day.

Jonathan didn't plan to get angry at home any more than he had planned to get angry at work. Now he feels guilty again, this time for having "lost it" with Sean. In fact, however, anger often occurs when we least expect it and for reasons that sometimes seem unpredictable.

Among the many hundreds of people who have shared their anger experience with me, I often hear statements like these:

> "I just found myself completely enraged and saying things to my boss I now wish I could take back."

> "Suddenly I just see red and seem to go from 0 to 60! Why is it that I can control my anger sometimes and then, pow, I just go off for a trivial thing? I don't get it."

> "It's kind of confusing, because I'm generally a fair person. But when angry I just want to punish him by withholding anything he really wants."

The fact that we don't know where it comes from leads many of us to simply give up on any possibility of controlling our anger. How can we stop such a powerful force when it comes out of the blue, without any warning? The truth is, we do get warnings. It's just that we're not attuned to them, so we miss our chance to halt the juggernaut, and our anger rolls right over everything and everyone in its path.

Fortunately, it doesn't have to be that way. If we knew what the juggernaut was made of, we could disable it before it could do any damage. In this chapter we'll take anger apart, examining its components so that we can see how it builds and where opportunities lie for heading it off the course that is not, as it turns out, inexorable after all. No matter how it's expressed or what the circumstances are, anger is always composed of the following five parts (triggers, thoughts, feelings, actions, and outcomes), which we saw in Jonathan's experience.

Triggers

Why do we get angry? You could probably write a long list of anger triggers, and you may already have read explanations of many common ones in other books. Losing your patience, such as when you're standing in a long line that seems to be going nowhere, often leads to anger. So does feeling as if your opinion or other contribution isn't acknowledged or appreciated. Injustice takes many different forms. Unfortunately, it takes so many forms that any list of anger triggers has to be endless. What triggers each person's anger is unique, based on what his or her childhood and life experiences taught that person to expect—from *him- or herself*, from *other people*, and even about *how the world should work.* When these expectations are not met, anger is often the result.

Jonathan expected his day to run smoothly. When clients and peers did not immediately return his calls, he became furious. When a FedEx package did not arrive on time, he found himself yelling at his secretary rather than politely asking her to look into it. Also, he rarely got done what he set out to accomplish because the standards he set for himself were so high. Then he had to stay at work late, which only exhausted him. Jonathan was raised by parents who held everyone to high standards and who often expressed disapproval when Jonathan failed to perform at the top of his class or team at school. Their motto was "No excuses—just do it."

If you got to know Jonathan, his standards might seem unusually high and rigid; you would never expect that kind of performance from others. Your own uniquely learned set of expectations for yourself or others about issues like table manners, courtesy on the road, or how others should respond to an invitation may be different from Jonathan's, because your childhood taught you different beliefs about what to expect. So, what triggers your anger may be very different from what triggers your spouse, best friend, or coworker.

Chapter 3 will help you explore and revise your anger triggers as you review which of your deeply ingrained expectations are realistic and attainable and which are unrealistic and should be discarded or modified.

Thoughts

While Jonathan's unrealistic expectations triggered his anger, his ongoing thinking or "self-talk" sustained his reaction and directed how he ended up responding. Consider these thoughts that ran through his mind in his first hour at the office, setting the stage for the remainder of his day:

"Today is going to be a real zoo. I'll never get all this done." (He immediately felt hopeless and exhausted, flopping down in his chair with a feeling of irritation and resignation.)

"Why can't people be considerate enough to answer their e-mails right away? This is inexcusable." (His immediate anger at others who had not answered their e-mails "quickly enough" fueled his first headache of the day.)

"If I don't do it myself, it just won't get done properly." (Feeling angry and overburdened, he criticized his secretary, which he later felt guilty about.)

It's easy to see that the mail on his desk, phone calls to return, and his secretary's statements did not automatically "cause" Jonathan's reaction. These events have no power to create any emotion. It was how Jonathan *thought* about these things that fueled his ire. Along similar lines, your own self-talk at this very moment (e.g., "This really makes sense," "This is really boring," or "I feel exhausted right now") will determine how you feel (enthusiastic, bored, sleepy) as you read on.

It follows that to change your angry response to a trigger you must change the way you think about it. You can't expect a different emotion with the same self-talk. If Jonathan wants to feel more calm and in control, he will have to keep two things in mind:

> Psychologists have found that certain kinds of negative thinking called "cognitive distortions" (e.g., "magnifying" a problem beyond the facts, "mind reading" others' thoughts and feelings without evidence) greatly contribute to anger problems as well as to depression and anxiety disorders. Treatment directed at learning to combat this thinking, called cognitive-behavioral therapy (CBT), has been found very effective in managing emotions while problem-solving a solution to life's challenges.

1. Anger-arousing self-talk becomes less available when it is challenged or just not practiced any longer.

2. Calm thinking is learned and becomes strengthened through repeated practice.

Chapter 6 will help you recognize cognitive distortions and other unhelpful thoughts that may be contributing to your anger. Chapter 7 offers ideas for challenging this anger-arousing thinking while learning new ways of viewing situations that triggered your anger in the past.

Feelings

When important needs like feeling safe and secure as being well as affirmed and accepted by others are threatened, your body immediately readies itself in a primitive, physical way called the "fight-or-flight response," the physiological component of anger, fear, and other intense emotions. The fight-or-flight response is an invaluable survival mechanism. The trouble is, though, that it kicks in whenever we *perceive* a threat. Self-talk that magnifies an upsetting situation will elicit this emotional response regardless of the reality of the situation. Jonathan's thoughts immediately created shoulder and neck tension that led to a pounding headache by the middle of his stressful day. Physical symptoms and even more serious health problems are an outcome of chronic and unresolved anger. "The Physiology of Anger Arousal" (in the box on pages 36–37) shows how your body is likely to react as you are becoming angry.

As you look over the box, think about how *you* physically react when angry. "Anger scaling" will be presented in Chapter 4 to guide you in recognizing the early signs of your anger so you can manage it before it builds to unmanageable proportions. Then Chapter 5 will offer powerful strategies to immediately dampen the fires of your angry reaction so that calm thinking can direct you to resolve the challenge you face.

Actions: Anger Expression

While some believe that they "just lose control" as anger is aroused, a major theme of this book is that you have choices in the way you react. Sadly, these choices often include one or more of the dysfunctional "faces" of anger described by the self-assessment questionnaire in Chapter 1. Before considering a more effective alternative, it's helpful to be able to recognize each of these unfortunate expressions of anger. The sidebar "Faces of Anger" (page 38) describes characteristics you can look for in yourself or another person.

Passive–Aggression

Being passive and aggressive sounds like a contradiction in terms—that is, until you experience someone who seems to do just the opposite of what you would like and then denies any negative motivation.

The Physiology of Anger Arousal:
Signs and Symptoms to Look for in Yourself

Heart and blood pressure	Heart rate and blood pressure increase to supply more oxygen to the brain and muscles. Pounding pulse may be observed in temples, wrists, throat, and chest. Most people cannot detect blood pressure changes, so a blood pressure cuff is necessary.
Respiration	Breathing rate will increase to get more blood to the brain and muscles. Look for shallow breathing, chest heaviness, breath holding, suffocated feeling, restricted/tight throat.
Gastro-intestinal (GI) responses	Stomach and GI system are emptying of blood as digestion slows or halts to free up blood for the brain and muscles. Look for stomach upset, queasiness, acid reflux, sometimes nausea and even vomiting, changes in bowel and urination frequency, including diarrhea and irritable bowel syndrome.
Musculo-skeletal responses	All of your muscles begin to tighten, poised to help you "fight" or "flee" from the situation. Notice particularly your shoulders, neck, forehead, jaw, and also tension in your arms and legs. As arousal continues, muscle soreness or pain may result. Poor posture or improper body mechanics (e.g., sitting in a chair with inadequate back support) contribute to muscle tension and discomfort.
Vascular changes/skin temperature	Blood vessels in the face, hands, and elsewhere constrict or dilate to control blood flow. Look for the face to feel flushed, warm, or hot (described by others as "red") and the hands to feel hot with anger, cold with fear. Many notice a general flushing, like heat rising in the chest and throat up to the face.

Senses more acute	Vision, hearing, smell, and touch all are more sensitive and magnified. Sounds, like someone's voice, seem louder. Pupils dilate to permit better night vision, which may change focus in daytime. Movements toward you or someone touching you may seem more threatening.
Blood chemistry changes	Adrenaline and cortisol are among the chemicals released into your blood to trigger the "fight-or-flight" response. Red blood cells become more "sticky" to increase your ability to clot in case you are injured. More fats and sugars are released by your liver into your blood.

Jonathan could be difficult to live with at times. Sean often expressed her own anger at his behavior indirectly, by doing things she knew would aggravate him. Going out with a friend so Jonathan had to feed the children and get them ready for bed or taking her time getting ready when Jonathan was downstairs fuming were among the ways she passively expressed her irritation. Sometimes, when he tried to hold her at night, she would turn away from him yet deny she was upset.

Passive-aggression is perhaps the most difficult face of anger to deal with because the other person withholds or obstructs what you want but denies anger. How can you resolve a problem the other won't admit exists?

Sarcasm

When angry, Jonathan often made cutting remarks to Sean. For example, when eating with friends, Sean enthusiastically described her new position at her company. Jonathan did not affirm her accomplishment, but instead threw in sarcastic comments and barbs like "Now Sean gets to play boss and tell a lot of little people what to do. I'm sure she's really looking forward to that!" Sean was confused by the edge she heard in Jonathan's voice. When later confronted, he denied he was angry or intentionally mean and accused Sean of being too sensitive. He never surfaced his real issue: Sean's job was already time consuming, and

Faces of Anger

Face of anger	Characteristics to look for
Passive–aggression	Withholds praise, attention, or affection. May "forget" or fail to follow through on commitments. Withholds intimacy when upset. Engages in actions known to upset the other person. Chronic lateness.
Sarcasm	Makes "humorous" or cutting remarks about others. Reveals embarrassing personal information to others or causes public humiliation. Uses a tone of voice and manner that convey disgust or disapproval.
Cold anger	Withdraws from the other person for periods of time. Avoids intimacy. Refuses to reveal what is wrong. Tends to avoid emotional discussion when angry.
Hostility	Conveys an inner intensity, raised voice—seems more stressed out. Acts time-impatient. Shows visible signs of frustration and annoyance with others who don't move fast enough or who fail to meet high expectations for competence or performance.
Aggression	Raises voice, is verbally loud and/or abusive. Curses, uses name calling, and blames. Has thoughts or mental pictures of hurting another. Acts out anger with touching, pushing, blocking, or hitting.

Jonathan was irritated that her new post would rob him of even more of her time.

At times the line between humorously joking *with* another person and sarcastically making a joke *of* the other's behavior may be hard to discern. Some individuals become masters at combining intellectualization and biting sarcasm as a way of letting off the steam of anger through the "valve" of intellectual riposte and "comebacks."

When you are the recipient of sarcasm, you may feel wounded yet not know how to interpret what was said or how to respond. Indeed, you can be made to feel that *you* are the problem because you just don't have a good sense of humor or because you're "so thin-skinned."

Cold Anger

In contrast to "hot" anger, cold anger involves a turning off, avoidance, or lack of responsiveness to another as a way of expressing anger.

Sean was generally patient. She grew up in a family where discussion of anger or any unpleasant emotion was discouraged in favor of keeping things on an even keel. She never heard her parents argue. When her expectations for a calm and loving home life were disrupted by one of Jonathan's outbursts, she felt angry and frustrated, yet unable to express her feelings directly. Instead she would often withdraw emotionally and physically, sleeping in the guest bedroom for days at a time as a way of punishing him for his actions and protecting herself. Her withdrawal only created more fuel for Jonathan's anger. At his next temper loss, this cycle would be repeated, and their problems were never addressed directly until they entered counseling.

It is not uncommon for both partners in a relationship to display cold anger. When one withdraws, the other reacts with a "quid pro quo" or equal and measured response. No response is less likely to resolve conflict than meeting cold anger with coldness.

Hostility

A kind of free-floating anger that has no clear object, hostility can be aroused by any situation that fails to meet the person's expectations. This venting of intense anger is often related to the level of stress in the person's life.

Recall Jonathan's behavior of impatience and free-floating anger when any person or situation did not measure up to his standards. Sean reported a major blowup when the family was preparing for a trip to the beach. Jonathan assumed the family would be packed and ready to leave by 9:00 A.M., despite the fact that the family had never been able to get up, dress, eat breakfast, and pack before 11:00 A.M. His unrealistic expectations not met, he began pacing and mumbling about his disgust as 9:00 A.M. came and went and the family was still getting ready. The trip was punctuated by Jonathan's outbursts at "incompetent" drivers, Sean's misreading of a map, and his sons' predictable wrangling in the back seat. Soon after "losing it," Jonathan would apologize, but his

Jonathan displayed many characteristics of what Drs. Meyer Rosenman and Ray Friedman have called "Type A" personality, which is believed to increase the risk of coronary disease:

> ➤ Time impatience (e.g., constantly looking at his watch and demanding "on-time" behavior from others).

> ➤ Polyphasic behavior (e.g., trying to do too many things at the same time, like channel surfing his television while also balancing his checkbook).

> ➤ Hostility (e.g., becoming agitated and irritable over "inefficient" coworkers, feeling restless, and easily becoming angered). Research has found this component is most associated with coronary disease.

intensity put a damper on the family's fun. Sean refused to talk to him for the first few hours of the trip.

Hostility often creates difficulties in personal, work, and family relationships because it is truly stressful for others who bear the brunt of loud, intense comments or behaviors that express impatience and dissatisfaction.

Aggression

Aggression clearly has the intent, through cutting words or actions like yelling, name calling, pushing, slapping, or hitting, to intimidate or hurt another emotionally or physically. In contrast, hostility is a more diffuse, intense emotional state that may even be directed toward objects and clearly lacks the focus of aggression (e.g., loudly bemoaning the "piece of junk" lawn mower that won't start). Jonathan was often hostile but occasionally crossed over the line into outright aggressiveness.

When you read the exchange between Jonathan and Sean that occurred in my office, try to put yourself in Sean's place as the object of Jonathan's aggressive behavior.

SEAN: Jonathan, I really do not want to plan another trip with you until you get control of your anger. It scares me when you lose it in front of the boys.

JONATHAN: (*raising his voice*) I can't believe you would think I'm the whole problem. I get angry because you are always late and a complete incompetent in managing the boys. You can't get yourself ready on time, let alone be a capable mother to them.

SEAN: I am a good mother, it's just that ...

JONATHAN: (*interrupting her, pointing his finger*) Look, I don't want to hear any more of this garbage. You're just trying to humiliate me here. I'm not the one with the problem. It's being married to you that's the problem.

Not only did Jonathan fail to acknowledge Sean's statement that his temper frightened their sons, but he quickly jumped into a verbal attack on his wife by raising his voice, interrupting, using abrupt hand

---

An Important Note about Violence and Abuse

It is a premise of this book that any touch that is unwanted is inappropriate, whether it be holding, blocking, restraining, or indeed hitting, whether by a man, woman, adult, or child.

If you've acted abusively, whether emotionally or physically, you should seek professional counseling with someone who will not judge or criticize you but will reinforce new anger actions, like those found in this book. The vast majority of my clients who verbally or physically intimidate or abuse are good people who have just gotten caught up in incredibly destructive behavior that creates pain for others who receive or witness these actions (e.g., children). Most important is to be aware of your level of anger in time to leave the situation in a "time-out" before your actions hurt another, as suggested in Chapter 4.

If you are the recipient of aggression, Chapter 9 will discuss how to keep your cool and protect yourself when confronted with aggression as well as the other dysfunctional faces of anger. Also, you should consider reading my book *Overcoming Anger in Your Relationship* (see Suggested Resources). You will learn specific ways to set and reinforce new boundaries for you and your partner to ensure unhelpful anger is derailed before it becomes a serious or dangerous problem.

thrusts and gestures, calling her "incompetent," and referring to her statements as "garbage."

Although Jonathan had never been physically violent with Sean and was not often this aggressive, it's worth noting that for some of my clients serious physical acting out can be triggered by an exchange like that between Jonathan and Sean. Research has shown that verbal abuse often precedes physical violence. It is a serious threat to any relationship.

If you behave aggressively, you likely regret these actions after the fact and have no doubt vowed to watch what you say and do in the future. Unfortunately, aggression can feel powerful and often does get the attention of the other person, thus strengthening it as a habit you may retrieve the next time you are really angry. Then another cycle of acting out, followed by regret and apology, begins. I encourage you to make a commitment to end this bad habit, and the chapters to follow will support your decision.

"So, How Do I Express My Anger More Productively?"

The five faces of anger expression just discussed have much in common, even though they vary from the indirect and passive to the all-too-direct flare of aggressive anger. They act out angry feelings in ways that frustrate or threaten others and often themselves become the focus for discussion. (Does "Your *anger* is the problem here" sound familiar?) Most important, they are unlikely to resolve the issue at hand because they prevent rational discussion of how both you and the object of your anger can get your realistic expectations met substantially. Believe it or not, you can learn instead to express your anger in a thoughtful discussion that can lead to resolution of the conflict or relationship problem before you. I call this alternative, productive face of anger "assertive problem solving."

Assertive Problem Solving

Drs. Robert Alberti and Michael Emmons describe "assertiveness" as a clear, bold, and information-rich statement of your position to another person in a way that is not threatening or aggressive. "Problem solving" has been described by many researchers as a way of finding the best solution to a problem, and includes:

➤ Defining the problem in behavioral language so that another person can understand it.

➤ Mutually brainstorming many possible solutions.

➤ Selecting the solution that both parties agree is best, after thoughtful discussion of costs/benefits.

Assertive problem solving combines assertiveness and problem solving to ensure that two people not only talk through a problem calmly but also craft a solution that satisfies the needs of both (a "win–win" solution). If this sounds like a wild promise, rest assured that the chapters to come will break down this process step by step so that you can acquire the skills you need to make assertive problem solving your normal face of anger—no matter how out of control your episodes of anger feel right now.

By following the steps to acquire those skills, Jonathan and Sean learned to transform an angry, unproductive discussion into assertive problem solving. The issue this time was whether Sally, Jonathan's 24-year-old sister, should stay with them for a while after the breakup of her marriage. Jonathan wanted his sister to come, while Sean had misgivings. The couple got off to a poor start, blaming and mischaracterizing each other, their voices and gestures becoming more and more aggressive.

SEAN: I know you won't listen to what I think and just do what you want anyway. You are so selfish when it comes to your family. Well, what about my feelings? I'm the one who will have to do most of the work if Sally comes.

JONATHAN: Sure, I never listen to you! Right away, all you can think about is yourself and not me or my sister. The reason I don't want to listen to you is I know you won't support me in this. I need to help Sally. Can't you get that?

After reviewing the basic steps of assertive problem solving as described in Chapter 8, I encouraged them to slow down the discussion, each expressing personal thoughts and feelings about the impending visit while the other paid close attention, without interrupting.

> SEAN: I'm afraid Sally might become dependent on us. I want to help her but not make it too easy for her to escape from responsibility. Jonathan, what do you think? [A clear assertion of her thoughts and feelings while inviting her husband's ideas]

> JONATHAN: I agree that we need to help her get on her own feet, and I'm just as concerned as you are about making her dependent. [Having really listened, Jonathan restates Sean's concerns, showing he understands her position.] I think we should offer to let her stay with us as a gesture of our support, but only for a limited time, say two months, while she looks for work here and finds an apartment she can afford. [Offers a solution that may meet both their concerns: to help, but to limit her dependency.] How do you feel about that? [Invites Sean's ideas for problem resolution.]

> SEAN: I'm glad you agree with my concern. Two months would be fine with me, provided we make it clear to her at the start. Also, I wouldn't mind helping her with some of her rent to encourage her to find her own place. [Agrees on Jonathan's solution, offers another idea.]

> JONATHAN: That's a great idea. Let's try to agree on time frames and how much money we'll give her. Okay? [Moves to final resolution of the problem.]

Notice the absence of accusation and criticism. They listened to each other without interrupting as they shared their ideas and feelings about this important issue. Each looked at the other when speaking and used a calm tone to restate ideas and offer new ones. As they problem-solved a solution, it was clear that each felt respected by the other.

Chapter 8 will guide your efforts at assertive problem solving, offering numerous ideas for communicating successfully while keeping unhelpful conflict to a minimum. Chapter 9 will give you a heads-up for remaining calm when others' dysfunctional faces of anger are really provoking you.

Outcomes

Every time we experience and express anger, a variety of outcomes result. Jonathan's daily anger-fueled headache is a personal outcome that adversely affects his efficiency and the quality of his life. The lack of intimacy in her marriage is an outcome of Sean's passive–aggression and difficulty in directly confronting issues with Jonathan. As you look over these examples, ask yourself if there are any that ring true for you.

Personal Outcomes

Because of the way you handled your anger, you end up with stomach upset, sleeplessness, or a feeling of being stressed out. Or perhaps you become so angry in trying to finish a task that you start making errors, costing you time and efficiency. Other personal outcomes might include having to repurchase an item that you broke in anger or just the discomfort of feeling that your life is not in control. The possibilities for personal pain are unlimited when anger remains unresolved.

External Outcomes

Obviously your anger can have an impact on others. If you lose your temper only occasionally, the impact will probably be only fleeting. Those who were the target or witness of your ire are likely to forgive your transgression as the type of human failing we all fall prey to every once in a while. But when you express your anger inappropriately over and over, the impact may be greater and longer lasting. It may change the way other people treat you, which can have effects that reach into every part of your life. Your outbursts at work may create so much frustration that coworkers avoid working with you on projects or your supervisors feel the need to reprimand you. Eventually, your livelihood, or at least your current position, could be threatened. Your community may no longer value the civic contributions you're so equipped to make because your temper makes you more of a hazard than a help. Friends who are tired of having relaxing get-togethers spoiled by your hurtful "kidding" may stop inviting you to join them. Your spouse may become less and less affectionate, no longer able to trust you to act with the kindness that reflects the love you profess. Maybe your kids no longer seek you out for help with homework or even a game of catch because they're afraid you'll snap at them in impatience and criticism. In total, you could find the relationships and activities that make life rich and rewarding falling away, leaving you isolated.

Far too many of my clients have ended up in this sad state with very little knowledge of how they got there. It doesn't have to be that way for you.

From Self-Awareness to New Anger Expression

To prove to yourself that your anger is not an uncontrollable juggernaut, accept a simple challenge for the coming week. Remember the five components of every anger episode: trigger, thoughts, feelings, anger expression, and outcome. Breaking anger down into these components will help you recognize how your own anger unfolds. Find a small notebook or pad of paper and keep it with you for the next week. Every time you experience an episode of anger, pull out your little journal and record what happened, using the Daily Anger Log found in Appendix 2 and illustrated on page 48.

Depending on the faces of anger that you typically use, it might be relatively easier or harder to identify the incidents that "count" here. Clearly, yelling at a coworker or employee is an episode you should record. But what about those times when you were "just kidding" throughout a lunch with colleagues or "just didn't feel like talking" to your wife? When you're just starting on an anger management program, the biggest hurdle may be recognizing and admitting when you're feeling and inappropriately expressing anger. To be sure you come as close as possible to recording all anger episodes, review the faces of anger described earlier in the chapter until you feel the "symptoms" are ingrained in your mind. Also pay as much attention as you can to the reactions of others. Sure, your instinct may be to shrug off comments like "That's not really funny, Stan," or to deny it and defend yourself when your wife accuses you of "punishing" her with aloof disinterest. Even if you yield to these instincts in the moment, try to look back on any incident that you reacted to by being angry or feeling threatened and record it in your Daily Anger Log even if you're not convinced it was an episode of anger or it seems small or only irritating or annoying.

Keeping a record of your anger is immensely valuable in furthering your understanding of its anatomy. The more familiar you become with exactly what happens to you during an episode of anger—what triggers your anger, the thoughts that jump into your mind in response to the trigger, the complexity of emotion that surges through you, the physical symptoms that you may have ignored in the past, to say nothing of the negative impact of your anger expression—the more alert you will be to anger that is rising within you. That's the first skill you need in learning to manage anger: self-awareness.

Keeping a record of your anger episodes also helps you begin to see the connections—from trigger to thoughts to feelings to physical symptoms to expression to outcome—and possibly to begin to break them. Carlos had been having temper flare-ups with his girlfriend, and when he returned to my office for a second session after recording his anger episodes over the intervening week, he expressed amazement at the number of times he had "caught" himself before his anger escalated. When his girlfriend held them up in leaving the house for a party, for example, he found himself beginning to pace and mutter to himself that she was "purposely" trying to make him mad. By then he had recorded enough episodes in his diary that anticipating making entries had become a somewhat automatic thought process. This process was enough to focus his attention on his thinking in that moment, and he quickly saw how absurd his interpretation of Mia's actions was. He began thinking of some alternative reasons that she might be late, such as that she wanted to look nice for him and for herself, and his anger immediately subsided.

If that turnaround sounds a little pat, it's because I'm pulling a single incident out of a sequence of events that took place over seven days. The fact is, it takes practice and habit to instill a new kind of thinking, the self-awareness that can make you stop in your tracks just long enough to cut off the escalation of anger. So, why not start now? Your anger log will become an effective tool for measuring your progress as you begin to implement the ideas in this book.

You have now completed the first step in your anger management program, "Understanding and Recognizing Anger." That's not meant to imply, however, that you now know everything you need to know about your own anger. Learning about this complex emotional experience will be an ongoing task; what you have now is the foundation for future self-awareness and self-control. In the rest of this book, you'll learn additional steps toward experiencing and expressing your anger more effectively. These steps are presented in the order in which you will use them to manage any triggering situation that comes up in your

Bryan's Anger Log: A Model

Bryan decided to use the ideas in this chapter to keep track of how often he lost his temper, which he defined as raising his voice to express criticism of another person. He used each component of an anger episode to make recordings like the following in a small notebook he carried in his back pocket.

Trigger: "Ann should have picked up the dry cleaning as I asked her to. I have a major presentation tomorrow and nothing decent to wear."

Thoughts: "I can't believe she could be so inconsiderate. She never comes through when it really matters to me. How selfish."

Feelings: I felt really angry. My face got hot, and my shoulders felt really tight.

Actions: I guess I got aggressive. I lost it, yelling at Ann and cursing. I wouldn't let her explain.

Outcomes: I felt really tense, and my headache started up. Ann told me she would not put up with another outburst and left the room. She refused to speak with me all evening, and I ended up apologizing again. I felt foolish to have lost it when I'm supposed to be trying to stay calm.

At the end of a week of recording, Bryan realized that he had lost his temper at least once a day—much more often than he had thought. His journal entries showed that he was very impatient with his wife, Ann, and often raised his voice and spoke to her aggressively. His review of the outcomes of his anger revealed that his way of getting angry was making things worse for himself and his marriage. Every time he got angry at Ann, he felt stressed and, a little later, extremely guilty, which made him feel depressed. At week's end, he decided to do something about his anger. The Daily Anger Log is found in Appendix 2. You can make copies of it or use it as a guide for establishing an anger notebook or to establish a file to record your anger using your iPad, iPhone, or computer.

daily life. Recognizing that your anger has been triggered and quickly dampening your arousal before you lose it therefore precedes figuring out how your unhelpful thinking is contributing to your ire and deciding how to communicate to resolve the problem.

"The Six Steps of Anger Management" shown below is an overview, a kind of "map" of the process you will be learning in the chapters to follow.

Ready to begin? Chapter 3 will help you recognize the kinds of situations that trigger the face(s) of anger you identified in these first two chapters.

The Six Steps of Anger Management

STEP ONE. Understanding and recognizing anger

First you will learn to identify whether or not anger is a problem for you or others you interact with. Then you will learn the components of your anger so you can recognize anger as it develops within you.

Chapter 1 helps you recognize whether anger is a problem for you.

Chapter 2 reviews each component of your anger so you can begin observing how you react to triggering situations that arise.

STEP TWO. Identifying and preparing for anger triggers

When others, objects, or the situation you are in do not fulfill your expectations, they may trigger anger as an emotional reaction. These expectations are often well learned in childhood and are derived from your experiences in getting or failing to get your significant needs met.

Chapter 3 reviews how predisposing childhood experiences shape your expectations for self, others, and life situations. Then you learn to identify and alter unrealistic expectations that trigger anger as you prepare for situations that have triggered anger in the past.

Being aware of your anger triggers permits you to predict and prepare for events that are likely to evoke your anger.

STEP THREE. Pinpointing your anger early on and dampening arousal	Once aware of triggers, it is important to keep track of body sensations that occur early on as your anger is escalating so that you can decrease or "dampen" your inner tension before it reaches levels where rational thinking is difficult. Dampening also helps you to manage daily stress that contributes to your tension level.	Chapter 4 teaches you to link the earliest signs of anger to new actions that permit you to control your face(s) of anger. You will express this information in a personal Anger Scale. Chapter 5 illustrates a variety of ideas for reducing your inner tension through regulating your breathing, muscle tension, and imagery. You will learn to quickly reduce anger arousal so that you can cope with the triggering situation more effectively.
STEP FOUR. Identifying and changing thoughts that fuel anger	You must learn to examine and change thinking patterns that fuel anger. This often includes developing new self-talk and images in your mind to view the situation	Chapter 6 teaches you to identify unhelpful self-talk and images that fuel your anger and guide what you do. Chapter 7 teaches you

	objectively and to craft a plan as to how to react.	to challenge cognitive distortions and to use self-talk and imagery to your advantage.
STEP FIVE. Staying cool under fire	Using assertive problem solving, you can communicate your needs as you defuse conflict and work out solutions to differences. This face of anger must replace the negative and unhelpful faces described in Chapter 2.	Chapter 8 reviews the mechanics of assertive, nonthreatening communication as a way of communicating with others who fail to meet your needs or frankly antagonize you. You will learn to defuse conflict and to resolve problems as the relationship is strengthened.

Chapter 9 gives you pointers on how to deal with each face of anger that others reveal to you, while maintaining calm control. |
| STEP SIX. Staying the course: Sustaining new behavior and coping with roadblocks | Getting new behavior started is easier than sustaining it. There are powerful strategies for learning and reinforcing new faces of anger so they become easily available to you when the going gets rough. When you face roadblocks or | Chapter 10 reviews powerful strategies from the human learning literature for practicing and strengthening your new anger skills, while rapidly getting rid of old habits.

Chapter 11 offers insights and strategies |

setbacks, it is important to reassess and adjust your efforts.

to end your resentments and decide whether or not to forgive others when you feel you have been treated poorly.

Chapter 12 helps you diagnose and quickly overcome setbacks that are likely to occur as you implement what you are learning about anger.

Step Two

Identifying and Preparing for Anger Triggers

NOW THAT YOU'RE LEARNING TO BE AWARE OF YOUR ANGER and how you express it, it's important to pay attention to the kinds of situations that trigger your ire. You'll find that you've developed expectations for how you and others should act and even for how the environment and things in it should operate. Anger is aroused when these expectations are not met. In Chapter 3 you'll learn to examine your expectations to be sure they're realistic and attainable.

3

Understanding Your Anger Triggers

What makes a situation aggravating? Some people calmly pass the time in the worst traffic jam, while others barely control their rage. Keeping her cool, your friend reframes others' nasty words as "their problem," while you would feel personally attacked in the same situation. Chapter 2 introduced the role of expectations, unique to each of us, in triggering our anger. Let's get personal. How do you think I should respond if you send me a gift?

Mail you a thank you note?

Call?

Is an e-mail sufficient? What about an e-card?

How about texting "Thanks!!!"?

What if I just enjoy your generosity but fail to acknowledge your gift?

If the situation were reversed, a simple thank you the next time we meet would suffice for me. But you may expect a different response. Who's right? And if our expectations are not met, how would we each react? Depending on our relationship and other circumstances, I might feel a bit let down, irritated, or downright angry if you didn't respond the way I expected. How about you?

In childhood, our parents and significant others shaped our expectations for how we, others, and the world around us should function. Some expectations—such as that others will say "please" or that we will not be physically abused—are commonly shared, while others are unique and may be puzzling to those people who don't share or at least know our background. Regardless of their origin, however, when our expectations are not met, one very common emotion we experience is anger.

You have only to think about the last time your anger was triggered to see that this is true. What set you off? Something someone said? Some action or behavior? Someone's failure to do or say something? Now think about what you were expecting to happen. Did what actually happened meet your expectations?

Jack felt his temperature rising as he crept through rush hour traffic again. Sure, it had happened many times before. But on a deeper level he expected the state to expand the highway system ("They sure get enough tax revenue from me to pay for it!") to accommodate increases in use. The fact that he saw evidence every day that it wasn't doing so really made him mad.

Nobody ever seemed to have time to listen to Tanya's long stories about her many ailments. Still, she kept imposing on anyone who would sit still long enough, and when they finally excused themselves and escaped, Tanya added them to her "list" and made a point of making nasty remarks about them to the next victim who came along.

Sandy was a modern woman—she really was. She loved the fact that her husband shared parenting duties equally with her (well, almost equally), that she was a bigger sports fan than he was, and that he cooked more of their dinners than she did. Why, then, had she started taking every available opportunity to snipe at him about his "so-called salary" and "going-nowhere job"?

In a word: expectations. We all have them—big ones, small ones, deeply ingrained ones, fleeting ones, ones we're well aware of, ones that surprise us when someone points them out. Thinking about the last time you got angry may already have revealed some expectations you take with you in all your interactions with others and all your handling of things and events. Maybe you expect everyone around you to be courteous, saying "please" and "thank you" and "excuse me" without fail. Or perhaps you expect your train to arrive on the platform at the time printed in the schedule every day. Are these expectations reasonable and realistic? Some people might agree with you that it's reasonable to expect a cashier to say "thank you" when you've made a large purchase but not to expect a "please" from someone who yells for you to "Get back on the curb!" when he sees you are about to get hit by a bus. It might be realistic to expect your train to be close to on time most days, but few would expect it to run with clockwork precision each and every day.

When you hold unrealistic expectations, you're setting yourself up for disappointment and anger by greatly increasing the odds that you won't realize your expected outcome. Jack's expectation that the state will expand the highway system may or may not be realistic, depending on the government and its resources. But to expect the state to stay on top of increasing needs to the extent that rush hour traffic jams never occur is undoubtedly unrealistic. Dozens of compassionate souls had listened to Tanya's laments for longer than most people would expect, yet it was never long enough for Tanya. Sandy expected her husband to reject traditional role definitions regarding housework and child care, but she wanted to keep them firmly in place when it came to breadwinning.

In contrast, the more realistic your expectations are, the more likely they are to be met and the less often your anger will be triggered. Jack could expect the state to respond to the need for more highways (he could even channel his anger into lobbying for such changes) without expecting to drive at 55 miles per hour all the way, every day. Tanya could expect lots of sympathy and attention from her closest relatives and could be grateful for the time that others spend listening to her without insisting on being the only one who was allowed to end a conversation. Sandy could tell her husband she wanted him to be the main breadwinner and take over some of the other traditionally female tasks herself, or she could leave the household arrangements the way they are and live with the equity in earning power too. These are not, of course, the only solutions that these people might arrive at. An infinite number of possibilities can come out of the assertive problem solving introduced in Chapter 2 as a positive alternative to the dysfunctional faces of anger. But most of them will have at their core a recasting of unrealistic expectations so that an angry response is not so inevitable. This chapter offers you the opportunity to identify your triggering expectations as a step toward managing your anger. In doing so you increase your sense of control and empower yourself in two ways:

1. You can "edit" or discard unrealistic expectations, permanently eliminating triggers that used to get to you.

2. You can better prepare for triggering expectations you are unwilling or unable to rid yourself of.

Research on stress tells us that increased control and prepared-ness make you more "resilient," that is, more able to adapt flexibly to a challenging situation. Resilience is at the heart of managing your anger and not letting it manage you.

Each of us has a unique set of expectations, but we all have expecta-tions for ourselves, for others, and for the events and circumstances we face every day. I should note that some of us, due to upsetting or even traumatic experiences in our childhoods, have developed a threaten-ing and somewhat negative view of the world around us and of people in general. We have all known someone who seems quite pessimistic and can quickly come up with the most negative interpretation of a situation before even giving it a chance to unfold. If you find it really difficult to shake off negative thinking or find it very difficult to alter your negative expectations into positive ones using the ideas in this book, you should consider seeking the help of a counselor who can help transform the negative beliefs that underlie this mindset.

Expectations for Self:
Are You Your Own Worst Enemy?

No matter how high you set your expectations, your performance will be shaped by a combination of your genes and what you have learned and practiced. Accomplishments are also influenced by your health status, fitness, nutrition, encouragement from others, and also factors beyond your control, like the weather.

When you expect yourself to perform beyond what is reasonable, anger becomes more likely. Do any of these situations ring a bell for you?

Physical Endurance and Performance

In exercise, sports, and other physical tasks, you expect more than you can physically deliver.

Out of shape and 50 years old, Jose begins an exercise program without professional advice, setting standards for lifting weights and running more appropriate to a man in his 20s. His workouts soon become frustrating: "I can't believe I'm so out of shape. I should be able to lift much more! What's wrong with me?" He carries his irritation with him like a dark cloud as he arrives home in a sour mood he denies having.

Sara rarely plays golf, yet expects to pick up where she left off, shooting at just above par. She is loudly critical of her game, cursing and muttering as she plays. It is so unpleasant that her friends often decline her golfing invitations, much to Sara's puzzlement. She would agree she is an intense competitor but doesn't understand how unpleasant her expression of her anger is for others.

Keiji, a weekend carpenter at best, remodels his basement without professional help. Deciding he will finish the job in time for Christmas, he soon falls hopelessly behind. Dreading the weekends, Keiji is irritable and impatient with everyone in his family, who wish he had never begun the project. He finds it hard to admit he will "fail."

You know you've set unrealistic expectations for your physical self when:

> ➤ You find yourself overly exhausted and/or stressed by the activity—to a point that it affects your enjoyment.

> ➤ You are injured or so sore you cannot carry out other important responsibilities.

> ➤ You begin dreading what you once enjoyed.

How do you set realistic expectations for the next time you approach a similar challenge? Consider these points:

1. As you approach a physically taxing task, realistically consider your current physical fitness based on the recent past. Forget what you used to be able to do, but objectively evaluate your strength and endurance lately and set standards for yourself that agree with these facts.

2. When taking on a task that requires certain skills, like home repairs or fixing your car, ask yourself before you begin how much hands-on experience you've had with this particular project. Do you have the necessary tools and supplies to set the stage for success?

3. Do you need the help of others and, if so, in what roles, to carry out the task in a safe and effective manner? Are you willing to ask for help?

Intellectual and Task Pursuits

No matter how smart we are, we need to study and practice to learn new things. Many of us set lofty goals for mastering new information, for completing tasks at work, and even for playing intellectual games (like chess or bridge), feeling angry and frustrated when we're not successful.

Josh decides he must make an A in his computer course, even though he has had little computing experience. Falling behind, he becomes angry with the instructor for going "too quickly" and embittered when he finally drops out in frustration.

Lali agrees to coordinate a major meeting at work, even though she has never planned an event of this magnitude. Resisting any offers of help, she forges on, becoming stressed and angry when things start to go wrong. At one point she blows up at an assistant, who complains to management, only adding to Lali's burden.

Telltale signs that you have set unrealistic expectations for yourself are the following:

> ➤ As you begin a task, you aren't sure you have sufficient knowledge, background, or experience to complete it successfully. You've been trying to rationalize that all will be okay, but deep down you have misgivings.

> ➤ You soon find that you're failing to meet goals you've set for yourself and must "catch up."

> ➤ You feel insecure and anxious or guarded that others may find out you're in "over your head."

Before committing yourself to any task, consider these points so that you don't set yourself up for a stressful experience and possibly an unsuccessful outcome:

1. How much past experience do you have with this task? How have you performed in the past? This is the best standard by which to predict the level and quality of your performance this time. If you have doubts about what's required, ask for advice from someone who is knowledgeable before you decide whether to take it on.

2. Examine your thinking about this task. Are you trying to please

or prove something to others? Is it worth it if you find yourself overwhelmed or robbed of time needed for other important life activities?

3. If you need help to successfully complete this task, be sure to ask for it. If it's too much for you to do alone, given other responsibilities, consider refusing to take it on.

Time and Speed

How fast can I mow the lawn, paint a room, get to work, or complete a project? Often we set time frames for ourselves without realistically appraising the task and possible roadblocks beyond our immediate control. When we don't perform at warp speed, we are angry and self-condemning.

You've agreed to an impossible deadline for a project at work and feel stressed and irritable as you work long hours and still fall further behind. Blaming the "stress," you deflect others' concerns that you're becoming defensive and grouchy.

Against your better judgment, you agree to take your friend to the airport during rush hour. Once stuck in an immovable sea of cars you are furious with him and yourself, but you hold it in, only to feel completely drained and moody when you finally arrive home.

Unfamiliar with the location of your friend's wedding, you wait until the last minute to leave. When you promptly get lost, you blame this predicament on your spouse for not remembering to bring a map.

We often set time standards for others and ourselves with little thought about the facts of the situation. Going shopping during Christmas week and deciding to take the expressway in the late afternoon, and then feeling angry when the inevitable lines and waiting begin, are examples of self-inflicted pain.

You know you've stretched the limits of time and set yourself up for a rushed, "winded" experience when you notice these things happening all too often:

> ➤ You find yourself wishing you had set aside more time to complete a task or had left sooner to get to a destination. You find yourself complaining of "too little time" or of being "rushed," forgetting that you are ultimately in control of your schedule.

➤ You feel anxious as you watch the clock and realize you're falling behind or get angry or impatient with others who fail to
meet your time expectations.

➤ Others have begun to comment that you're late in getting things
done or "last minute."

Consider these ideas for becoming more realistic about time and
speed:

1. Before setting a time threshold for yourself or others, ask yourself why it's so important to meet a certain deadline. Some situations
are objectively time critical. You don't want to be late for a wedding
or a business meeting, and it's common courtesy not to keep another
person waiting when you've agreed on a time to meet, for whatever purpose. But do you *have* to paint the kitchen this weekend? Is this the best
day to get started on your taxes when April 15 is a couple of months
away? *Must* you lose 10 pounds by Christmas, or should you just make
a couple of positive changes in your diet and see what happens? Even if
the kids are pressing you to set a definite date to go to Six Flags, can't
you make your plans at the last minute, based on what you've gotten
done during the week and how you feel on Friday? Many of the tasks
and events we add to our schedules just aren't time sensitive. They can
wait.

2. Review your past experience with this task or activity and how
long it took then. If you have no past experience with it, ask someone
who does know how long it might take. Set a time frame based on these
facts and give yourself some "wiggle room" (if travel from your office
to the airport usually takes at least 50 minutes, for example, consider
giving yourself an hour to get there feeling refreshed and calm).

3. Is being late worth upsetting yourself or others, who may not
be as invested in getting a trip, a project, or another goal accomplished
in the time you set? If you're depending on another person, make sure
you mutually agree on the time frame; otherwise, don't count on the
other performing as you wish.

4. Is your time frame for an activity affected by factors well beyond
your control? For example, if you're depending on supplies or materials
being shipped or planes, trains, taxis, or public transportation being
on time, consider realistic expectations in light of the time of year (e.g.,

holidays, thunderstorm season) and conditions (e.g., weather, rush hour).

Success and Failure

Our needs for recognition and self-actualization are fulfilled when we achieve our goals. If we set daily and longer-term goals that are practical and comfortably achievable, we greatly increase our odds for success. Unfortunately, the same needs may drive us to set very high but unattainable goals, only leaving us feeling angry and frustrated when we don't achieve them.

Mario is never satisfied. In an excellent relationship and making more money than he ever dreamed possible, he constantly drives himself to further build his stock portfolio so he can "retire at 40." When the market loses value, a predictable reaction to economic ups and downs, he gets angry and blames himself. His fiancée complains that Mario is often irritable and preoccupied with counting, measuring, and comparing.

Mariah drives her staff to succeed, no matter what the cost. Wanting to achieve senior management before she hits 30, she demands that others be as willing to give up evenings and weekends as she is. Her quest to be successful takes its toll. She feels little joy in her daily life and is often moody and irritable. She has begun spending her limited free time alone, just trying to recover.

What's wrong with setting high goals for achievement? Having a vision of where you're headed is necessary to achieve any worthy goal. But when you set a high standard, it's important to determine that it's realistic and worth the costs. Can you relate to any of these signals that you're setting yourself up for discouragement?

> ➤ You and others around you pay a high price for achieving the goals you set. Long hours, barely met deadlines, much agonizing, and conflict occur all too often.

> ➤ When you do attain a goal, you devalue it, immediately resetting a new standard in a never-ending derby of accomplishment.

> ➤ Like Mariah, the enjoyment of your daily life takes second place to achieving outcomes. Remember that you're likely to spend most of your life in the daily *process* of achieving your dreams,

not in achieving them. I like the phrase "Most of life is a journey and not a destination."

What can you do if you are too success driven? Consider the price you're paying when you drive yourself or others beyond reasonable expectations:

1. In setting standards for success, consider the cost you or others will pay. You could be successful in coaching a winning soccer team for your children, only to have them hate soccer because you've driven them so hard to "win."

2. Set a goal that is at or just above what you've attained before or that a knowledgeable source tells you is reasonably attainable. Once it's achieved, you may push your goal up a notch until you find the limits of what you can expect to accomplish. Psychologists call this "successive approximations," taking small steps toward your goal and feeling good about each accomplishment. This is much more likely to create enjoyment for you or others you work with than setting blue-sky objectives that end up being unattainable and exhausting.

When Others Fail to Meet Your Expectations

In childhood you learned what to expect from others and how to behave in response. Because your early experiences were likely somewhat different from those of others, your expectations may not be shared universally. When you *conclude* that someone else has acted outside of these expectations, whether factual or not, you're likely to experience anger.

Manners and Social Etiquette

Whether you were raised with butlers and maids or "on the street," your experiences engraved a kind of inner rule book that defines the social behaviors appropriate for various occasions. When others violate these unwritten rules, you may find yourself angry, sometimes wondering why.

Edward grew up in a family where following the rules and respecting parents were enforced by strict discipline. He is immediately irritated when good friends fail to correct their son for calling Edward by his first name. He often sees children acting "ill-mannered" in public and has found himself admonishing the parents for their laxness.

Charlotte is often aggravated by the "poor manners" of her coworkers. She is quick to criticize others who hang up the telephone without saying good-bye, end e-mail in a perfunctory manner, or fail to express their appreciation for her work.

Telltale signs that you may need to reexamine your expectations for others' courtesy and demeanor include the following:

> You often find yourself irritated or disappointed with others in matters of protocol and decorum. Others are not polite enough or act "improperly" (e.g., "rude" or "lacking manners") when you are clear as to how they should behave.

> Conflict with another person often revolves around something he or she failed to do to express appreciation, courtesy, or respect for you or others.

While your beliefs about manners and customs aren't "wrong," you need to recognize that differences in background, culture, and experience may cause others to view "correct" social behavior through a different lens. How much power do we have to change someone else's attitudes about manners, parenting, or anything else? When others violate your expectations for "civilized" behavior, consider these realistic options rather than stewing or acting out:

1. Revise your expectations to take into account the background and culture of the person who has offended you. Our country is filled with people of different backgrounds who reflect a kaleidoscope of customs and ideas, many of which do not agree with your rule book.

2. Take into account the age and experience of the other person. For example, the teenager who seems to be rude or unkempt may reflect a youth culture that you can empathize with if you just remember your own youthful dress and behavior.

3. If you must say something, consider whether the outcome you're expecting is realistic (e.g., to change someone's thinking or to

teach him a lesson?). Ask for what you want with facial expression, tone of voice, and words that make it a "polite request," not an indictment of the other's actions.

Affirmation and Intimacy

You can quickly feel irritated or rejected when friends or family fail to act in ways that seem supportive or intimate enough. No matter what others intend to communicate, however, it's your expectations, even if unrealistic, that determine whether you're satisfied by their efforts.

> ➤ How and how often should your partner approach you in a loving manner?

> ➤ What constitutes an intimate, romantic evening?

> ➤ How often should friends, siblings, or grown children telephone, write, or communicate with you?

Shannon often accuses her husband of being "cold" and "unromantic," castigations that inevitably lead to arguments once her husband defends himself. Lately she's been expressing her cold anger by sleeping in the guest room, and she's begun threatening a separation she has no intention of seeking. She recognizes she can't "make" her husband change but seems caught up in a continuing struggle for his affirmation.

Tyrone is angry again with his two brothers. They rarely call, and he has to initiate every get-together. He recently blew up at his brother Akeem over something "silly," when the real issue is that he feels hurt and disaffirmed. He has begun thinking of breaking all ties to his brothers.

Do any of the following attitudes or actions seem familiar?

> ➤ You often find yourself questioning others' commitment to you. You conclude that others have let you down or have not contributed as much to the relationship as you have.

> ➤ You feel hurt or rejected when others fail to initiate communication or activities with you or fail to be as attentive, affectionate, or intimate as you expect.

> ➤ In your closest relationships, conflict often revolves around your

unfulfilled needs for attention or affirmation (e.g., "Why can't you be more loving/affectionate/involved with me?").

While it's conceivable that others may not love or care for you as much as you care for them, it's also possible that you simply express affection and intimacy differently. Given that you're powerless over everyone else, you have two basic choices:

1. You can hold on to expectations that are rarely or never ful-filled and react by suffering silently, acting out your hurt and anger, or just writing others off.

2. In contrast, you can identify and communicate your expecta-tions in a calm, problem-solving manner (see Chapter 8). When the other person is unable or unwilling to change, you must adjust your expectations if the person is important to you. As a last resort, you can decide the relationship is just not worth all the effort.

Equity and Fairness

Based on our morals and beliefs, we each have expectations as to what is fair and just. The problem is that others often don't agree with us. An employer who lays off a small number of employees to preserve the jobs of the rest feels justified in doing the "greatest good." But if you were one of those laid off, after many years of service, you might feel angry and embittered by what you saw as unfair treatment.

When your internal standards are violated, the "symptoms" may be feelings of guilt when you let yourself down and anger when others fail to act "fairly."

Chen left work two hours early to take his friend Sam to the air-port. When Chen later asks Sam for a ride to pick up his car, Sam declines, stating he just can't leave the office early. Hanging up the phone, Chen blows up: "I finally ask this guy for a favor and he can't even take off a half hour early. What a sucker I've been." He vows to wait for Sam to do him a good turn before having anything further to do with him: "The ball's in his court."

Is Chen's behavior rational? His implicit expectation is that because he does something for Sam, he can now expect Sam to reciprocate in a manner Chen deems fair. Chen is often disappointed when others don't come through for him in ways he considers equitable.

Consider these signs that a focus on equity is stressing your relationships:

➤ You find yourself comparing what others have received or how hard they've worked to your own experience, frequently concluding you've been treated unfairly. It's hard for you to overlook any situation that doesn't seem "fair."

➤ When what you receive in material terms (e.g., a raise at work, a gift) or effort (e.g., another offers to help you out in return for your good deeds) doesn't seem equitable, you feel angry and have a hard time forgetting about it. Unfairness makes it hard for you to carry on as if nothing is wrong, and relationships with family and others often suffer as a result.

Using Chen's situation as an example, try to craft expectations for others with the following points in mind.

➤ *Others may not reciprocate as we would or at all. We are powerless over what anyone else does in response to our actions.* In the previous example, when Chen chooses to give, he clearly expects he will be given something of equal value in return. He is very aware of how much, what, and to whom he "gives," as if toting up a score. Is it reasonable to expect an equal return? Perhaps others see what Chen does as a wonderful gesture that is given with no strings.

➤ *Each of us may differ in our expectations as to what is fair and reasonable behavior within the relationship.* For example, Chen set the standard for a fair exchange, believing that Sam "owed" him a ride home. Perhaps Sam's idea of a "good turn" is different. For example, Sam offered Chen some extra tickets to the opera, which Chen declined and discounted because he is not interested in listening to "two hours of singing in Italian."

➤ *If an expectation is that important, it should be communicated in an unambiguous manner: what is desired and why.* Others are not mind readers and may not divine that the behavior in question is so critical to the relationship. Sam may not have a clue as to how important it is that he take Chen to get the car. If it's so important to you, make it clear or understand there is a good chance your expectation will not be fulfilled. I have too often seen important relationships ended because of unrealistic and poorly communicated standards for equity.

Further, think about the risk in placing important relationships on the line by imposing these "make or break" standards. After all, when *you've* forgotten something important to a friend or family member, is it because you don't care or because you're a fallible human being?

Intrusion and Annoyance

Sometimes others act in ways that are just plain annoying to you, violating your expectations for peace or smooth functioning.

As you try to catch up on your summer reading at the beach, a family nearby is talking loudly and permitting their kids to play rap music at a decibel level more appropriate to a jet engine. You find yourself irritated and imagine smashing the offending boom box into a thousand pieces. You finally pack up and leave in disgust, a nice day ruined by the "selfishness of others."

Your best friend talks slowly and in a circular manner. You expect him to quickly get to the point. As your irritation rises, you find yourself interrupting him or changing the topic. Also, long, pointless meetings, women who wear too much perfume, and others who waste your time with incorrect answers are among daily annoyances that sometimes drive you wild with irritation.

What really sets your teeth on edge? What do you find that you "can't stand" in your day? Who and what is most annoying, and how do you react? Look for these signs that your expectations may be getting the best of you:

> ➤ You frequently find yourself annoyed or impatient with how others act. Loud voices, noisy children, annoying mannerisms (e.g., nail biting, humming, knuckle cracking) set your teeth on edge. You find it hard to ignore these unwelcome intrusions.

> ➤ Your own activities (perhaps with family or friends) are affected adversely when you can't just let go of an intrusion beyond your control. For example, the noise made by a large family at the table next to you makes you so irritable you ask your spouse to quickly finish so you can leave the restaurant. Your spouse thinks you are overreacting and ruining the evening.

Does what you can't stand really affect the quality of your day? Examine your expectations:

Rational Belief: Other people will continue to act in ways that fulfill *their* needs. As soon as I accept this truth and stop trying to impose my expectations on others, I can be at peace with what they decide to do, even if I disagree with it.

Try out this mantra when the chips are down:

"I am powerless over everyone but myself. What they say, do, think, and feel is their right as long as it doesn't hurt others. It is not my job to be a parent, teacher, police officer, spiritual leader, or critic—that takes time and robs me of energy. I can problem-solve how I decide to react to what they do or just accept what I cannot change. Either way, I can be calm. Either way, they will continue to do what they choose to do."

1. Can you really expect the world to fit into your plan? Will teenagers, long-winded speakers, and long lines disappear in your lifetime? Is it realistic to assume that other people, individually or as a group, will always act in ways that are calm, less intense, reasonable, or relaxing?

2. Ask yourself if there is anything you can do to change the situation. If not, change your thinking, problem-solve an alternative way of coping (e.g., earplugs to block out raucous sounds, a paperback book to read in long lines), or leave. You likely can continue to enjoy the beach, remain a member of that committee, and continue your friendship with a loquacious friend by accepting those things you cannot change, while problem-solving those you can.

Aggression and Abuse

Voice tone, manner, or actions that seem threatening or outright scary clearly violate the expectations of most of us and should not be permitted. It is a realistic expectation that you should not be subjected to threatening or abusive words or actions. My book *Overcoming Anger in Your Relationship* (see Suggested Resources) shows a "ladder" of behaviors ranging from contemptuous statements ("What is the *matter* with you!!??"; "Can't you do anything right—duh!!?"), negative labels (e.g.,

"How *stupid* of you!"; "You are a cold b——— ") to threats of violence or any physical action (e.g., getting right up into your face, blocking you from leaving, holding on to your arm, hitting) that is unwanted. Any statements or actions on this ladder can lead to serious outcomes for the recipient. Chapter 9 will give you lots of options to derail this behavior early on or to leave if it seems dangerous.

How Things Should Go in the World around You

I could give hundreds of examples of the environment and things we depend on occasionally letting us down, but here are just a few:

> Your new car won't start two weeks after driving it from the showroom. You're late to work, and your spouse has already left with the other vehicle.

> Your clothes dryer breaks down the day after the appliance serviceman told you it was operating perfectly. You have a week's worth of clothes to launder and little time to deal with this right now.

> You have planned a lawn party for a large number of guests who are due to arrive at 6:00 P.M. It has begun storming, and the weather report suggests more of the same all evening. You're picturing too many people crammed into your living room, ruining the evening.

No one would likely enjoy such outcomes, but many would feel calm disappointment and would soon be strategizing an alternative plan. Others would seethe inside, falling prey to the mistaken expectation that things we use and the environment itself will work just as we wish.

One of my clients was arrested for assault at our regional airport for verbally abusing a gate attendant when an aircraft arrived late. She had been delayed on two previous flights that week and expected the winter weather conditions to clear up: "Well, I just couldn't take another delay. I told myself this just wasn't going to happen to me again. These airlines treat you like [expletive], and I had to let them know I won't stand for it, so I let the attendant have it. Now I'm facing this charge, and I can't believe this is happening to me."

Most of us have never lost it to the extent we are charged with assault, but we can all relate to this woman's frustration. She fell prey to one of these irrational expectations, implicit anytime we lose it in our relationship with the things and environment around us. Do you share any of these common expectations?

"My needs will be fulfilled in an orderly, predictable, and scheduled manner."

"Good weather will prevail, and cars, buses, trains, and airplanes will work well and arrive on time."

"Every electronic and mechanical object that I own will work smoothly and last forever."

These expectations are absurd, right? But the next time you feel irritated in a traffic jam or curse at a computer that fails, you have just adopted an irrational expectation, whether you put it into words or not. Here are some alternatives:

1. Think about your past experience with this object or situation and state one or two realistic expectations and a plan to resolve your needs (e.g., "Of course my tires were eventually going to wear out. I need to put on my emergency blinker and call AAA for service"). Or how about "Computers fail all the time—so what else is new? This is just a particularly bad time, and I need to think of a plan to get this work finished. Maybe I can rent a laptop for the weekend while this one is being repaired."

2. Going into a potentially problematic situation, develop a plan for coping with reasonably likely problems (e.g., "There's a small chance of rain this Saturday. What could we do to get the guests under cover if it rains? Let's see … "). In situations where delays or setbacks are almost the norm, state a realistic expectation at the beginning and keep restating it when things go south. "Look, I knew it was not uncommon for luggage to get lost. It's actually not really lost, just sent to the wrong airport. I need to chill out for a while and then find out where to report it."

Changing Your Expectations, Changing Your Outcomes

The sidebar "Expectations That Trigger Anger" (page 74) briefly summarizes each category of expectation that can trigger your anger.

Now that we've illustrated what "causes" anger for others, what about you? Using the sidebar as a guide, can you now identify your personal expectations that "set you up" for repeated episodes of anger? Can your unrealistic but well-worn expectations be changed or eliminated once and for all?

Transforming Your Expectations

Because unmet expectations fuel anger, discarding or revising those that are unrealistic reduces the odds that your anger will be triggered. It is kind of like removing old cans of gasoline from your garage to reduce risk. You can clean out your garage in an afternoon, but how do you successfully alter expectations you may have spent a lifetime learning?

First, identify expectations that are frequently unmet and associated with your anger. Examine the situations that have triggered your anger over the last few months. If you have a hard time remembering, take a few weeks to record anger episodes using the Daily Anger Log as found in Appendix 2.

Who or what is the object of your anger? Examine what happened that you blamed for your anger. What were you expecting that failed to occur? For ideas, you might look over the sidebar about expectations. In every case you will reveal an expectation if you fill in the blank in this sentence:

"I/He/She/They/It should have _____."

Your "should" will reflect an unstated expectation. Does this expectation apply to just one person or situation, or would it apply to others, making it more general and worth changing?

From what you've learned in this chapter and the following two questions, is this expectation unrealistic and therefore unnecessarily triggering your anger?

1. Based on your past experience with yourself, the other person, or a thing, how often has this expectation been met up until the present? If rarely or never, the expectation, even if reflecting lofty ideals, is unrealistic. Past experience is the best predictor of future outcomes.

Expectations That Trigger Anger	
Expectations	Your anger is triggered when:
Expectations for yourself	
➤ Physical endurance and performance	➤ You can't physically carry out a task or sport as smoothly or as competently as you expect.
➤ Intellectual and task pursuits	➤ You don't meet high standards on tasks and don't receive the grade or result you expected.
➤ Time and speed	➤ Things are not done quickly enough, you don't arrive on time, or others are late.
➤ Success and failure	➤ You set high goals that are not achieved as well as you expected, always trying to achieve more.
Expectations for others	
➤ Manners and social etiquette	➤ From your perspective, others act in a discourteous, ill-mannered, ungrateful, or disgusting fashion.
➤ Affirmation and intimacy	➤ You are not loved, nurtured, or paid attention to in a way you expect by someone who matters.
➤ Equity and fairness	➤ Others are unfair, fail to acknowledge your contribution, receive an unearned reward, or fail to reciprocate a good deed you've done for them.

Expectations	Your anger is triggered when:
➤ Intrusion and annoyance	➤ Others make noise, interrupt you, or somehow intrude on your thoughts or activity.
➤ Aggression and abuse	➤ Another person uses unwanted verbal or physical actions that are threatening or even dangerous.

Expectations for things in the world

➤ How devices, electronics, and machines should work	➤ Electronic devices/machines or your car breaks down or fails to deliver as promised.
➤ How things should be organized	➤ Highways, government agencies, your place of work, or your home is not run "right" and seems too disorganized to suit you.
➤ How activities should unfold	➤ Travel is delayed, or events do not go as planned. Traffic, construction, or an accident blocks you from getting someplace quickly.
➤ Weather and environment	➤ Just when you planned on an outdoor activity or trip, the weather turns bad and spoils it.

2. Is the desired behavior relevant or important to the person from whom you expect it, and/or have you clearly communicated what you expect with a polite request? If not, your expectation is unrealistic and unlikely to be realized.

Mary said about her husband:

"I haven't spoken to him in days and often find myself cold to him when I'm mad. This time I got angry when he interrupted me again in front of our friends. I go to tell a story about our trip, and he corrects me and then ends up telling it. What was I expecting? Well, he should have been respectful enough of me to give me an opportunity to speak without taking over, interrupting. [Violates her expectations regarding courtesy and manners.] As to how often he lets me finish? Almost never. But I guess I've never clearly told him just how important it is that he stop this behavior. I always thought that if he really cared about me he would just know how I feel. I shouldn't have to tell him." [Mary's expectation, while a social ideal, is unrealistic because she hasn't clearly communicated it to her husband or gotten his agreement to work on changing his behavior. Until she does, a realistic expectation is that he will interrupt her again in the future.]

Previewing and Planning

Based on the facts as you know them from past experience with yourself, the other person, or the thing that irritates you, "preview" an expectation that is most likely to be fulfilled, whether it agrees with your heartfelt beliefs or not. Remember, others don't necessarily share your ideals and values.

As you prepare for an encounter with an old trigger, take a few minutes to *preview* by stating the new, realistic expectation to yourself. Now develop a *plan*: specifically how you will react when this expected behavior or event occurs. Try to think of some ideas to help you cope:

> *Preview*: "Given that I'm leaving at peak rush hour, it will likely be stop-and-go."
>
> *Plan*: "I'll catch up on the news or listen to that book on tape I've been meaning to get to."
>
> *Preview*: "Since we're going to discuss raises for the upcoming year and the company is not doing well, I guess I better prepare myself for a small increase."
>
> *Plan*: "I don't like it, but let me think about some other perk or accommodation I could ask for that might fly with my boss."
>
> *Preview*: "Heather has been 15 minutes late for most things the

whole time we've been together. She will likely be late, and so what? It's just not worth getting into the old argument."

Plan: "I will let her know one time when we need to leave, then check my e-mail or get some correspondence done while I wait. There are certainly things about me she puts up with."

In each of these cases the person gets prepared for what is *likely* to happen by previewing the fact-based likely outcome; this realistic expectation then leads to problem-solving a plan for coping. When the expected outcome occurs, this person can think, "Here it is. I've expected this and am prepared for it."

You might also find imagery useful, vividly picturing in your mind the situation as it is expected to unfold, including how you will handle it differently than in the past (e.g., picturing yourself in the likely congested traffic, listening to the radio or an audio book you've brought along, just in case). This rehearsal in your imagination implants an inner map to guide your behavior when the situation actually arises.

When an unwanted event catches you by surprise, as is often the case, it helps to identify your expectations as soon as you realize you're becoming angry. Very often you'll find you can surface a "should" that reveals an unrealistic expectation that is getting to you.

Let's say your car won't start on a cold morning: "I can't believe this **!*!! car has never been right. I'm so angry I can't stand it. I'll never get to the office! [Anger welling up.] *Wait a minute–what am I expecting?* This car should always run, even in the coldest weather, and the battery should last forever? This isn't the end of the world. Let me figure this out. ... I'll call AAA and let them deal with it. In the meantime I'll call the office and let them know I'll be late. It's just not worth getting so upset over."

Whether evoked suddenly or building slowly, you will not understand and effectively manage your anger until you bring

> **"Are you saying I should lower my standards?"**
>
> Ideals and expectations are different. Ideals reflect how things *should be*, based on your personal standards, your beliefs and values. A realistic expectation prepares you for what is *likely to happen*. What is most likely is what has happened before. Don't lower your *personal* standards, but adopt realistic ones for others.

your expectations to the surface and, if necessary, revise them. In any case, you must recognize that your anger has been triggered so that you can intervene before an unhelpful face of anger is expressed. Chapter 4 will help you learn the specific skill we'll call "anger awareness."

Just for Practice

Look over the sidebar "Expectations That Trigger Anger" to reflect on your own expectations that may be setting the stage for your anger. Ask yourself these questions:

> ➤ When was the last time you were really angry or intensely frustrated with yourself? What task or activity were you engaged in? As you think back, were your expectations for yourself realistic, based on your past actual experience with the activity? Can you think of more realistic personal expectations if you were about to pursue the same task right now?

> ➤ Who have you been angry with in the recent past? For each situation you can recall, ask yourself what the other person did or said that triggered your anger. Ask yourself what the other person "should" have said or done that would have halted your anger.

>   • Is this "should" (expectation) realistic, based on how this person has acted in the past? Remember: a reasonable expectation is what he or she actually did the last time in a similar situation, not what you think the person ideally should have done.

>   • If you were in each of these situations now, preview a more realistic expectation. If you really want the other person to meet your idealistic *should*s, can you think of a plan to positively influence this person to change, keeping in mind you are powerless over everyone but yourself? Chapter 8 will offer lots of ideas for communicating what you need effectively.

> ➤ Can you recall the last time you kind of "lost it" with a thing, like a car, computer, or other device that seemed "stupidly made," defective, or out to get you (e.g., "It let me down just when I needed it most")? Or a time you got angry when the environ-

ment "failed" you (e.g., the weather caused you to be late to an event or a vacation week was "ruined" by cold temperatures)? While it may seem foolish in hindsight to have gotten so aggravated at such things, reevaluating these episodes may help you revise your approach in the future.

- What happened and how did you react? What was your implicit expectation, the "should" that was not stated but was beneath the surface of your emotional reaction? Try to identify it by completing the following sentence: "This [what happened] should never have happened because I believe that [your belief about how the thing or situation should have worked]."

- Is your expectation realistic (e.g., if you just bought a television, you expect it to work) or unrealistic, based on past experience in the world as it is (e.g., after owning a computer for two years you are appalled when it breaks down, or you can't believe a summer storm delayed your trip)?

- If this sad event were to occur in the next five minutes, what realistic expectation could you state in your mind, and how would you plan to cope with the situation differently?

Step Three

Pinpointing Your Anger Early On and Dampening Arousal

ONCE YOU'RE AWARE THAT YOUR ANGER HAS BEEN TRIGGERED, it's critical to take steps to reduce your anger arousal before it escalates to a level where calm thinking and acting are difficult. Chapter 4 teaches you to be aware of the earliest physical signs that you're getting angry so that you can catch yourself before it's too late. Chapter 5 instructs you in ways that will then quickly reduce body tension and relax your mind so that you can calmly make decisions.

4

Anger Awareness

Once I get really angry I can't seem to control what I say. It's like another person takes over and I say things that really hurt."

"Why is it that I repeat the same old mistakes when I'm really upset? I know that withdrawing and being spiteful is totally unhelpful, but I do it anyway."

Most people are not cognizant of having any real control over their anger. The face of anger that gets them into trouble seems to occur with little warning, as if happening *to* them. Now that you've read Chapter 3, you know that anger doesn't really make sneak attacks; it arises when your expectations are unmet. You also know that you can reduce the frequency of anger episodes by transforming unrealistic expectations into more realistic ones. But all of us tend to retain some unrealistic expectations, and we can expect anger to flare when these expectations are unmet. We can also expect anger to flare sometimes when perfectly reasonable expectations are not met. In either type of situation the trick is to recognize that anger is starting to rear its head so that you can control it before it controls you.

In this chapter I'll show you how to spot the early warning signs of anger, a prerequisite to dampening the flames before it's too late. I'll also show you some factors that can greatly intensify the level and quality of anger expressed but that you may not connect directly with your anger because they occur during the hours and even days before your anger erupts, not directly beforehand.

Remember the physical sensations of anger arousal listed in Chapter 2? When anger escalates, we're flooded with these feelings at the same time that our senses are becoming magnified, making clear thinking and emotional control much more difficult. At some point we reach what I call the "danger zone," a level of fight-or-flight arousal where resilience, our ability to adapt to challenging events, is at its lowest ebb. At this point the unforeseen unmet expectation can trigger an intense reaction because our coping resources are depleted. When resilience is low, we're less able to "inhibit" our inner impulses in favor of calm reasoning.

Being aware of your level of arousal as you seek to modify or eliminate anger intensifiers is at the heart of managing your anger. These points can be summarized in two goals that are critical for anger management:

1. Taking steps to eliminate or modify anger intensifiers helps you remain at a low level of anger arousal so you can cope better when a triggering event occurs.

2. Learning to be aware of the physical sensations of increasing anger arousal permits you to address your anger at a low level, when you can still cope calmly and thoughtfully.

Eliminating Anger Intensifiers to Increase Resilience

Sleep, stress, substances, diet, and overall health will all affect your resilience, both on any given day and over the long term. You might be particularly quick to anger following a sleepless night, or your resilience level could be chronically low due to poor sleep habits in general. Being under especially great stress at any one time depletes the resources you can devote to calm problem solving, and ongoing high-stress levels can have far-reaching effects on your health and well-being. Overuse of substances like alcohol and caffeine can put stress on the body, as can poor dietary habits. But you also need to be alert to the fact that too many cocktails could spur an unnecessary fight with your spouse that evening, too much coffee one morning can rob you of the patience you need for a midday meeting, and skipping a single lunch can leave you too depleted to remain alert to anger that has been triggered in you. Because change can take time, I urge you to examine these elements in your life right away. Following is a summary of the effects these factors can have on your resilience, as well as some suggestions for recognizing a problem with anger intensifiers and how to resolve it. Each anger intensifier begins with an "S," making them easy to remember.

The Five S's

Sleep

Getting sufficient sleep restores our ability to think clearly and respond calmly. Sleep deprivation tends to make people more irritable and less resilient. Research indicates that the average adult needs just over eight hours of sleep to perform well, while teens and kids need much more. Lack of exercise, an inconsistent sleep schedule, unresolved stress, certain medications, overuse of alcohol, medical problems like sleep apnea, and poor sleep habits (e.g., too much light in the room) are among factors that can interfere with a good night's sleep.

Stress

The pioneering work of Dr. Hans Selye introduced the term *stress* to describe the body's physical reaction, the "fight-or-flight" response, as it adapts to change and stimuli like noise and crowding. At high-stress levels you are likely to be more irritable and less resilient. Too many tasks, unrealistic deadlines, any significant life change (including "good" events like vacations and moving to a new home), uncertainty, worry, and a low sense of control increase stress, pushing you closer to the danger zone when an unforeseen trigger occurs.

Substances

Alcohol, caffeine, and other substances we ingest can dramatically intensify our emotions. Unlike the popular wisdom, alcohol doesn't reliably make you feel happy and relaxed. If you're already some-what irritated, sad, or anxious, alcohol will likely intensify your feelings because it depresses centers in your brain that ordinarily permit you to control (inhibit) your emotions. In fact, research shows that in fully three-fourths of couple violence one or both partners has been drinking alcohol. Caffeine increases your tension level and can escalate irritation and stress. Some drugs purchased over the counter (cold remedies, for example) can boost tension, so it is important to check for side effects. Many illegal drugs either reduce your ability to think clearly, boost your emotions, or are specifically linked to aggression (e.g., cocaine).

Sustenance

Adequate and proper nutrition is necessary to maintain resilience and lower emotional intensity. When you skip meals like breakfast or lunch, your blood sugar level plummets, increasing your level of irritability and fatigue and reducing your ability to think clearly. Many nutritionists believe that too much sugar or junk food may increase the likelihood of mood swings that can affect your ability to cope consistently with the next trigger that arises. Eating well-balanced meals and ensuring you are getting necessary vitamins and minerals boosts your resilience so you can cope with whatever comes along.

Sickness

When we are ill or coping with pain, our resilience is reduced. Having a headache, stomach upset, or the aches and pains of a bad cold or flu focuses our inner resources on getting well, leaving little extra energy to cope with aggravating events. Some of us have chronic painful or debilitating conditions (e.g., low back pain, fibrositis, migraine headaches) that may tax our coping resources and distract us from being able to focus fully on important aspects of a triggering situation. Pain and discomfort increase our arousal, can create irritability, and generally reduce our ability to think clearly. Also, our mood can affect how we react.

An Ounce of Prevention . . .

Removing anger intensifiers is like removing all combustible materials from in front of an open fireplace. You can never tell when a spark will be catapulted into the room, so why take any chances? Todd came to anger counseling following a "blowup" that frightened his wife and young son and left Todd ashamed and confused. Arriving home after a "stressful" day in his public relations job, he found "toys strewn about the floor," dinner not yet prepared, and his wife, Sandra, playing on the floor with their four-year-old son. "Appalled" at Sandra's "disorga-

---

A Word about Anger and Mood

Two forms of mood disorders can lead to irritability and in some cases contribute to full-blown anger. If you or others have noticed that over the past two weeks you are sad, feel hopeless about your life, do not enjoy the things that used to energize you, are avoiding people, are distractible, notice appetite changes, have serious problems sleeping, or have thoughts of suicide, you may be suffering from clinical depression.

If you or others notice you've been feeling remarkably "up" or "high," stay up late and can't sleep because you're so filled with energy, talk rapidly or in a pressured manner, seem to have one idea after another that you can barely keep track of or have been engaging in risk-taking behaviors (e.g., gambling, risky business deals, substance abuse), you may be experiencing bipolar disorder.

In either case, you should see a health professional to further evaluate these symptoms and perhaps propose a program of treatment. It will be hard for you to manage your anger successfully if your underlying mood is not addressed. See Suggested Resources for ideas to better address mood issues.

---

nization," he lost it, screaming at her and at one point shaking her by the shoulders "to get my point across." As his son cried in fear at Todd's sudden explosion, Sandra quickly took the child to a neighbor's home. Apologizing to his wife was not sufficient; she demanded he get some help because his anger was "totally unacceptable."

We began by discussing what happened that day, from when Todd got up in the morning until just before he lost it. It soon became clear that the strewn toys and lack of dinner were merely the immediate triggers, unmet expectations that provided the spark for his loss of control. As is often the case, a number of anger intensifiers had contributed to Todd's rising anger and lack of resilience by the time he finally arrived home.

Sleep

Up late the night before, preparing for an important presentation at work, Todd had gotten only five hours of sleep, which left him "kind of irritable and exhausted" as the day began. He told me he rarely got more than six hours of sleep and often less.

How about you? If you have any doubt about whether you typically get enough sleep, record the times you went to sleep and woke up for a week or two. Also jot down any times you were aware of waking up in the middle of the night. If you're getting less than eight solid hours of sleep on a regular basis, investigate the factors mentioned above that can interfere with sleep. Try to slowly move your bedtime earlier, say by 15 minutes each week, to gradually reset your sleep "clock" to a regular bedtime and awakening time. If sleep continues to be a problem, consider discussing diagnostic and treatment options with your physician. Many sleep problems can be helped by ideas found in the Suggested Resources.

Stress

Todd's day was very stressful. He arrived at the office late, still irritated at the traffic backup on the expressway. Todd was faced with "too many accounts" to manage, yet was being pressured to take on more. Just keeping up with phone calls and e-mails was overwhelming, and every day felt like a juggling act as he tried to balance these demands. Too many tasks (adaptations) and too little control over his schedule had greatly increased Todd's stress level.

He admitted his blowup with Sandra was not his first anger episode that day. A "critically important" PowerPoint slide presentation had been marred by equipment malfunction, which Todd blamed on a technical subordinate who had left for the day. Immediately "overcome" with rage, Todd had to "stuff" his anger and ended up with a severe headache by midafternoon.

Stress gives rise to so many different symptoms that it would be difficult to diagnose your stress level based on the answers to a few simple questions. But if you often feel overwhelmed, nervous, anxious, or behind schedule, there is a good chance you're under too much stress. At the very least, list the obligations you feel you're faced with on a regular basis and then try to prioritize them. Are there any you can drop altogether, delegating them to someone else or just leaving them undone? Can you try to leave yourself some true downtime—time to relax and read a diverting book, take the dog for a peaceful walk in the woods, or whatever calms and refreshes you—every day, even if it's just a few minutes? If you need more help than these simple measures, consider taking a stress management workshop or seeking a therapist who specializes in stress treatment and look over ideas found in the Suggested Resources.

Substances

Using coffee as a misdirected way to cope with his stress, Todd consumed at least six cups prior to his drive home. He often felt "wired" but had never associated his increased tension with caffeine.

Take an honest look at how much caffeine you consume (don't forget caffeinated sodas as well as coffee and tea) every day, how much alcohol you drink, how many cigarettes you smoke, and any illegal substances that you indulge in. Though they may seem to do something positive for you at the time, there's a price to be paid in resilience later. If alcohol is becoming a problem, it is wise to see a specialist or clinic for an evaluation to determine what level of treatment, if any, would most help you. The Suggested Resources offer recommendations for learning more about the impact of alcohol.

Sustenance

Rushing to complete the outline for his presentation, Todd had skipped lunch, relying on the coffee and sweet roll he had for breakfast to sustain him. He often either skipped lunch or ate at his desk, trying to keep up with work as he "wolfed down" his food.

Your body needs regular fueling so that your energy doesn't

Rule of Thumb:
When Is Alcohol a Problem?

When it begins to create problems with others, with your health, or with your efficiency at work, no matter how much you consume. Even if you and your partner have only two glasses of wine or a few beers and you find arguments tend to occur more or only when drinking, either give up the alcohol completely or try to set a rule/boundary: no personal or inflammatory discussions when drinking. If you find your partner violating this, call a time-out using a "stop" phrase, explained toward the end of this chapter.

become depleted. Too many of us today gulp down a cup of coffee for breakfast, skip lunch, and then are exhausted by late afternoon. Even if it's minimal, be sure you refuel regularly throughout the day so you don't suddenly find your resilience on "empty" when you need it.

Sickness

While not ill at the time of his blowup, Todd reported that he usually felt more irritable when he was sick with a cold or flu. Having a chronic low back problem, he often found himself impatient with others when his pain levels flared up.

If you have chronic health problems, you're already at a resilience disadvantage. You should be extra-alert to anger triggers when you have a cold or flu. If chronic muscle pain or headache is the problem, consider discussing with your physician a referral to a pain management specialist. If a mood disorder is present, seek professional guidance.

By the time he arrived home, Todd was clearly poised for the blowup he now regretted, having made choices earlier in the day that intensified his anger arousal while lowering his resilience. Todd and I made a commitment to help him get better sleep and to reduce stress by reorganizing his day. He met with his supervisor, who agreed to eliminate two of Todd's most stressful accounts and to provide him with additional administrative support. Todd agreed to spend at least 45 minutes eating lunch away from the office and to reduce his caffeine intake drastically by mixing decaf coffee with his regular blend.

But we were still faced with a dilemma. Like most people I know, Todd was just not good at noticing his escalation from tension and irritation to full-blown anger. He was great at recognizing when he was "furious," but that was often too late for calm thinking to prevail. We decided to focus on *anger scaling*, linking the early signals of rising tension and irritation (the first feelings of anger) to new actions that would reduce anger arousal early on.

Creating a Personal Anger Scale

If you're like most people, you can't recall off the top of your head what body change occurred first, second, and so on the last time you got angry. You just know you got angry. But when and how did it begin? By examining the prelude to your anger in closer detail, you can construct an anger scale that reflects your personal pattern of anger arousal. This sequence of body changes as anger escalates is different for each person, but it always includes one or more of the symptoms of "fight-or-flight" anger arousal shown on page 36.

I asked Todd to describe the physical sensations he experienced at each significant (clearly noticeable) increment in his anger. Then each numbered stage was linked to "desired behaviors" Todd would initiate when his anger reached that point in the future.

Following is Todd's anger scale, which uses the numbers 0–100 to identify each stage of Todd's anger arousal, as an example.

Use the following steps to scale your anger, as Todd and I did for his. First, review your Daily Anger Log (Appendix 2) to reveal anger sensations you recorded as you got angry over the past few weeks. Keep these in mind as you also do the following: [Note: A blank Personal Anger Scale that can be copied may be found in Appendix 3.]

1. *Start by focusing on a state of complete relaxation.* I asked Todd to close his eyes and take a few minutes to lean back and get relaxed, imagining himself in a place where he felt completely at peace.

"Let's see," Todd started. "I can't think of much relaxation lately, but I do know the most relaxed and safe I can remember feeling is when we lived with my grandmother when I was in high school. I can picture her backyard and sitting out there in the summer evenings just talking to her. She would always have iced tea for me. I can still see the lightning bugs around us as it got dark. I loved her house."

While Todd reacted emotionally just by imaging a scene vividly, you may have difficulty recapturing this relaxed state the same way. If so, I suggest you use one of the dampening strategies found in Chapter 5 to get as relaxed as possible so you can experience exactly how your body feels.

Then I asked Todd to focus on how he was feeling physically, considering the parts of his body from head to toes, paying particular attention to his face, shoulders and neck, chest, breathing, and stomach.

"My face feels cool," Todd said, "and I can't feel any tension in any part of my body. My breathing is slow and relaxed. My head doesn't hurt, unlike the past week. I just feel kind of light and free of tension. It feels great to recall that time. My mind is free of any thoughts other than enjoying the moment."

Todd's Personal Anger Scale: An Example

Ratings	Physical sensations	Desired behaviors
0–20	Muscles relaxed, face feels cool, and my breathing is slow and easy.	I need to stay aware of my body and my thinking.
21–40	I'm beginning to notice shoulder tension and can feel a headache starting.	I will manage my tension by sitting down, loosening my muscles, and taking some deep relaxation breaths.
41–60	My face feels hot, and my shoulders are really tense. My head is pounding, and breathing is more rapid.	I will cope by [Todd lists two or three anger management ideas to be found in the later chapters of this book]. If I hit a "50," I will leave the situation.
61–80	I'm standing up and pacing. My fists are clenched, and all the previous sensations are really intensified.	I will tell the other person this "feels intense" and leave the situation [a "time out"] until I return to a "40" or below.
81–100	I find myself moving closer and in the other person's face, shouting and cursing. My face feels "on fire," and my chest is pounding.	I should be gone.

We then filled in "0–20" on the blank scale using what we had learned.

    2. *Now select a recent occasion when you ended up really angry*, using your Daily Anger Log for examples. Use your log to recall your physical sensations. In addition, you can use imagery to reconstruct your physi-

cal reactions to a recent anger episode. Pick a recent episode. When you have a scene in mind, begin by imagining it vividly, trying to "see" and "hear" in your mind's eye the events that led up to the peak of your anger. You will focus on the physical sensations you notice first and at each noticeable increment in your anger arousal as the prelude to your anger unfolds.

Because Todd's blowup was fresh in his mind, I asked him to begin by imagining the *first signs of irritation* that occurred the day of his blowup, the first changes in how his body felt. Rather than beginning with the blowup, where his anger was at its peak, I asked him to focus his attention on his anger arousal during the prelude, from the point when he first noticed feelings of tension or irritation. I told him if he really got into imagining the scene he might feel body sensations similar to those he felt in the actual situation. Or he could just recall how he felt.

"Well, I guess I was kind of tense when I got up that day," Todd recalled. "I hadn't slept well and woke up with a headache. As I get into it, my muscles were kind of tense across my shoulders. I can picture myself rubbing my shoulders like I sometimes do to loosen the tension. I began thinking about all the things I had to do at work that day." As Todd elaborated on how he felt as he imagined the scene, we filled in "21–40" on the blank scale.

3. *Imagine the next significant increments in your level of anger arousal as you fill in each of the succeeding stages of the scale, ending with your anger at its peak.* Todd continued focusing on his day as his irritation built, noting the body sensations present at each escalation of his anger: "Things only got tenser when I got to the office. I'm picturing seeing my desk full of unfinished work and a million Post-It notes about calls I need to make. My technician comes in to discuss my upcoming presentation and doesn't seem prepared but minimizes any problems. My face is feeling hot, and my head is really beginning to pound." Todd then described the other physical sensations recorded under "41–60."

I then asked him to continue recalling his day, focusing on what happened next to significantly increase his anger and on how his body felt. "We get to the presentation room," he said, "and it becomes clear to me the damned projector isn't working right. We've based the whole thing on the slides, and I am really furious. My heart is really beginning to pound, and my face is really hot. I just left as soon as the presentation was over and sat in my office." The physical sensations Todd continued to describe were entered under "61–80" on his scale.

Then we focused on the peak of his anger, just before and during the blowup: "Well, I just sat there for a while, thinking how angry I was at Debu [the technician] for letting me down. I drove home in awful traffic and walked through the door, only to find nothing was done, dinner not ready, and Sandra just looking at me. I just lost it. My face felt on fire, and I was standing and shouting at Sandra about what she hadn't gotten done: How could she be playing when dinner should have been ready? What did she do all day? Stuff like that. My thoughts were just racing with these kinds of things as I yelled. I hardly remember grabbing Sandra by the shoulders, but I know I did."

These physical sensations, entered on his scale at "81–100," occurred as Todd clearly entered the danger zone of intense arousal that made clear thinking impossible.

Linking Anger to New Actions

Todd's anger scale shows new, desired behaviors we agreed upon linked to each stage of his escalating anger. If he notices shoulder tension and the beginnings of a headache ("21–40"), this is his first signal to reduce his arousal, using various techniques described in full in the next chapter—sitting down, calming his breathing, noticing his tension, and so on. By intervening at this first anger sign, he asserts control over his anger. Now he can calmly consider what he is expecting (is it realistic and practical?) and take time to problem-solve the situation using the ideas in the remaining chapters. Meanwhile, he can also try to eliminate any anger intensifiers he's identified, taking steps to reduce a stressor, taking a break to eat lunch, and so forth.

If Todd fails to intervene and finds himself at the next level of anger (41–60: head pounding, face really hot, breathing faster), he must immediately take steps to curtail his tension. If he reaches a 50 or greater, I recommended that he immediately leave the situation, if at all possible, so that cool thinking could direct his actions.

Calling a Time-Out

Many people I've worked with have wished, in hindsight, that they had just stopped responding before saying or doing something they later regretted. But how do you just stop responding and leave when others want to continue a heated discussion without insulting them or making things worse?

I recommend using a *stop phrase* that gently defuses the situation, permitting everyone to save face:

> "This is important, but I need some time to think about it."

> "This feels intense for me. I need to take a break to think it through."

With your partner or family members, you can agree on a prearranged stop phrase like "I need a *break*" or "I need to *chill*." All agree in advance that the "time out" will be honored, and under no circumstances should the "stopping" party be followed or in any way intimidated into continuing discussion while anger is flaring. It may help to agree on a place in the house where each can go to be alone for at least 30 minutes to dampen anger and rethink the situation before discussion resumes on a calmer note.

You can communicate this without labeling or putting down the other person, thereby defusing the tension. Compare the possible impact of these two approaches.

> *Be creative: Design your own format for scaling.* The format of the scale is optional, as long as it links increasing stages of anger arousal to new anger actions. Many of my clients use the image of an "anger thermometer," visualizing the mercury rising from 0 to 100. Or you might use colors to designate your level of arousal from cool blue or green for the "relaxed" end of the scale to hot red at the top of your scale. Any other medium is fine as long as you find it easy to recall and to associate with various levels of anger intensity.

Threatening approach: "You are obviously too angry to discuss this now," or "this isn't getting us anywhere because you are shouting."

Conflict-defusing approach: "I need to take a time out to collect my thoughts. I'll be back to discuss this [describe when]. Thanks for understanding."

When you cannot physically leave a triggering situation, you can stop verbally reacting and learn to "go inside" for a while to regain control. Todd, for example, could not just leave when he was playing a central role in a business meeting. While others were talking, he learned to sit down, lean back, loosen his muscles, and employ relaxation breathing, while repeating a calming thought tied to each breath as described in Chapter 5. Just knowing he was approaching the "danger zone" was immensely helpful in directing what he did next. A formula for halting anger arousal called "STOP" will tie this together in Chapter 7.

What Goes Up Can Come Down: Managing Your Anger Arousal

Anger scaling not only provides you with physical data that signal when your anger is escalating but also gives you a goal: trying to reduce your tension so that your body feels more like what is described for the next step down on your scale. While seeking the relaxed body state described for "0–20" is an ideal, any time you can slow down your arousal and reduce your anger tension to the next lower level, you have essentially derailed your old anger pattern and regained some measure of control. The farther down the scale you can go, the better.

One final note. At first you may not be able to quickly recall your anger scale when you're in a triggering situation and your anger is escalating. No matter where you are on your scale when you remember to say to yourself, "Wait a minute—I'm getting angry; what level am I at?" it isn't too late to take steps to dampen your arousal. Often you'll catch yourself when you've already advanced into the danger zone, but you'll still have time to use a stop phrase and get out of the situation so cool thinking can prevail. The more you practice using your scale, the more quickly you are likely to remember to pause and reflect on your anger level. Chapter 10 offers numerous ideas for making anger scaling a new "habit."

No matter where and when you catch your arousal escalating, you must learn to immediately "dampen" your fight-or-flight arousal to the next lower or better level. Chapter 5 offers enough ideas for reducing your arousal that you are likely to find one that feels right for you.

5

Dampening Anger Arousal

"Just relax."

"Calm down."

"Chill out!"

Very few phrases have an effect that's so far opposite what was desired. If you've ever been told to relax, calm down, or chill when you were angry—or, for that matter, worried or aroused in some other way—you know that at the very least such directives have no effect on your arousal at all. In fact, they often make things worse. That's because trying to shift into a tranquil gear once you've been aroused is extremely difficult to do; it goes against every physiological response you were armed with at birth. Being treated as if you should be able to stop being furious at the snap of someone's fingers is only infuriating.

In this chapter I'll give you a choice of methods for dampening your arousal and returning to a calm, rational state once you've spotted the signs that your anger has been triggered and is escalating out of your control. Not everything works for everyone, so you may have to experiment. It's important that you be able to put your relaxation technique into action quickly and somewhat automatically. Not only do different measures work for different people, but they may work in different situations, so consider making more than one your own.

Sasha couldn't believe how often her anger escalated into high numbers on her anger scale. An employee she supervised had filed a complaint, alleging that Sasha was "too intense, impatient, and sarcastic." This was not the first employee who had complained; some had even asked to be transferred to another supervisor, an embarrassment to Sasha and a stain on her otherwise outstanding record. Her anger was triggered by high expectations for others to perform "with just as much commitment as I have." She was often angry and disappointed when her staff would not remain after hours or took sick leave. After all, she never balked at a "full day's work."

Sasha's first noticeable body sensation (at 21–40 on her scale) was muscle tension in her shoulders and neck. When she noticed this early anger signal, we agreed she needed to immediately dampen her arousal in ways that were practical and quickly effective. Also, we decided to address anger intensifiers by reducing her stress, curtailing caffeine use, and taking short breaks to practice relaxation at her desk. Of course, we also reviewed a stop phrase she would use to leave the situation if her anger arousal rose to a 50 or above. We began with the first and most crucial step for dampening arousal: control of breathing.

The Breath of Life: Diaphragmatic Breathing to Manage Arousal

Virtually every relaxation technique or meditation regimen reviewed by Dr. Herbert Benson in his pioneering book *The Relaxation Response* focuses on breathing as the foundation for dampening arousal. If you've ever participated in Lamaze training or practiced yoga or meditation, you already know the power of breathing to regulate your internal state. How does breathing affect arousal?

> ➤ As your brain "listens" to your self-talk and perceives a threat, stress chemicals are released and your breathing rate increases. This is because your brain signals your lungs and diaphragm to send more oxygen out to your muscles and up to your brain so you can "fight or flee."

> ➤ While breathing is involuntary and controlled by a part of your brain stem (just try not to breathe and see what happens), breathing is also under voluntary control, unlike your heart, blood vessels, or gastrointestinal system. By trying to slow your breathing rate to simulate how you breathe in deep sleep (slow

and rhythmic), you signal your brain to bring the rest of your physiology in line with your relaxed breathing pattern.

> ➤ This kind of breathing involves loosening the muscles of your stomach so that your lungs are free to fully expand into the abdominal cavity, permitting a truly deep breath. You breathe like an opera singer, deep and from the diaphragm, which is called "diaphragmatic breathing." You will immediately experience a reduction in "fight-or-flight" arousal, lowering the intensity of your building anger.

I've developed a method for this deep breathing that you will learn to link to your first signal that anger is escalating. This change in your breathing, which I call "signal breathing," not only immediately dampens your arousal to the next lower level on your anger scale but is also useful for managing daily stress, an anger intensifier.

Sasha was skeptical when I said I was going to teach her to relax using "signal breathing." How would she find time in her busy schedule to do anything more? I reassured her that once she learned the method, it would take no more than a few minutes, two or three times each hour and whenever she noticed her first signal of anger. I asked her to practice each day for about two weeks. She decided to practice in the evening to help her unwind. The idea was to get her to achieve a deep state of relaxation at home using a more extended relaxation breathing exercise. Then the signal breath would become the key to unlocking what she had learned at home when she needed it most, at the office and in other stressful places. Here is the method we used.

Signal Breathing

Breathing Diaphragmatically

Loosen your clothing and sit or lie down so that all of your muscles are fully supported by the chair or cushion beneath you. Place your hands on your stomach, just below your rib cage. Now loosen your stomach muscles and let your lungs expand into the abdominal area, noticing that your hands are moving outward as you take a full breath. Just practice doing that for a few minutes, taking regular full breaths.

Many of us are so used to breathing shallowly that this new sequence of actions is hard to follow. If you're having any trouble, practice at home as Sasha did and place a magazine on your stomach as you lie on your back. As you inhale, watch the magazine rise. When you lie down on your back your breathing automatically reverts to diaphragmatic, so it is a good way to get the feel of it.

The Signal Breath

Now take a diaphragmatic breath that is very full, letting your stomach expand without unduly raising your shoulders. Hold the breath momentarily and then, as you very slowly count down in your mind from ten to one, let the breath go slowly through your slightly pursed lips. You control the exhalation by letting the air escape very slowly. If you exhale quickly with your mouth open, you will accomplish very little. The key is to exhale over a minimum of about 15 seconds at first (worth timing when you begin), gradually increasing to 20 or more seconds as long as it's comfortable. As you let go of your breath, feel the tension inside letting go as you focus on leaning back and:

> ➤ Smoothing your forehead.

> ➤ Loosening your jaw.

> ➤ Dropping your shoulders (let them naturally drop down as much as possible).

> ➤ Letting your arms go limp.

It's important to practice signal breathing every day, making an effort to sit down, lean back, and loosen your muscles. When the body sensations of rising anger (above 30 on your anger scale) signal the need to dampen your arousal, *always begin by sitting down* (this is usually, but not always, possible). When you are seated (or lying down), proprioceptive sensors within your body signal this more relaxed position to your brain, and you immediately begin to relax. You can no doubt recall times you sat in a comfortable chair or lay down and started to feel sleepy, even though you had been alert minutes before. Conversely, standing up and moving about signals your brain to sustain or even increase your current level of arousal. Also, you are much less likely to "lose it" with aggression when seated, and the other person is likely to be less threatened by your actions, defusing the situation. Next take one or two deep signal breaths every 20 minutes or so. If this sounds like a chore, remember, you have to breathe anyway; I'm just asking you to change *how* you breathe. Many clients have told me it's easy to do this if they can just remember to do it.

Sasha and many of my other clients have found the Premack Principle helped them remember to do the exercise by linking this new behavior to an existing action that occurs often. Because Sasha talked on the phone often, we agreed that she would take a deep signal breath and lean back as well as she could every time she was about to make a phone call. The telephone now became a signal for her to dampen her arousal. As a reminder to take her breath, she taped a picture of her and her husband on the beach at Maui, a place in Hawaii she associated with relaxation (one of the few relaxing holidays she could recall). It worked. She found herself leaning back and trying to remain relaxed at other times as well. Now her desk was becoming associated with her newfound goal of slowing down and adopting a more relaxed pace. With each call that used to stress her out, we now inserted a moment to refresh and relax.

Tensing Your Muscles to Relax: A Paradox That Works

Your muscles prepare to "fight or flee" by tensing, poised for action, when you're stressed or angry. Ahead of his time, Dr. Edmund Jacobson, a physiologist in the 1920s, discovered that a deep relaxation response could be achieved by teaching patients to discriminate between tension and relaxation. His approach was very simple. The patient was instructed to tense a series of muscle groups for 10 to 12 seconds each, typically beginning with the hands and fingers and concentrating on how the muscles felt. Upon releasing the tension, the patient focused on the internal sensations associated with relaxation.

Various techniques for progressive muscle relaxation have been developed over the years, often coupled with diaphragmatic breathing, relaxing self-talk/instructions, and imagery. This one is simple to learn and has been very effective for my clients.

Progressive Muscle Relaxation

Your goal is to notice the difference in how each muscle feels as you compare tension with a loosening of the muscle. You tense each muscle group for 10 to 15 seconds, to a point where you can feel the muscle quiver. Try this right now by making a fist that's tight enough that your hand shakes. Do two repetitions for each of the muscle groups listed below.

Note: If you have a muscle disorder or chronic pain problem, check with your doctor before proceeding.

Take a small breath at the end of the tensing period (usually after about 8 to 10 seconds of tensing), then let go of the tension and your breath at the same time. Like the signal breath, this reinforces the link between release of tension and exhaling. Notice how the sensations within your muscles change when letting go of the tension (e.g., "I can feel my arms becoming numb as I let go more and more").

I asked Sasha to sit in a comfortable armchair that fully supported all her muscles, including her neck (very important). Her feet could easily touch the floor so that her legs did not hang off the chair. We began with her hands and fingers, with the following direction:

> "Tense, making your fists as tight as you can, noticing how the muscles feel. The muscles should almost quiver [after about 15 seconds]. Take a breath and then let go of the muscles and your breath, noticing how the muscles feel as they relax. Now tense the muscles again [two times in total]."

Here is the sequence that I taught Sasha. Others are certainly possible, but you might start with this.

1. Make fists to tense both fingers and hands. Now tense. Notice how your hands feel, so tight and tense. Hold it for about 15 seconds. Then take a breath and completely let go of your muscles as you exhale, releasing the tension. Notice the relaxation flowing into the muscles—how they feel now. Now repeat this a second time.

2. Push down your forearms (into the arms of the chair) to tense your forearms and upper arms (same routine as for fists).

3. Raise your shoulders up to your ears (a severe shoulder shrug).

4. Push your head back into the back support to tense the muscles of your neck. Forcefully push your tongue up against the

roof of your mouth to tense the anterior (front) part of your neck and throat area.

5. Raise your eyebrows as high as you can and feel the pulling of your forehead muscles. After two repetitions, pull the muscles down in a forceful frown (eyebrows in a V shape).

6. To tense the small muscles around your eyes, squint forcefully as if bringing your cheeks up to your eyebrows.

7. Open your mouth as wide as you can without causing pain to tense the jaw muscles. (Caution: If you have jaw pain or notice a "popping" sensation when you chew or open your mouth wide, you may have a medical problem called *temporomandibular joint syndrome*, or TMJ. Check with a dental professional or physiatrist before tensing your jaw as described.)

8. Squeeze your arms against your rib cage while tightening your chest (pectoral muscles).

9. Pull in your abdomen as if toward your spine as tightly as you can, holding the tension.

10. Arch your back, tensing all the muscles from up under your shoulder blades all the way to the base of your spine.

11. Tighten up your buttocks as tightly as you can, as if holding in a bowel movement.

12. Tense your upper legs by pushing your feet, flat on the floor, down forcefully. You should immediately notice your thighs tensing to the point where they shake.

13. Tense your calves by extending your legs off the floor and raising your toes as if trying to touch your knees.

14. Curl your toes (scrunching them) while tensing your feet and toes as much as you can.

Practice this sequence every day for at least 20 minutes until you learn exactly how each muscle group feels when fully relaxed. When you notice tension at work or elsewhere, sit down (if possible), take a deep signal breath, and then focus on letting your muscles quickly drop down into the relaxed position you've learned. Just as the athlete, with practice, learns how to move his or her muscles to sink a putt or pitch a softball almost without thinking (called "muscle memory"), you have now "practiced" how to reproduce the relaxed state with your muscles.

I asked Sasha to take a deep signal breath when she first noticed her shoulders tensing up (her first anger signal) at work. Then I asked her to let go and try to recall and reproduce just how her muscles felt when completely relaxed. I suggested that each time she exhaled, her muscles would become more and more relaxed, just as she had practiced at home. When she had a hard time at first reproducing the relaxed state, I encouraged her to actually tense and then let go of any muscles she noticed were tightening as her irritation and stress escalated—right at her desk.

Once you've learned progressive muscle relaxation you'll be much more aware of tension in parts of your body and better able to "catch" your anger early on. Also, you can now employ *part or whole-body tensing* to quickly release tension throughout your body.

Once Sasha was comfortable with the sequence, I taught her to tense and relax multiple groups of muscles at the same time, a powerful and immediate way to dampen arousal. For example, one afternoon she found herself overcome by "intense rage" when one of her staff failed to begin an assigned report and then called in sick. Discovering the report would not be ready for distribution on time, Sasha rose to an 80 on her scale and felt like the top of her head was about to explode. She returned to her office, blocked all calls, and sat down, leaned back, and began signal breathing. She was having little luck dampening her fury, so she began tensing all the muscles of her upper body at once, coupled with a deep breath, then releasing the tension after about 20 seconds. This physical release helped her dampen her arousal to under 50, but it took three or four repetitions. She accomplished this by simultaneously:

> ➤ Making fists while raising and tightening her shoulders as much as she could.

> ➤ Pushing her upper arms against the sides of her chest while tightening so that her pectoral (chest muscles) tightened.

> ➤ Pulling her stomach muscles in.

> ➤ Squinting and trying to tighten as many facial muscles as possible.

While this may not look pretty (but who's going to see you, any-way?), it's a powerful way to immediately let go of escalating tension. Obviously, other muscles could be tensed as well, including the back and legs for a "whole-body" relaxation.

Autogenic Phrases: Making Your Intentions Real

Progressive relaxation uses muscle memory to dampen arousal on command; autogenic relaxation uses the power of suggestion. If you begin to focus your awareness on a part of your body, stating repeatedly in your mind how that part feels when completely relaxed, your mind begins to produce these sensations. Your mind knows how relaxation feels; you just need to instruct it to take you there. Autogenic relaxation—"auto" refers to self and "genic" refers to change, from the Latin—is easy to learn and requires that you do two things:

1. Focus your full attention on each part of your body as you mentally state a phrase that depicts how that part feels for you (based on past experience) when completely relaxed (e.g., "smooth and cool" or "warm and loose").

2. Repeat the phrases four times, stated softly and slowly and tied to a *moderately* full breath, as you further open up your awareness to those sensations.

I asked Sasha to sit comfortably and to close her eyes as she focused her full awareness on each part of her body, one at a time. Once focused on the part (e.g., her face), I asked her to slowly take a deep breath as she stated softly in her mind, "My face feels cool ... and calm," tied to the cadence of her slow rhythmic breathing: (*inhale*) "My face feels cool ... (*begin exhaling*) and calm." I told her to expect these relaxing sensations to occur at their own pace and to try not to "force" them to appear.

Autogenic Relaxation Sequence

Inwardly state each phrase four times, slowly in your mind, tied to a moderately full and comfortable breath. If your experience tells you that rather than feeling "warm and heavy," your arms feel "light and cool or numb" when relaxed, that is the phrase you should use. The following list is a place to begin developing your own list of autogenic phrases.

"(*Breathe in*) My arms are warm ... (*breathe out*) and heavy.

"My shoulders are limp ... and loose.

"My neck is loose ... and relaxed.

"My scalp is smooth ... and relaxed.

"My face is cool ... and calm.

"My chest is light ... and loose.

"My breathing is free ... and smooth.

"My stomach is limp ... and loose.

"My back is loose ... and relaxed.

"My legs are loose ... and relaxed.

"I am calm ... and relaxed."

This method is well suited to dampening anger. Once you've practiced the full sequence daily for at least two weeks, you can apply all or part of it to rapidly quell rising tension in specific parts of your body, no matter where you are (e.g., at a meeting, during a dinner party, in the middle of an argument).

Sasha's shoulder tension and "face feeling hot," early sensations of anger arousal, were now a signal for her to sit down and begin signal breathing. Sasha reported that sometimes her angry self-talk seemed to counteract the relaxing impact of the breath. I asked her to calmly state an autogenic phrase appropriate to shoulders and face, tied to gradually trying to slow her breathing, thus accomplishing two goals:

1. The phrase evoked a powerful relaxation response when stated repeatedly, just as when she had practiced it. Trying to say the phrase more and more slowly helped her to reduce her breathing rate, thus calming her further.

2. Because it occupied her mind, the phrase blocked out upsetting, anger-arousing self-talk.

Sasha became skilled at signal breathing without calling attention to herself. While the other person was talking, she would inwardly state an autogenic phrase ("My face is cool ... [exhale breath slowly] ... And calm"), trying to lean back and let go of her anger, particularly at times when her negative self-talk began to escalate.

With practice, you'll find you can quickly reduce your arousal by focusing an autogenic phrase on body tension, no matter where you are. My clients often report using a phrase, tied to ever-calming breathing, while in traffic, in stores when children or noise is irritating, while on a stressful phone call, and almost anywhere irritation or stress starts to escalate.

Imagery: Opening a Mental Window to a More Peaceful Reality

Everyone knows how vivid the imagination can be. A dream can seem perfectly real when you first awake, and re-creating a special occasion in your mind conjures up all the sights, smells, and sounds you perceived at the time. You can use your capacity to make the imagined real to dampen anger arousal. Imagining a situation vividly can evoke emotions similar to those you would experience in reality, just as it recalls the sensory experience. That's why imagery is part of so many relaxation programs. It's also why merely imagining a triggering experience can heighten your anger hours or even days after the actual event occurred, as discussed in Chapters 6 and 7, and why, conversely, positive imagining can set the stage for reacting to a trigger in a new, calm fashion.

Sasha reported that she would often daydream and found herself soothed by happy memories. I told her that we could make good use of her ability to imagine and taught her an imagery method that included the following steps.

1. Set a goal for the emotional experience you wish to evoke. For dampening, you might wish to feel some combination of peaceful, serene, calm, relaxed, safe and secure, confident, in control, and soothed. Sasha decided to focus on calm and confident as her emotional goal to replace irritation.

2. Close your eyes as you concentrate on your goal, suggesting to yourself that you will recall a time and experience when you felt that way. Let thoughts and images come until a well-formed scene appears in your mind's eye. If you cannot recall a scene from your past experience, then your creative mind can construct a place where you would feel the way you wish (e.g., the middle of nowhere, floating on a cloud, resting in a beautiful garden). Either way, this becomes your relaxation image. Sasha came up with a scene from her childhood: "lying on the beach at Casey Key, Florida, during summer vacation."

3. Using each of your senses, imagine this scene as vividly as you can, incorporating each sense separately until you have a complete image. Make sure you're lying down, sitting or floating in the water (e.g., a hot tub) in a physically inactive, calm position in your scene.

4. Notice *what you can see* around you, the colors and hues. Look up at the sky, off toward the horizon, and so forth. Sasha focused on the "blue sky and puffy clouds, the green hues of the water and glimmer of sunlight on its surface" as she filled in the visual aspects of the scene.

5. *Hear the sounds* around you like the babbling of a brook, the sound of wildlife, the wind, and any sounds likely to be present if you were in this situation in reality. For Sasha the sounds of the "waves washing in and out" and of the "breeze, softly blowing" were predominant in her image.

6. *Feel the temperature* on your face and elsewhere. Notice *how your body feels* as it is lying or seated comfortably (e.g., the sand beneath you). Sasha focused on feeling the "wind on my face" and the "warmth of the sun."

7. Be *aware of any pleasant smells* that are a part of your scene. There are direct pathways between smell and the part of your brain that experiences emotions. That's why a perfume, certain foods, and "bad smells" evoke a powerful emotional response in us. Take advantage of this and imagine pleasant and comforting smells (e.g., "mother's bread baking," flowers, freshly cut grass). The "salt air and the smell of suntan lotion" made the scene more real to Sasha.

You can practice using this relaxation or "resource" scene on a daily basis until you develop a facility for vividly imagining and capturing the emotions evoked. Often there will be a portion or fragment of the scene, a particular color or hue, a face or an object that will particularly stand out or capture the essence of what you're imagining. I call this an *image fragment*, a small but primary element of the entire scene. Once you've practiced imagining the entire scene enough times, this image fragment can come to quickly evoke the emotional responses associated with the entire scene.

Sasha focused on one key image fragment ("the green hues of the water") of her beach scene to quickly capture the mood of the scene while sitting at her desk at the office: "I'm noticing my shoulders getting tight, my face getting warm (*cue to relax*). Time to take a deep and slow signal breath as I imagine the *green hues of the water at Casey Key.*"

Distraction That Can Be Helpful

We don't typically think of distractions as beneficial. But distraction can serve a purpose in managing your anger: interrupting your focus on inciting self-talk, thus dampening arousal a different way.

Almost any strategy that works to refocus your attention on something that is more neutral, dull, or mind-occupying can be useful to reduce anger arousal. Consider these possibilities that might work when other dampening strategies are not quite bringing down your arousal.

Slowly count down from ten to one as you let go of tension and exhale a deep relaxation breath.

Repeat a poem, hear a calming refrain from a favorite song, or repeat a phrase that has spiritual meaning for you (e.g., a psalm, a passage from the Bible, Torah, or Koran).

Concentrate on a mind-occupying task like trying to remember a grocery list, planning a party, or something as dull as counting the number of panes in the window across from you.

Sasha decided that the most calming yet distracting activity she could engage in when it was hard to get control of negative self-talk was to hear the words of the James Taylor song "You've Got a Friend."

Because the song was associated with a very positive time in her life and the lyrics were calming and reassuring, Sasha found she could quickly dampen her arousal as she heard and visualized Taylor singing it. Just going into a potentially aggravating and stressful meeting humming the song seemed to remind her of what she needed to do to remain in control of her arousal.

Dampening the Fires: An Integration

It's well beyond the scope of this book to review all the ways you can achieve the relaxation response. I've reviewed five strategies that are particularly useful in dampening anger, but you may discover others, including versions of meditation, self-hypnosis, and yoga. All have in common the reduction of "fight-or-flight" arousal as you quiet your mind and refresh your body.

But how do you decide which dampening techniques to use and in what order? While almost any one or more of the five strategies will likely interrupt your anger-arousing self-talk and help you refocus instead on relaxing yourself, I recommend that you try the following sequence first.

1. Sit down and lean back to signal your brain to begin the relaxation response as previously described.

2. Once seated or while standing, take one or two deep signal breaths, using the distraction technique of counting backward from ten to one as you slowly exhale each breath through your lips. This immediately initiates a dampening.

3. Then you have the option of using some combination of the other dampening techniques as you try to slow your breathing to a more moderate pace (breathing in and out to a slow count of five).

Sasha usually combined an autogenic phrase with her image fragment of "green hues," signaling the deep relaxation she achieved when imagining her resource place (the beach scene):

"I'm sitting, and I take a couple of deep signal breaths to let go. Then I begin hearing the phrase 'My shoulders are limp and loose' or 'My face is cool and calm' as I try to recall the feelings of being at the beach by imagining the green of the water. In my office I can do this pretty quickly. When in a meeting or elsewhere, I just daydream a bit as I keep slowing my breathing and hearing the phrases. It really works, and soon I can refocus completely on my work. When I have to continue to pay close attention to what's going on, I focus on hearing the phrase as if in the back of my mind, sitting with my muscles as loose as possible and taking an occasional signal breath very privately. No one knows I'm dampening but me."

4. When it's really hard to let go of your anger, take a "time out" and go to another location (recall the "stop phrase" in Chapter 4) for at least 20 minutes. At that time, part or whole-body muscle tensing and relaxing can be effective to physically help you let go. You can combine this with deep breaths as you "tense" a portion of your body, then exhale away the tension as you let go of your muscles and your breath at the same time. As you return to the "action," you might continue to hear an autogenic phrase, while keeping your breathing at a moderately full pace.

You may need to experiment a bit to find the best "first steps" to use to recall and implement dampening, particularly when in the middle of an intense situation. For me, my primary anger signal is a tight feeling in my throat and chest. Just remembering to sit down (or if already seated, to lean back and deliberately loosen my muscles) seems to best launch the other steps of dampening if used immediately when I notice my muscles getting tight. Chapter 10 will offer more ideas you can use to make dampening more automatic whenever your anger or stress is rising.

Once your arousal is lowered to below 30 on your anger scale, you can begin to review your thinking, perhaps asking: "What am I expecting that may be unreasonable, and am I thinking about the angering situation in a way that will solve my problem?" Dampening helps you regain emotional control, derailing your rising anger arousal, but it does not solve any problems in relating to people or resolving a task. Chapters 6 and 7 focus on the next step of anger management: identifying and changing unhelpful thinking that, up until now, has fueled your anger.

Just for Practice

Learning to dampen your anger arousal is such an important step in managing your anger that I strongly recommend daily practice until you master the basics. Each of the dampening ideas in this chapter is effective in reducing arousal, but I always start my clients off with practicing the signal breathing method. Practice daily for at least two weeks or until you can notice a significant change in your tension level just by taking one or two signal breaths. Find a comfortable place to practice, free of distraction.

Then work on learning each of the dampening strategies in whatever order you like. Experiment with a combination of strategies as suggested in this chapter to find the right methods for you to use quickly and effectively. In all cases, try to sit down as a first step of dampening, as this becomes a first signal to begin the process of slowing down your arousal.

With a small investment in time compared to the costs of living with high stress and escalating anger, you will soon be proficient in asserting control over your arousal. Also, keep in mind the anger intensifiers in Chapter 4 (the "Five S's") and find ways to modify or eliminate any that are still present in your life. This is like inoculating yourself so that the next trigger that arises won't have the same impact it's had before. Remember: Keeping your arousal at moderate levels all the time greatly increases your resilience when the next unforeseen anger trigger comes along.

Step Four

Identifying and Changing Thoughts That Fuel Anger

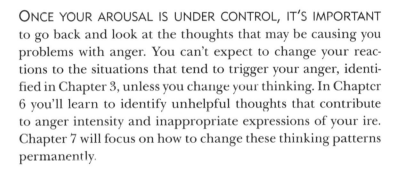

ONCE YOUR AROUSAL IS UNDER CONTROL, IT'S IMPORTANT to go back and look at the thoughts that may be causing you problems with anger. You can't expect to change your reactions to the situations that tend to trigger your anger, identified in Chapter 3, unless you change your thinking. In Chapter 6 you'll learn to identify unhelpful thoughts that contribute to anger intensity and inappropriate expressions of your ire. Chapter 7 will focus on how to change these thinking patterns permanently.

6

Recognizing Thoughts
That Fuel Anger

Three people waiting for a delayed flight at the airport notice a young boy and girl playing rambunctiously at the gate while their mother ignores them and reads her newspaper. Randall thinks of his rowdy grandchildren, smiles indulgently, and says to the kids, "It's really hard to wait for a plane to get here, isn't it?" Sidney wonders why mothers are so permissive these days, stands up with a loud sigh, and moves to the opposite side of the waiting area. Laura thinks it's outrageous that "these kids are being allowed to impose on everyone here, when we're all trying to deal with this totally incompetent airline to begin with." She fixes her glare first on the children and then on their mother, back and forth, over and over, for about 15 minutes, until the boy steps on her foot. Then she jumps up, stalks over to the mother, and hisses, "Could you *please* control your children?"

How we react emotionally to what's going on around us depends on the thoughts we allow to enter our mind in response. Those thoughts reflect our expectations for the situation. Should children's liveliness be tolerated in most settings? Should mothers try to ensure their kids don't bother the adults around them? Should strangers be able to read your mind and know when you just can't take another irritation? Obviously you'll react differently based on which expectation you hold.

As noted in the first chapters, when your reaction to challenging events is a face of anger that creates problems for you or others, it's time to examine your thinking. No matter how well you're able to dampen your arousal once your anger is triggered, if you don't try to cut down on the number of times it's triggered, you'll be expending needless energy every day on damage control. Fortunately, there's a proven method for learning to identify and in some cases alter thinking that contributes to unhelpful levels of emotion, whether depression, anxiety, or anger. It's called *cognitive-behavioral therapy (CBT)*, and it addresses two forms of thinking:

> *Self-talk*: Self-talk includes the words in your head that can seem like an inner conversation with yourself, including comments, interpretations, and directions to act in a certain way. John thinks, "I know Mary will be upset with me when I get home," and immediately feels defensive and irritable. Erin comments to herself, "I will not put up with another criticism at work." When her supervisor tries to discuss a "mistake," Erin explodes in anger.

> *Images*: These are the mental movies of events that have already happened (you picture and "hear" your supervisor "unfairly" criticizing your work) or might occur in the future (visualizing yourself successfully confronting the same supervisor). Just like self-talk, images immediately evoke emotions typical of how you would have reacted to the real situation. For example, you can probably recall times you've lain in bed imagining an aggravating event from your day, only to find your body tensing up and your anger rising.

Understanding the self-talk and images that are promoting your anger can help you change those ways of thinking and the inappropriate anger that results. Chapter 7 will give you the tools you need to alter your current thinking to achieve this goal, but first you need to identify your problematic self-talk and imagery.

Self-Talk: How Are You Thinking Today?

It's almost a cliché for psychologists to ask, "So, how did you feel about that?" While identifying your angry feelings early on is important, examining your self-talk is critical to understanding why you're feeling this way in the first place. Let's explore self-talk a bit more.

The Nature of Self-Talk

Most of our thinking seems to come as a stream of words that describe or interpret events or direct our actions. This stream seems so automatic that we're hardly aware of how unbroken it is. But try *not* to think and you'll have some idea of how constantly the mental gears are grinding. Most of us, in fact, find it difficult to clear our minds without special training in yoga, meditation, or another technique for gaining inner peace. Yet we need to eradicate certain types of thinking if we are to get control of the mental triggers for anger. "I find that I can't seem to control my thoughts," said one of my clients. "As soon as I feel taken advantage of, I feel like an automatic pilot takes over. I start cursing to myself and keep running the unfairness of it all through my mind. Why can't I get a grip sooner, before I end up losing it?"

Most cognitive-behavioral (CB) therapists believe that you learned to think in much the same way that you learned external behaviors like speaking a language, driving a car, or playing a sport. In most cases you were exposed to models like parents, teachers, and peers who showed you, by their example, how they thought about situations. In other cases you were formally taught how to think in school, by your religion, or by parental discipline. Sometimes you just made it up as you went along. But in all cases your self-talk became automatic when it was repeated over and over until it became a "habit," like how you automatically hold your tennis racquet or write your name.

This leads to an important point: If you learned these thinking patterns, it's logical to assume you can unlearn them by practicing new thoughts until they're so ingrained they take over. The old thoughts just collapse from disuse. But how do you identify self-talk that is fueling and/or misdirecting your anger?

Self-talk that misinterprets the facts of a situation to make it seem more threatening or unmanageable is called a *cognitive distortion* by CB therapists. Cognitive distortions come in many flavors. Some make a situation seem worse than it is, and others create a problem out of whole cloth. But they all have one thing in common, captured by the following important rule.

> *Rule of thumb: When self-talk is not based on facts, both current and historical, it is distorted and probably contributing unnecessarily to anger or other unpleasant emotions.*

A "fact" is an event that can be seen, heard, or otherwise sensed by both you and others. While two people may vary in their report of events, such as how fast a car was traveling before an accident, they probably won't disagree that two cars were present and an accident occurred. In contrast, their opinions about speed or who was at fault are not facts but interpretations based on each person's point of view. When we move beyond the mere facts into interpretations as to how others think or feel or why they do what they do, we may get it wrong.

Of course, some facts are not pleasant, like finding out that you are ill or getting temporarily laid off at work. This leads us to a second important rule, a corollary to the first rule.

> *Rule of thumb: When the facts are not pleasant, any thinking that further contributes to uncomfortable feelings or misdirects your actions should be identified and replaced.*

These thoughts are making the situation you face worse. For example, telling yourself that your illness is ruining every part of your life or angry thoughts that tell you to just quit an otherwise good job because you got one bad performance rating are clearly not helping you cope with what you're facing. So even if you believe they are based on reality, they are counterproductive and should be replaced.

Let's apply these two rules—"thoughts should be based on facts" and "thoughts based on facts should not make the situation worse"—to Luis's thinking when his brother fails to attend his 50th birthday celebration "without even calling to decline." The thoughts that are particularly crucial to understanding Luis's anger and actions are in italics.

Luis assumed his brother Pablo had received the mailed invitation. When Pablo failed to show for the party, Luis thought: "He *didn't even care enough* to call us. How rude. Not having him there *ruined the entire night* for our parents and my aunt who came in from California. It was *unforgivable*."

Does Luis's self-talk agree with the first rule of thumb? Upon further questioning I learned that neither Luis nor his wife was certain that Pablo had received the invitation, and they had no factual knowledge of Pablo's reasons for absenting himself. The thought "He didn't even care enough" to come is clearly a distortion. The only known fact is he was not present.

The corollary rule applies also. The unpleasant fact is that Pablo didn't come and Luis and others felt disappointed. But I further learned from Luis's wife that most present at the party commented that they had had a great time. Luis's thought that the entire evening was "ruined" is clearly an exaggeration that adds to his anger. Furthermore, telling himself that Pablo's actions were "unforgivable" made it harder for the two brothers to work this out. These thoughts clearly made the problem worse for all involved.

Applying these rules of thumb will enable you to discern quickly whether your thought is distorted and therefore unhelpful. I have also listed in the sidebar (page 120) specific examples of cognitive distortions that violate the two rules, fueling or misdirecting anger.

Which Cognitive Distortions Are Part of Your Self-Talk?

Can you identify these distortions in your own self-talk? As you read examples of each distortion, think of your recent episodes of anger. Do any of these distortions sound familiar? Pay particular attention to the underlined words, which are the key phrases capturing each distortion. Ask yourself the questions to determine which distortions are often part of your own self-talk.

Personalization

It's easy to accept a compliment or take credit for a rewarding outcome. In contrast, you may become angry when someone says or does something that seems directed negatively at you. But sometimes your assumption of negative intent is not justified by the facts. Do these examples sound familiar?

> We can all relate to this one: As you drive to work, someone pulls into the lane ahead, and you automatically think, "I can't believe he deliberately cut me off. How inconsiderate." Is that person deliberately cutting you off? It's possible, but his actions may have nothing to do with you. More than likely the other driver is just trying to get to work and chose to switch lanes without thinking.

> "This kitchen is a complete zoo. These kids will do anything to make my life miserable." Were the children really trying to fuel their mother's ire or just absorbed in play and not paying attention to the mess they were creating?

Ask yourself: When you think another person has a negative or malicious intent toward you, are there factual statements or actions to support your assumption? Or are there less threatening reasons for the

Cognitive Distortions That Fuel and Misdirect Anger

Personalizing: Without factual evidence, you believe that another person's statements or actions are directed toward you. You may feel personally attacked.

Catastrophizing: You magnify or exaggerate the negative impact of another person's actions or an event well beyond the facts. You "awfulize" the situation.

Forecasting: Without any basis in fact, you predict that a situation will turn out badly, without looking fairly at all the possible outcomes.

Polarized thinking: Not focusing on all the positive and negative aspects of a situation or thing, you see it in extremes (e.g., success/failure, bad/good). You think in overgeneralized terms (e.g., always, never, any, every).

Mind reading: Without asking, you assume you know how another person thinks or feels or what that person's motives are.

Labeling: You use name calling or inflammatory descriptors (e.g., "incompetent," "zoo," "farce," "nightmare") to describe another person or situation.

Filtering: You focus your thoughts on the most upsetting or threatening things that happened without looking at neutral and positive events that might belie your negative view.

Thresholding: Setting an arbitrary limit for what you can stand or will tolerate, you feel justified in being more intense or punitive when another person "crosses the line."

Blueprinting: You instruct yourself as to how you will act, often focusing on getting even or punishing another person.

other's behavior (maybe the person was distracted, hungry, or irritated by something else that happened) that have nothing to do with you? The principle of "enlightened self-interest" applies. Others have little time to plot how to make your day miserable or to judge you because they are likely focused on getting their own needs met (e.g., "When is lunch?"). Their self-interest is likely to trump any concern or focus they might have regarding your plight.

Catastrophizing

Blowing things out of proportion, you exaggerate the negative impact of an event well beyond what is factually likely, as in the following scenarios:

> When a meeting is canceled, John returns to his office and escalates his anger with the thought "Canceling this meeting at the last minute has <u>destroyed my whole day</u>."

> "This is the <u>absolute worst traffic I've ever seen</u>. I'll never get to the doctor's office on time."

> "Stephano was the <u>worst kid</u> on the playground today. He'll <u>never get invited to play with any of those kids again</u>."

Ask yourself: Considering current and past facts, are you exaggerating the negative impact of something that didn't go as planned, using overly dramatic or pessimistic language? Instead, consider a more likely result based on past experience and then problem-solve a plan to deal with it.

Forecasting

Without factual evidence you foresee a negative future outcome and immediately begin to feel irritable or apprehensive. Like a "self-fulfilling prophecy," making negative predictions about the future may lead to self-defeating actions (particularly a negative face of anger that contributes to the negative outcome you dread). Can you see yourself in situations like these?

> Madison's thoughts fuel resentment before she learns of her raise for the upcoming year: "I just know that <u>we're going to get the</u>

short end of the stick when raises are announced. Management will fund their own stock options, and we'll get what's left over."

As Nathan sits in the middle of a traffic snarl, he predicts, "We'll never get out of this mess. I'll be late for my meeting, and my boss will be really furious."

Ask yourself: Are you predicting that something negative will happen before the fact? Is there a factual basis for your prediction? In fact, none of us can reliably foresee what will happen next. Focusing on the most unfortunate possible outcomes evokes upsetting emotions that may be unwarranted. We end up angry and upset no matter what the future actually brings. Instead, consider and plan for a range of *factually probable* outcomes.

Polarized Thinking

Think of two extremes or polar opposites, like "never" and "always," "all" or "nothing," "good" and "bad," and you have the essence of polarized thinking. Rather than focusing on what actually occurred at a given point in time, you characterize another person's actions or events as fitting into one extreme (e.g., total success) or the other (e.g., an abysmal failure):

"This whole project has been a disaster—a total failure. Nothing has gone right."

A mother thinks that her daughter is completely out of control: "Kathy never does what I tell her anymore."

And I probably don't have to tell you how polarized politics has become and how angry so many voters are at one party or the other: "The Republican Party today is totally evil; only the Democrats have purely good intentions," or "The entire Democratic Party just wants to tax and spend, tax and spend!"

Ask yourself: Are you looking at a situation or person in an all-or-nothing, extreme manner, not considering the more probable middle ground? Thinking in extremes immediately makes any situation seem less resolvable, making you feel less in control. As a result you may feel overwhelmed and threatened, and this feeling can push your anger arousal to levels where rational responding is more difficult. Instead, think about what actually happened at a specific point in time (e.g., "<u>Today</u> the project didn't go well"; "Kathy misbehaved <u>this afternoon</u> more than usual").

Mind Reading

Without evidence, you assume what others think or feel or you decide on their motives. If you assume others have malicious motivation, your actions may be defensive or even aggressive. Do the following examples sound familiar?

> "I <u>know she hates</u> me and <u>would do anything to ruin my career</u>. Her questioning me in the meeting only confirms it."

> "It's <u>more important to please her mother</u> than to stand up for our marriage."

> "<u>Holly just loves to argue</u>! She is <u>just looking to complain</u>."

Ask yourself: Are you assuming you know another person's thoughts, feelings, or needs without asking about them? The most damaging aspect of mind reading is that your assumptions, which may be inaccurate, guide your anger and actions. Remember the mantra from the computer world: "Garbage in, garbage out." Instead, consider how rational your assumption is and check it out with the other person only if it seems reasonable and important.

Labeling

Assaulting yourself with critical labels ("stupid," "foolish," "hopeless") only increases your frustration and may rob you of the energy and self-confidence necessary to think through a problem. Name calling, cursing, and put-downs in your thinking about others may fuel your anger and set the stage for verbal insults you may later regret. Negative labels that dehumanize another person frequently precede aggression. It's easier to hurt someone you have thought of as a jerk, a moron, or a monster than a fallible human being with whom you disagree.

Labels can be applied to a situation too, fueling your anger and making it harder to endure. For example, thinking of your delay at the airport as an "endless nightmare" may reflect your feelings about a truly difficult situation, but these emotionally charged labels often make the situation worse than it needs to be.

> Erik's self-talk is filled with an entire repertoire of put-downs and epithets for drivers who are "<u>morons</u>" and "<u>imbeciles</u>." The problem is that Erik's thoughts often get translated into the spoken word, and lately he has started spewing a stream of cursing and invective witnessed by his wife and children.

> Lacey calls her office "<u>that loony bin</u>," her apartment "<u>this hellhole</u>," and her four sisters "<u>the witches' council</u>." She started out using these labels for witty effect when talking to her friends, but lately her humor has taken on an edge, and she's starting to resent these places and the people who populate them.

Ask yourself: Do you curse, name-call, or use harsh labels in your thinking about other people or situations? How often do you use this language in front of others? Instead, focus on their behavior without labeling the person: "I feel angry when Charlie <u>leaves his toys in the living room</u>" versus "Charlie is a slob, and his room is a disaster!").

Filtering

From among the mostly neutral as well as the positive and negative things that happen, you focus on the most upsetting events, filtering out information that belies your negative view. Do you think the way these people do?

> Mara sits at her desk, steaming as she dwells on a colleague's criticism of her report. She excludes from her thoughts the other positive comments this person has made and offered in the past.

> Lev keeps focusing on an argument he had with his wife prior to arriving at the office: "I can't believe <u>how nasty she was</u>." His mood is irritable, and he is cold and distant to his office friends. He fails to consider that his wife has been ill, is not sleeping well, and that her actions are unusual for her.

Ask yourself: Do you find yourself more readily focusing on upsetting events than neutral or positive events as you look over your day?

Do you look for the "cloud" as opposed to the silver lining? Is the glass always half empty rather than half full? Instead, look at the entire picture: Are there other, less threatening facts about the person or situation beyond what you didn't like or expect? Is this behavior typical for this person or unusual, perhaps provoked by one of the "Five *S*'s" and thus quickly forgivable?

Thresholding

You set an arbitrary limit for what you will tolerate or how far you are willing to go in solving a problem. When other people or circumstances violate this preset limit, you may feel justified in becoming angry, like these people:

> "Nobody should have to put up with this," said Jake. "I <u>can't take another criticism</u>. <u>One more insult</u> and I know I'll lose it."

> "I've done <u>all I can do</u> to resolve this," Seiko proclaimed. "Now the ball is in her court to make an effort."

Ask yourself: Are you setting a limit for what you can "stand" or tolerate that fails to reflect your personal strengths and past coping abilities? You've no doubt coped successfully with worse things, like disappointments or losses, haven't you? The biggest problem with thresholding is that you're powerless over what others say or do and over many circumstances (such as the traffic and the weather) that may be included in your self-imposed limit. Is it really necessary to set yourself up for more aggravation when the limit is breached?

Negative Blueprinting

Many who act out with unfortunate faces of anger think about what they're going to do hours and even days ahead. Like the plans to a building, blueprinting thoughts describe the actions to follow, sometimes in graphic detail:

> "<u>I'll tell him just what I think about how terrible he is as a dad, right in front of his family</u>. When they hear what I say, he'll be completely humiliated, and he deserves every minute of it."

"<u>When she gets home, I'm not speaking to her</u>, no matter how much she apologizes."

Ask yourself: Do you sometimes find yourself planning the details of how you can get even or hurt another person who has triggered your anger? Think ahead. A day after you act out this plan, will the problem you have with this person be resolved or made worse? What's the possible consequence to you if you carry out what you've "blueprinted"?

Imagery

Imagination is a powerful facility, as you learned in Chapter 5, where we talked about how to use soothing imagery to help you relax. But imagery can contribute to anger and unhelpful behavior as well. Images likely to arouse your anger could focus on past, present, or future.

Re-Creating Past Events

Resentment is a kind of chronic anger that continues long after provocation. You may continue to picture an upsetting event, mentally "hearing" what was said and even feeling the physical sensations you experienced, months or even years later. If you selectively focus on the most threatening details of the scene, your anger may actually grow beyond its original intensity.

> Wendy is still angry about her sister's wedding three years ago. Not invited to be a bridesmaid, she becomes even more resentful every time she vividly imagines the wedding. Her resentment in turn strengthens her resolve to avoid discussing her grievance with her sister.

Ask yourself: Do you find yourself vividly reenacting past grievances in your mind? Do you notice an impact on your mood and tension level as the upsetting scenes unfold? Instead, ask yourself the purpose of again imagining an upsetting event. Are you resolving your resentment or fueling it? If you want to resolve it, consider thinking through new solutions to this problem and playing each out in imagery to see how they feel to you. Chapter 11 will offer concrete ideas for identifying and resolving your resentment.

Images in the Present

When an anger trigger has just occurred—a few minutes or even a few hours ago—you may find yourself imagining what you found unacceptable, rearousing your anger when you need calm reflection to resolve the situation. These anger-provoking images may come along with self-talk that whips you up again too.

> Najid's supervisor just gave him an "unfair" annual review. Najid imagines his supervisor's "smug" face and "judgmental statements" as he tries to resume work at his desk, and he gets more and more agitated. Suddenly he finds himself bursting into his supervisor's office and losing it. Security is called, and he is asked to leave the building. His problem is now much worse because of mental pictures that have influenced his reality.

Ask yourself: When you're faced with a triggering situation, is your imagery merely reviewing, perhaps in condensed form, the most upsetting parts? What could you imagine that would help you relax and think through the situation right now (a relaxing scene, as noted in Chapter 5, or past ways you coped *successfully* with situations like this)?

Predicting the Future

Imagery can also be focused on provocation that hasn't occurred yet. As you vividly imagine a threatening future outcome (such as someone taking advantage of you), your brain immediately instigates anger arousal, which may then affect how you actually react to the person or situation (you are already irritated the next time you approach the imagined situation, *creating* a problem that may not have otherwise occurred).

> Colin dreads going to his wife's family reunion because he has never felt accepted. As he imagines his father-in-law ignoring him, he feels angry and vows "not to take any disrespect from anybody." By the time he arrives at the gathering, he is defensive and irritable, distancing himself from those he meets. His images have set the stage for the "lousy time" he ends up having.

Ask yourself: Do you find yourself focusing your imagery on what could go wrong or be threatening before you actually enter a situation?

Is there any basis in fact for the provocative picture you're painting in your mind? If there is, then consider imagining new behaviors that might resolve the problem, a much better use of your time.

Images also can focus on what you will say or do to act out your anger or resolve it.

Imagining Anger Actions

Similar to "negative blueprinting," imagining a behavioral reaction creates a kind of "cognitive map" that will likely guide what you end up doing.

> Chantal is furious that her husband is late "again" for family dinner and failed to call her with an explanation. As her anger escalates, she pictures herself glaring at him and refusing to talk or accept an apology. When he arrives, she finds herself acting out what she imagined, and the couple spends a few days not speaking to each other.

Ask yourself: When angry, do you sometimes imagine how you'll express these intense feelings? If so, are your images of positive coping, or do they seem to inflame your anger and direct you to a negative form of expression? Are you also imagining the realistic consequences/outcomes of each scenario you play in your mind? This gives you an opportunity to "try out" in imagery possible solutions to conflict without risking actions that you can't undo.

Time for a Rewrite?

Now that you're familiar with thinking that's likely to fuel and misdirect your anger, pay close attention to your self-talk and imagery as you notice the earliest signs of anger arousal. Ask yourself the questions I've suggested in the previous sections as a guide to evaluating whether your thinking is contributing to the problem or helping to craft a solution.

Your thinking "script" has no doubt been written in your childhood and throughout your life as you were exposed to powerful models and had life-changing experiences. But as well learned as it is, you can change it. Just as the playwright edits the dialogue in a play that doesn't quite work, you can learn to be the editor of your inner dialogue, challenging irrational self-talk and revising images that provoke an unhelpful face of anger.

Chapter 7 gives you the editing tools to craft new self-talk as you rebut and replace anger-arousing thinking. You'll learn to use the power of imagery to accomplish new goals for experiencing anger. So get out your "pen" and get the creative juices flowing as you turn to the next chapter.

7

Rewriting Your Script
New Thinking for New Solutions

Nick: "Sure, I now realize that Jen isn't purposely making us late everywhere we go just to make me mad. I can usually catch myself when I start thinking this and stop myself before I get too angry. But every time we're about to go somewhere and Jen isn't ready when I expect her to be, the cycle starts all over again. Maybe we don't end up in huge fights as often as we used to, but Jen still isn't happy about this, and I guess I'm not either."

Forest: "My company seems to have no concern for any of us. Guys are laid off and we are not told about it—they just don't show up for work. I just can't help thinking that I should begin to get my résumé out there, but what if I can't find anything? I know I will get paid less—what if I can't pay the bills? They are not getting any less; that's for sure! I get so angry at them and myself for not having more computer skills. I know I'm just making myself miserable, but I don't know how to get this off my mind."

Aidan: "Rory is doing everything in his power to break up his mom and me. All he seems to care about is himself, and Gerry lets him get away with it. If she really cared enough about our new marriage and could let go of babying her son, this relationship would stand a chance. I'm not overreacting to Rory as my wife complains during our many arguments about him. I'm beginning to think she cares more about placating Rory than me! This kid is totally out of control!"

Even after you've successfully identified many of the distorted thoughts and unrealistic expectations that tend to fuel your anger, it doesn't take long to realize that knowing what's steering you wrong and changing your course are two very different accomplishments. Forest's "forecasting" and "catastrophizing" set the stage for irritability and arguments with his wife when he can't get his mind off his fears. Gerry's husband, Aidan, catches himself "mind reading" when he claims to know what Gerry and Rory are thinking—their motives and feelings. Each of them has learned about how cognitive distortions can inflame their stress and anger, but that doesn't mean they won't indulge in "mind reading" or "forecasting" tomorrow or the next day. You can tell yourself to stop "labeling" someone in your life, but the picture of that person that you carry around in your head can be tougher to erase. You may be able to identify thought after distorted thought in your anger episodes, but if every eradicated distortion seems instantly replaced by a new one, it may be that you've failed to identify one underlying thought or expectation that is feeding all the rest. Or you might be able to stave off the anger you feel when sniped at by a relative or an old friend but unable to rid yourself of resentment over past offenses and transgressions.

I'd be glossing over the truth if I told you that changing the distorted thoughts and unrealistic expectations that fuel anger is an easy task. The mind is a brilliantly complex organ, capable of infinitely complicated thought patterns. It's no simple matter to figure out exactly which thoughts are triggering anger in which ways, in particular settings, with certain people. To make your job even more difficult, anger thoughts that have been repeated many times become "automatic," like any habit. No wonder those counterproductive images and self-talk tend to keep popping into your head despite your awareness of the harm they are doing.

Fortunately, cognitive-behavioral therapists have devised effective methods for sorting through and replacing the self-talk and imagery that exacerbate anger. These methods require commitment and patience, however. Repetition over time—practice—is necessary to install new thoughts and images in place of old ones, and it may take tenacious digging to unearth all of the expectations and self-talk habits that keep your anger erupting. Please don't give up if you don't get instant results. Old mental habits die hard, but they *can* be conquered. You'll undoubtedly see some positive change quickly. Tips for practice that will take you the rest of the way are included at the end of this chapter.

Rewriting your script calls for a two-pronged approach. First, you'll need practical ideas for shutting off the old anger thinking and shifting to rational new thoughts on the spot, whenever your anger is triggered. The more you use these techniques, the more your old thinking will be edged out and replaced by new, positive automatic thoughts. Second, each time your anger gets the best of you, you should reconstruct what happened in writing once you're clear of the triggering situation. This postmortem will help you learn from your mistakes, laying a new mental foundation that you can draw on the next time a triggering event occurs. The foundation will be made up of new self-talk and helpful images that you've constructed and practiced and that you'll remember the next time you're faced with a similar provocative situation.

Each goal supports the other. New thinking is being learned and practiced so that over time you've replaced old habits with new thoughts that are more likely to occur spontaneously. You get angry less often and handle it better when you do.

Through cognitive-behavioral methods like the ones in this chapter, you use the power of the mind to unlearn the negative messages you've unwittingly taught yourself. To remind you of the intellectual power that we all have over our anger, we'll call the act of challenging your thinking a "rebuttal." As in a debate, one side (the new-thinking you) disputes the validity of the arguments made by the other side (the old, automatic-thinking you). Also as in a debate, certain simple rules for rational thinking determine which side wins. As a result of the debate, you discard self-talk and images that violate those rules and craft new, rational self-talk and images that you will then practice.

Learning a New Inner Dialogue: Replacing Counterproductive with Productive Self-Talk

If we could all just "be more rational" on command, the world would probably be a pretty tranquil place. The truth is, however, that emotional arousal tends to cloud reason, making it hard to think straight when you're angry. That's why I recommend learning a sequence of four steps that, with practice, will guide you to consistently craft effective rebuttals—on the spot or in written practice afterward. Your ultimate goal is to *stop* unhelpful thinking, replacing it with helpful, rational thoughts, so the acronym STOP should help you remember this sequence of steps.

The STOP Method

Step 1. Stop!

As you'll recall from Chapters 4 and 5, you can't think clearly if you're flooded with anger sensations, so stopping your rising anger permits you to think things through. The first step in your rebuttal of anger thoughts is to stop your anger from escalating. First, use a forceful inner voice to derail your arousal and current thinking: Say to yourself, for example, "Stop!" or "Chill" as you take steps to dampen arousal. With practice, this inner stop word will become associated with an interruption of anger arousal and the cessation of anger thinking and will become more and more effective. Sometimes an image helps to interrupt your anger thinking (e.g., as you forcefully say "Stop!" you see or hear an image associated with stopping or interruption, such as picturing a bright red stop sign or hearing the voice of an authority figure in your life).

Next, sit down and lean back if possible, take a deep signal breath, and then follow with progressive relaxation, autogenic phrases, or whatever works to calm you down.

If you're in the midst of an intense discussion in person or on the phone, an internal stop phrase might not be enough. You may need a "time-out," as you learned in Chapter 4 when you reach 50 or more on your anger scale: Say, "This feels intense right now and I need some time to think," or merely excuse yourself for a brief time (e.g., say, "I need a drink of water," or take a rest room break) before you can rationally address your thinking.

Step 2. Think

If you've responded as desired to your own "Stop!" command, you've given yourself at least an instant of breathing space. Into this void, let one or two thoughts rise as you consider the triggering situation. Anger is almost always accompanied by self-talk that focuses on what seems unfair or hurtful, an unmet expectation, how upset you are, or how you are going to react, so it shouldn't be hard to uncover a thought that is fueling your anger. From the examples at the beginning of the chapter, Nick might have thought about Jen, "She does this just to drive me crazy!" or "Our friends are going to be really ticked off that we're late—again." Or Forest might find himself thinking: "I'll lose my home and everything we have saved for" as he again forecasts that he will be laid off.

Aidan may "personalize" his stepson's actions with "He came in late just to keep me up another night," or "This kid will put off his homework just to irritate me." Sometimes the thoughts that surface after you've halted your anger arousal are so clearly irrational or otherwise inappropriate that you may find them laughable once you look them square in the face. But not all automatic thoughts are so obviously irrational. You'll want to challenge each thought by comparing it to the "rules of thumb" and examples of cognitive distortions discussed in Chapter 6 and captured by the following three questions. These questions are worth memorizing because you will use them often to evaluate your thoughts in short order. Memorize the underlined key words.

> ➤ Is it <u>based on observable facts</u> (e.g., is there factual evidence in the present or past to support my assertion)?

> ➤ Is it <u>giving me good ideas</u> for calming myself and resolving the problem I face?

> ➤ Is it <u>free of cognitive distortions</u> (as listed in Chapter 6)? By reading over this list a few times you can begin to recognize a distortion as soon as it pops up in your thinking (e.g., "That's 'personalizing' or 'mind reading' and I need to change it.").

If you answer no to any of the three questions, your thinking is likely making the situation worse and should be discarded forcefully (e.g., "That's catastrophizing and completely unsupported!" or "This is only making it worse—let it go!").

Step 3. Objectify

Now that you've banished thoughts that failed your test, you need to replace them with new ones. Your new thought should be based on objective facts about the person or situation in the present or past that make you feel more comfortable. As you'll recall from Chapter 6, a fact includes actions or events that can be seen, heard, or experienced with other senses. The following guidelines should help:

> ➤ Focus on *realistic expectations* for this person or situation based on past behavior (e.g., "Of course she's late. The fact is she's often late, and I can't change that"; or "So what else is new? He always seems to need the last word. I choose to give it to him").

> ➤ Place an *unpleasant situation* in the *context of current and past factual events* that are more acceptable to you. For example, look at other things the person has done or said that seem more positive (e.g., "She usually is very helpful" or "At least he's a lot of fun to be with, even if he is late"). *Similarly, reevaluate a stressful situation* in the light of past facts (e.g., "This is the first time in 10 flights my bags have been lost").

> ➤ Review less threatening *facts that help you understand* another person's actions (e.g., "Bill has been under a lot of stress since his son became ill" or "She is new to the job and needs some understanding right now").

> ➤ Review your own *strengths* that can help you cope with this situation, like how well you coped with a loss or stayed calm in the face of a true emergency (e.g., "This is nothing compared with getting through the layoffs last year. I can handle this").

You're limited only by your creativity in finding a more positive yet rational view of the situation. As soon as you've rethought the situation, your feelings of anger are likely to dissipate.

Step 4. Plan

Changing your thoughts will certainly help you manage your emotions, but a fully rewritten anger management script should include self-talk for planning how to handle similar anger triggers in the future. What will you substitute for getting angry—or inappropriately expressing your anger—when you encounter an injustice, inequity, or other problem? Don't let your self-talk end with a new logic regarding what you can expect from others. Maybe it's not rational to get livid at your spouse for being late to every dinner engagement, but what do you do about the fact that this behavior still inconveniences you? It may no longer make sense to whip yourself into a lather over the favoritism you imagine all your relatives extend to your brother, but how do you mend the rift that has existed between the two of you for years—or just get through the holidays without gritting your teeth? You must act differently to obtain an outcome different from the one your uncontrolled anger produced, and deciding what that should be is the subject of Chapter 8.

For now, though, know that a good plan is *specific* and describes *actions* you will take (e.g., "I'll improve my attitude" is vague, versus "Tomorrow, right after the meeting, I'll offer to problem-solve the glitches in the project"). It is *under your control* (e.g., if your plan depends on another person changing first, revise it), and its *outcome can be measured* (e.g., either you get through the afternoon without yelling at your kids or you don't).

Having a plan increases your sense of control and will actually reduce any anger arousal that might potentially be triggered. To increase this benefit, use productive self-talk to further your specific goal:

> ➤ Forest works on an action plan to prepare for the real possibility that he could be laid off. He decides that rather than catastrophizing about all the bad possible outcomes, he will write down ideas for networking: friends, past coworkers, and supervisors he can call on to learn of possible job openings should he lose his position. By writing these fact-based and helpful ideas in his notebook he feels more in control. He is making a plan for what he will do should his unwanted job loss occur, rather than making himself miserable with negative forecasts of doom and gloom.

> ➤ Aidan decides his best plan is to discuss all discipline with Gerry before making decisions on how to cope with Rory. By including Gerry before the fact of discipline, he is getting Gerry to "buy" into the plan and thus be more invested in enforcing the decision. This reduces conflict between Aidan and Gerry and ensures a united front with Rory.

The STOP method should be used as soon as you notice anger arousal at "41–60" (e.g., shoulders beginning to tighten, face starting to become hot) as you've learned from your anger scale in Chapter 4. To illustrate how to use the STOP method, look over Aidan's STOP protocol, shown on pages 138–139.

While a STOP can resolve the immediate problem and derail anger arousal, it may not be enough to solve the underlying problem, and it didn't point to a future plan or the self-talk that could help him fulfill it. The insight required to complete these steps toward anger management often comes only from reflection and the distance that a little time after the event provides.

The Written Rebuttal: Practicing for the Future

It's hard to consider your thoughts thoroughly when you're angry. But by writing out what happened *after the fact* you can examine each part of your anger, from trigger to action. Then you can craft new rational thoughts and actions to practice for the next time you're faced with this triggering situation. Taking this writing step will reveal a lot more about the dynamics of your anger than you can hope to get on the spot, and therefore it's a good way to troubleshoot. Using the STOP method while angry doesn't prevent the same triggers from continuing to set you off as time goes on.

If the idea of writing down everything that happens every time you get angry seems onerous, understand that it's not only revealing but also serves as another form of practice that will turn your new anger actions into new positive habits. The more you practice, not only by rehearsing when your anger is triggered but also by scripting your anger episodes ahead of time, the more likely you will be able to quickly recall these new thoughts when under fire. After all, you wouldn't expect your golf game to improve simply because you had read a book on perfecting your swing or by just deciding to try harder; you know you would have to learn a specific new approach and then practice it. Since you can't instantly produce a real-life trigger to practice with, written practice is the next best thing. My experience and much clinical research on cognitive-behavioral therapy tell us that written practice really works. Keep in mind, too, that writing everything down with the goal of making changes in your self-talk in one situation (e.g., with your spouse at home) may make it easier to think more rationally in similar situations

The "STOP" Model for Managing Your Anger: Aidan's Example

Stop:

> ➤ Tell yourself in your loudest inner voice to "Stop, right now!" Picture a bright red stop sign or someone's face who could get you to stop.

> ➤ Take a deep signal breath, sit down if possible, and lean back/ loosen your shoulders and arms.

> ➤ If the other person gets louder, you get softer. You are in control.

> ➤ If you can't reduce your anger below "50," take a "time-out" using your stop phrase (leave the situation for at least 20 minutes).

Think:

> ➤ What self-talk is most upsetting right now? *Rory doesn't like me and will do anything to undermine my relationship with Gerry.*

> ➤ Answer the three questions:

>> ➤ Is it a fact? *No. I have no idea what is inside that kid's head. He has never said he wants me gone.*

>> ➤ Is it calming you? *Not at all. I am getting more furious with Rory and his mom for letting him get away with things.*

>> ➤ Is it giving you good ideas for getting what you want? *No. It is only making me hate this kid.*

> ➤ If you answer no to one or more of these three questions, your thinking is the problem and you should change it.

Objectify:

> ➤ Think of the facts that can affect you! Try on these or make up some yourself:

>> ➤ *Rory can't control me—only I can, and I choose to not let him pull my strings any longer.*

> ➤ *Wait. Stop right now. If I let him get to me, I lose and Gerry will get mad at me. I control how I react, and I choose to stay calm. Regardless, Rory will be 16 and sometimes do things I don't understand or like. So what? I am the adult.*

➤ Think of a less threatening reason the other acted the way he or she did, like these:

> ➤ *He is 16 and is clearly self-absorbed. So was I at that age. He is more interested in what he wants to do than in making me miserable.*

> ➤ *He may have been in a bad mood today. The more I think about it, the more I realize he was up late trying to ace his chemistry final. He is usually in a much better mood.*

➤ Ask yourself: Is this trigger really worth my losing it? Try on some thoughts like these:

> ➤ *This is really not that important. By tomorrow he and I will probably have forgotten about it. It is just not worth getting so charged up about.*

> ➤ *How is Gerry likely to react if I complain about Rory again? I think I know. She will probably react the same way she always does and be very disappointed in me. Do I want that?*

Plan:

➤ Now problem-solve a plan to stay calm and approach the situation differently:

> ➤ *I will take a few signal breaths and focus on relaxing my shoulders. This is just not worth getting upset.*

> ➤ *I will sit down with Gerry and Rory and work out a contract as to how we expect him to behave and the rewards and consequences of his actions.*

elsewhere (e.g., at the office), adding to the benefits you receive for your labors.

I've developed a vehicle for the written rebuttal, called an "Anger Analysis." Nick, the man you heard complaining about his wife Jen's lateness at the beginning of the chapter, used the Anger Analysis to figure out why he kept getting so angry and what new self-talk he could use to change that. Nick came to see me when Jen threatened to separate because of his "constant hostility and put-downs." Minimizing Jen's concerns, Nick blamed his anger on stress at work. When I wondered if he could remember some of his actions that occurred as he angered himself, he told me he just didn't pay attention: "My anger just overwhelms me—I don't recall what I do I get so mad."

After asking Jen what behaviors she defined as "hostile," Nick entered into the left side ("What happened") of an Anger Analysis form (shown on the next page) each episode when either he or Jen observed one of these actions. This analysis is designed to help you reconsider the ways you thought, felt, and acted during an anger episode. For his "Thoughts/self-talk" Nick tried to recall self-talk that stood out in his mind as his anger escalated.

When convenient, he filled in the right side ("What you would like") and had the opportunity to set new goals for how he would like to think, feel, and act the next time a similar "lateness" situation arose.

The Anger Analysis is also a handy way to keep a log of your anger episodes so you can track your progress over time. On the following page is one of Nick's completed Anger Analyses.

When Nick showed me the completed left side of his analysis, I guided him in rebutting his self-talk and setting new goals for feeling and acting by filling in the right side, as you've seen. Let's review how he did it.

Camera Check

I asked Nick to try to view the triggering situation through an objective lens: What would a video camera have recorded if it had been present? A camera records exactly what was said or done, thus helping you separate the objective facts from your interpretations (e.g., a camera will not record guesses, assumptions, interpretations, or labels for things—just what occurred).

While Nick's initial view that Jen "purposefully made me late" fueled his anger, his "camera check" found Jen upstairs putting on

Nick's Anger Analysis	
What happened	What you would like
Situation (who, where, what happened):	Camera check:
Jen purposefully made me late to dinner with our friends.	*A camera would see my wife getting ready. I can't see her thoughts or motives, so how do I know it was on purpose?*
Implicit expectation:	Realistic expectation:
We should arrive at our destination at least 15 minutes early to ensure promptness.	*Based on past experience, we are likely to arrive no more than 15 minutes late to most things.*
Thoughts/self-talk:	Rational self-talk (think, objectify, plan):
1. *We will be incredibly late, and our friends will be upset with us!*	1. *Forecasting. Fact is I ended up getting there on time. In the future, I need to be calm, take a signal breath, and read the paper until she's ready.*
2. *Jen is doing this to me on purpose ... she knows I can't stand to be late. She's taking every single second she can to make us late.*	2. *Mind reading. Fact is she likes to look nice, and that's the likely reason she took longer than I did to get ready. I'll try not to mind read and personalize this. I will sit, do my breathing, and if she is still not down at a reasonable time I'll let her know I'm taking the other car.*
3. *Only a moron could continue being late, again and again.*	3. *Labeling. Fact is that I love Jen and she is probably smarter than I am. This has to do with style, not intelligence. I'll follow my plan (#2 above).*

What happened	What you would like
4. *I can't stand this ... she will never change.*	4. *Stop the Thresholding. I can stand it; I have stood it before and will again. Jen is not as time-focused as I am. In fact we are rarely more than 15 minutes late and I will survive. Is it worth ruining the day?*
Angry feelings/body sensations: *I feel furious, and it's hard to catch my breath.* Rate feelings (0–100): *90*	How I would like to feel: *Disappointed but calm. Try to slow my breathing to a regular, rhythmic pace.*
Behavior/face of anger: *Paced, cursing to myself. I also yelled at Jen to get ready and spilled coffee on myself I was so upset.*	Desired behavior/face: *Calmly let Jen know when we have to leave one time. Sit and read paper. Relax, take a few signal breaths, and lean back.*
Outcome: *I felt like a fool for losing it again. We ended up getting there on time, but with Jen stressed and upset with me.*	Desired outcome: *A calm and relaxed evening before and during the ride to the restaurant. ...*

clothes and makeup. A camera couldn't "see" Jen's thoughts, so Nick's threatening supposition that she was *purposely* late is "mind reading," not supported by any evidence.

Realistic Expectations

He also set a realistic expectation to be no more than 15 minutes late in most cases, based on past experience. Just resetting and stating this rational expectation really helped to reduce his anger the next time he and Jen prepared to go somewhere.

Rational Self-Talk

Nick then wrote a rebuttal for each of his core thoughts, using the STOP format already discussed. He just omitted the first step, because there was no need after the fact to "stop" and calm down. As you look over his rebuttals, you can see that each used the three steps: think, objectify, and plan. To illustrate, let's take his first thought in reaction to Jen's lateness: 1. *"We will be incredibly late, and our friends will be upset with us."*

Think. Each rebuttal began with Nick thinking through whether his thought was rational using the three questions (key words again underlined) I asked you to memorize, found in the previous section. He then noted which distortion(s) it represents.

> ➤ *Is my thought <u>based on observable facts</u>?* No. It was not a fact that they would be late or his friends would be upset, because it hadn't happened yet.

> ➤ *Is it <u>giving me good ideas</u> for staying calm and getting the situation resolved?* No. In fact, it contributed to more irritation, pacing, and complaining, thereby making the problem worse.

> ➤ *Is it <u>free of cognitive distortions</u>?* Having become familiar with the cognitive distortions in Chapter 6, he quickly decided it wasn't. This thought is an example of forecasting.

Nick concluded it was an irrational thought and needed to be replaced now and in the future. He wrote in the cognitive distortion the thought represented: "forecasting."

Objectify. Nick decided to think of one or two objective facts to state in his self-talk to rebut the irrational thought. He decided the main fact is that they ended up getting there on time and his friends were the ones who were a bit late. To put Jen's behavior in context, he noted that she was very caring about his needs in virtually every other way.

Plan. Nick planned to practice dampening (Chapter 5) the next time he found himself waiting for Jen to get ready. His plan was to remain seated and to read the paper while using signal breaths as needed. If he began to upset himself, he decided to remind himself of his new realistic expectation and to use the STOP rebuttal method to immediately challenge any upsetting self-talk.

How I Would Like to Feel

Since getting angry and feeling that his breathing was getting out of control was upsetting and self-defeating, Nick decided to work toward feeling disappointed (which, given his nature, was realistic) but calm and to try to slow his breathing to a stable and comfortable pace. By focusing on this goal, he felt he had a realistic standard to strive for and to assess how he was doing.

Desired Behavior/Face

To envision more effective solutions to react to Jen's lateness in the future, Nick used problem solving, thinking of as many new ideas as he could muster, recording the best on the right side.

Desired Outcome

Finally, Nick considered the outcome he would like to achieve by changing his thoughts, feelings, and actions the next time he faced this kind of situation. Visualizing the outcome you want next time is the surest way to make it happen. Note that his desired outcome seems practical and attainable if he just keeps his anger in check.

Look over how Nick rebutted each of the three additional thoughts (numbers 2–4) using the STOP method. It's best to complete the left side of an Anger Analysis soon after an anger episode so you can clearly recall what happened. You can then practice filling in the right side to build your skill at rebuttals when you have the time. After you have completed five to ten of them, you will likely notice that much of your unhelpful self-talk is repetitious, so you won't have "hundreds" of irrational thoughts to challenge. Soon you will be able to immediately rebut these thinking "traps" on the spot, using the STOP method, which you have repeatedly practiced in writing, saving yourself a lot of grief.

Most important, as you practice new thinking, you will notice that your former irrational thinking occurs less as your newly practiced self-talk starts to become more automatic.

A copy of the Anger Analysis, suitable for reproducing, is available in Appendix 4. Keep some copies handy so you can begin to log your anger episodes.

Stress Inoculation: Another Method for Using Self-Talk to Manage Anger

Another way your self-talk can be redirected toward helping you manage your anger is called "stress inoculation." Cognitive-behavioral therapy researcher and therapist Dr. Donald Meichenbaum has shown that we manage each stage of stressful situations much better when we use positive self-talk to guide our actions. Dr. Raymond Novaco has applied Meichenbaum's ideas for "stress inoculation" to anger management, by viewing an anger episode as comprising four stages:

1. Preparing for provocation

2. Dealing with impact and confrontation

3. Coping with increased arousal

4. Reflecting on performance

In stress inoculation you create a series of self-instructional thoughts that help you cope with each stage of anger arousal, like those found in the sidebar on page 147.

Preparation

Sometimes you just know you're likely to be triggered because you got angry the last time under similar circumstances or with the same person. When you have this heads-up, previewing one or two ideas for how you will act as you enter the situation can set the stage for success. Look over the statements for "Preparing for a Provocation" in the sidebar for some ideas to help you create preparatory self-talk that feels right for you.

Nick decided to prepare for the possibility that Jen would be late the next time they were invited out. For preparation he decided to think repeatedly about the more realistic expectation that she would be up to 15 minutes late, based on past experience, while reassuring himself with a preparatory self-instruction: "Any lateness gives me a perfect opportunity to catch up on the sports section. The later she is, the more I catch up."

Impact and Confrontation

Unfortunately, you can't always predict when you are about to be provoked, but the remaining stages of the inoculation method are applicable to every anger situation. This next stage, impact, occurs when you are first aware that your anger is rising, using the anger-scaling model of Chapter 4 (e.g., you notice that your fist is getting tight or your face is becoming hot, your anger "signal").

For example, if Nick noticed his chest starting to get tight, he decided to take a deep signal breath and then focus on a helpful self-instruction linked to each slow and calming breath: "This is beginning to get my chest tight. Time to focus on my plan. I will sit down, take a signal breath, and tell myself "I'm in control and I choose to be calm."

Coping with Increased Arousal

When you notice that you are at a 40 or above on your anger scale, you need to bring on the heavy artillery to stay in control. Sit down, if possible, take your signal breath, and focus away from what is happening outside you by directing your attention to dampening your arousal (e.g., while the other talks, you can be focusing on new thinking). If your arousal keeps rising, you will have to leave the situation with a "stop" phrase as described in Chapter 4, so time is of the essence. Self-instructions can be directed at specific parts of your body that are reacting to your arousal, like the following:

"My shoulders are getting tense. I need to focus on recalling them feeling loose and limp as I take another deep signal breath."

"My face is getting hot. Each time I take a breath I can feel the coolness and exhale away the heat."

"My voice is getting loud and my jaw is tight. I will lean back and let go of a little more tension and intensity each time I exhale."

Self-Instructions for the Regulation of Anger

Preparing for a provocation

> ➤ This may upset me, but I know how to deal with it.
> ➤ I can work out a plan to handle this. My plan is to "_____."
> ➤ Remember, stick to the issues and don't take it personally.
> ➤ I can take deep breaths for relaxation and think more clearly.
> ➤ Easy does it. I am in control.

Impact and confrontation

> ➤ Stay calm. Just continue to relax.
> ➤ As long as I keep my cool, then I'm in control of the situation.
> ➤ There is nothing to be gained by getting mad.
> ➤ What difference will this make in a week or a month?
> ➤ If I stay calm, I can think clearly.

Coping with arousal of anger

> ➤ My muscles are getting tight. That's my signal for a relaxation breath.
> ➤ It's just not worth it to get so angry.
> ➤ Time to take a deep breath and slowly image _____ (e.g., color blue).
> ➤ My anger is a signal to use my problem-solving skills.
> ➤ Try to reason it out. Focus on behavior (e.g., what I/he/she wants).

After the confrontation

> ➤ I could have used a calming phrase. Let me rethink how I could have handled it better.
> ➤ I started to lose it. My signal breathing kept me in control. Way to go.
> ➤ The more I try to get my point across when angry, the louder I get. Next time sit, breathe, and think.
> ➤ Okay. I blew it this time, but now let me focus on when and how I lost it so I won't make the same mistake next time.
> ➤ That's over. What can I learn for next time I get in this situation?

As Nick's chest felt tight and his breathing was more restricted he knew he was rising above a 50, so his self-instruction addressed how he would like his chest and breathing to feel: "Each time I exhale I am letting go of heaviness and tightness. Each time I breathe in the cool air, my chest feels lighter and looser."

Reflecting on Performance

After you have reacted to provocation, think over how you handled the situation. Rather than thinking you really blew it if you reacted with an old face of anger, cut yourself some slack and consider what you learned that can be applied next time. If you did well, don't be bashful. Give yourself positive credit.

The next time Nick waited for Jen to get ready, she complimented him on controlling his temper and being more reasonable. He noticed how differently their evening turned out when he took steps to cool his anger and to think more rationally. His reflection was positive and constructively critical: "I did a much better job thinking before I said anything. My signal breathing and statements were really helpful. At one point I got up and began pacing, and this immediately got me tense, above a 50. Next time I need to stay seated until Jen comes down and really work on keeping my muscles relaxed."

Once you develop self-talk for each of the four stages of anger, jot it down on a 3" × 5" card to keep in your wallet or purse so you can read it regularly until it becomes automatic. This is a way of reinforcing the belief "I can handle this; I am prepared," making triggers seem more manageable.

Many of my clients have told me that just one self-instructional phrase worked for them. A young Navy lieutenant about to be dismissed from flight training because of his temper would hear the phrase repeatedly "I'm cool—I'm in school." By repeating a phrase continuously during a difficult moment, you stay focused on your game plan, while blocking out automatic negative self-talk.

New Images: Creating a New Reality

While imagery can trigger anger and provide directions for unfortunate action, helpful images view a past, current, or upcoming provocative situation through a less threatening and more helpful lens. Like a map that visually directs us to the right destination, imagery helps us rehearse a new way of thinking and acting, without having to actually experience the situation. Imagery is like a "free ride." You get to try out new behaviors and see how they seem to feel and work without risking "real" failure. Also, many research studies show that imaginal rehearsals are almost as effective as actual practice in preparing us for "real-life" situations.

Reframing Triggering Images

When your imagery fuels anger, it's probably focusing on the most upsetting aspects of the past, present, or possible future, while not including more neutral or positive details. By focusing on less upsetting facts about the situation, you can often dampen your anger.

Imagine *other times that your experience with the person, object, or situation has been better.* This places your negative experience in the context of other encounters and reframes your perspective. For example, Nick could picture Jen looking ravishing as she walks into the restaurant or focus on picturing her kindness to him when he was laid up with a broken ankle.

Reframe *the upsetting situation as a small part of your busy life* by focusing on one or two things that are really important to you. For example, Nick felt much different when he focused his imagery on Jen's receiving positive medical results after a biopsy that had worried both of them. This led to the self-talk "My anger over Jen being late is a tiny annoyance compared to Jen or our kids being sick."

Reframe into the future *how important the upsetting situation will be one month or one year from now.* Can you imagine it will continue to affect your life even a week from now, let alone a month or year? If it will still be affecting your future life, it is really important and should be problem-solved using the ideas found in Chapter 8. It's more likely that what triggers you today is really meaningless as a predictor of your future, and this "reframe" should help you see that. For example, Nick found it impossible to picture Jen's being 15 minutes late to a dinner having any negative consequences for their future. It really was trivial in the grander scheme of their life together.

Redirecting Your Actions with Imagery

When you vividly picture how you will act in a situation before the fact, the likelihood of this picture "coming true" is increased. For example, think of times you successfully used imagery to prepare for giving a talk, fixing a piece of equipment, or redecorating a room.

You can capitalize on the power of imagery by closing your eyes and imagining how you'll react differently the next time you're confronted with a trigger.

1. Picture the situation, with others present, and all relevant details and then how the other person or object is likely to act.

2. When confronted by the trigger, vividly imagine various ways your words and actions could be different using the ideas you've learned in this book and your own creativity and then imagine the likely outcome from what you know about the other or the situation.

3. Notice how you feel as you try out new behaviors. Pick a set of actions that seem most comfortable and most likely to help you remain calm, while being more effective than your past efforts. Picture a more positive outcome.

Nick tried to imagine how he could handle Jen's lateness differently. He pictured himself sitting comfortably reading the sports section of the paper while listening to his favorite Sinatra CD as he waited for Jen. When he imagined her coming down 15 minutes late, he pictured telling her she looked nice and calmly suggesting they leave.

Building on what we've discussed about imagery in Chapters 5, 6, and this chapter, Chapter 10 will provide additional ideas for using imagery to firmly establish your new anger actions. When they become habits, you no longer have to focus on exactly what you're thinking. These new, adaptive actions will begin to occur quite naturally. Another benefit of imaginal practice in handling provocative situations is that they lose their power to arouse your anger the more you practice them. Just as we resolve a fear by repeatedly "exposing" ourselves to the thing we fear, your anger arousal to anger triggers is bound to lessen the more you practice coping.

From Thoughts to Actions

Now that you've learned to identify and replace irrational thoughts that fuel and direct negative faces of anger, you must also be able to communicate your way through conflict while keeping your own goals in mind. Chapters 8 and 9 focus on ideas for achieving assertive problem solving, first discussed in Chapter 2. This ideal face of anger permits you to communicate in a nonthreatening manner when difficult issues arise with others and you feel under fire.

Just for Practice

You won't change your automatic reaction to triggering situations without practicing new thinking. So how do you begin? These two chapters on the role of thoughts in arousing and directing anger offered numerous ideas for identifying and transforming your thoughts. To help you practice these ideas, initiate the following plan:

1. Pay attention to your anger over the next few weeks using your Daily Anger Log. When you notice a physical sign that your anger is escalating or you or another person notices an unwanted face of anger, fill in "what happened" on the left side of a blank copy of the Anger Analysis. Keep the forms handy (e.g., in a desk drawer at the office, on top of the refrigerator) and try to record as soon after the anger episode as possible so the events are fresh in your mind.

2. Using what you learned about identifying and rebutting irrational thoughts in these two chapters, and using Nick's example as a guide, fill in the right side of the Anger Analysis at a convenient time. Use the STOP method when crafting a rebuttal to each listed thought. Each rebuttal should decide if the thought is distorted and, if so, review objective facts and decide on a plan.

3. If you're aware of imagery that seems to be associated with your anger, is it helpful in calming your emotions and directing you to resolve the challenge you face? If not, create a new image of calm reacting that clearly details how you would use new anger actions to react to the situation or solve the problem. Imagine the scene vividly, using each of your senses. The more you imaginally practice the scene, the greater the likelihood that what you rehearsed in your mind will influence your actions the next time you're in a similar triggering situation.

4. For the situation you recorded in your Anger Analysis, use the stress inoculation method to prepare one or more self-instructional

phrases you could use if faced with this situation again. Write them down on a 3" × 5" card to keep handy in your wallet or purse.

5. Remember that practice makes perfect. So keep at it. The more Anger Analyses you do on paper, the easier it will be to remember and use the STOP method on the spot, when you most need it. In fact, you'll probably have to use it less than now because your new thinking is gradually replacing the old.

Step Five

Staying Cool Under Fire

RATIONAL THINKING AND REALISTIC EXPECTATIONS WILL GO a long way toward helping you stay in control of your anger, but they can't eliminate the conflicts and differences we all encounter in the real world. Chapter 8 explains how to use assertive problem solving, introduced in Chapter 2, to handle your own anger when these conflicts arise. Chapter 9 shows how to use the same tools when others are angry with you.

8

Assertive Problem Solving
Expressing Anger Constructively in Conflict Situations

Ben: "I begin to make a point, and my wife starts raising her voice, telling me I'm losing it again. When I try to defend myself, she cuts me off and gets really furious with me. I can't stand to be cut off like that, and it only makes me angrier. But I still manage to control myself. Unfortunately, Maria doesn't hear anything I say at that point."

Relationships are interactive. Conversations are unpredictable. Life is complicated.

These are the facts of life that make anger management a challenge. Most of us can learn to catch ourselves in an anger-provoking thought; we can even uproot deeply planted expectations that have been serving us badly for years. With practice we can catch our anger in that split second before it bursts into flame and take action to turn down the heat. All of these skills should be helping you reduce the number of really damaging anger episodes you have, and in fact you should find your anger flaring less often altogether. You've come a long way.

But what do you do with the problems that are still triggering your anger? Some may be based on unrealistic expectations that you can't quite shrug off. Your upbringing and the accumulated experiences of a lifetime can't always be exchanged at will, like last season's wardrobe.

Maybe you're still irked by the rudeness you encounter everywhere you go, even though you know it's a rougher, more rushed world than it was when you were young. You don't "lose it" at the grocery store and on the phone with "customer service" anymore, but you sometimes arrive home at the end of the day feeling beaten down by the uncivilized behavior of our modern civilization. How can you resolve this problem?

Other times your anger may be fully justified by the facts of the situation and your thoughts about them. What you're running into—maybe a bully at the office or a teacher who shows flagrant favoritism in your child's classroom or the vandals who are destroying your neighborhood—would make anyone mad. As you know, losing control in response to these injustices not only fails to right the wrong but usually ends up hurting you in the bargain. So what do you do instead?

You use assertive problem solving, the only face of anger that is appropriate in all situations, is constructive, and makes you look good, too. I told you a little bit about this skill in Chapter 2, and in Chapter 7 I showed you how it's the natural endpoint of the STOP method that starts with dampening arousal, continues through thought evaluation and adjustment, and then turns to planning for action.

Righteous anger in the form of assertive problem solving is what helps you meet your needs and expectations. Instead of secretly plotting to force the office bully out of the company, maybe you find him a lateral move that will tap his talents but keep him on projects that require little collaboration. Rather than writing venomous threatening letters to the principal, you might decide to talk to the teacher to find out whether she's even aware she is showing favoritism. In response to the neighborhood vandals, you don't drum up a vigilante group or sit on your porch with a shotgun across your lap but contact the local police about how residents and law enforcement can work together to protect your homes.

Assertive problem solving can also help you resolve the less dramatic—but no less important, at least in the aggregate—conflicts that occur every day, like the one described at the beginning of this chapter. Controlling your anger doesn't have to mean ending every conflict in a standoff, the problem that triggered your anger still hovering over you like a dark cloud. You can be heard, even though you're angry. You just have to make sure that how you communicate isn't designed to trigger the anger of the person you're in conflict with.

Angry Faces in Communication: What to Avoid

Your work so far has concentrated on turning inward, learning to recognize your own physical, mental, and emotional cues so that you can head off anger before it takes control of your behavior. In the real world, though, you'll often have to use these skills while under fire. Other people and the events going on around you will be vying for your attention. Those you're trying to communicate with may very well not only have opinions of their own that are begging to be heard but also be angry themselves, making it all the more difficult to keep your wits about you.

When your anger arousal is escalating up your scale, your customary face of anger may be magnified. If you tend to be passive when angry, you may find yourself completely shutting down so that resolution of differences becomes impossible. Or your facial expression, words, and gestures, and even the volume and tone of your voice may be magnified into a face of hostility or aggression. You may come across as more irrational or hotheaded than you wish, losing the listener's attention entirely or triggering a negative face of anger in defense.

In any case, your message is lost, and a relationship may have been stressed or even damaged. So, when anger is rising on both sides, how do you get your message across in a way that defuses anger and focuses on resolution of the differences?

In this chapter I will show you exactly how assertive problem solving works as a strategy for successfully communicating your ideas, feelings, and needs in even the most provocative situation. Sometimes, of course, your efforts at communicating effectively are challenged by others whose anger expression is so provocative or downright threatening that you must take steps to defuse the situation. Chapter 9 will give you ideas to stay calm when each angry face is used against you.

The first thing you need to do toward learning assertive problem solving is to become fully aware of which unproductive faces of anger you tend to use in your daily communications. If you don't remember what each face looks like, go back to Chapter 2 and review the descriptions there. In general, though, do you tend to express your anger actively and directly or passively and indirectly? Would you call yourself a shouter or a shunner? Do you strike out or brood? You may still prefer not to think of yourself as fitting any such "label," and naturally your mode of behavior (and everyone else's) is much more complicated than that. But it's important to see your anger-communication style with a clear eye so that you know what you'll need to work on to get to assertive problem solving.

See if you can recognize yourself in any of the following descriptions. We'll start with the active and direct faces of anger, hostility, and aggression, because they are so intrusive and coercive that they often cause more immediate problems than the other faces. Passive faces of anger can be just as infuriating (sometimes more so), but because they are often intended to express ire without suffering the consequences of doing so, they sometimes allow the angry person to escape repercussions—at least for the time being.

Hostility and Aggression: Unwelcome Faces at Any Time

Hostility and aggression seem like strong words, so most of us would prefer to disown them. But if your anger tends to come out in one of these intense ways, those who bear the brunt of it are not too likely to let you do so. If you've ever been the target of someone else's hostility or aggression, you know it's hard to ignore, especially since people who express their anger this way often make demands on the person they're angry at.

Try to recall the last time another person became hostile or aggressive toward you. The person's *voice* was probably loud or intense in some way. If you were talking to a friend who became hostile or aggressive, maybe his or her tone became brusque, condescending, or downright rude. How did you react? Many people feel intimidated, defensive, or threatened when someone speaks to them that way. As your defenses become aroused, you're not too likely to open-mindedly consider the other person's point of view, are you? Do you notice that you sometimes also raise your own voice in response?

Hostility and aggression also come out in *body language* that includes scowling, staring, or grimacing at you. Abrupt and forceful gestures, such as finger pointing and hand waving, and other distracting movements—maybe the person shakes his head to communicate disagreement as you talk—may make it hard for you to keep your cool. Have you noticed that these body communications can be just as threatening to you as harsh words?

What happens when someone, say a coworker, really gets in your face, maybe *pacing or moving closer* to you when angry? Research has found that we all have a space boundary for comfortable communication, which varies across cultures. When another person invades your comfort zone or "personal space," how do you feel? Physical touch like making a fist, blocking, holding, hitting, or in any way touching you is very likely to arouse your "fight-or-flight" reaction (see Chapter 4), leading to serious repercussions for both parties.

In short, the way a hostile or aggressive person talks to you, gestures, and moves when angry is likely to make you stop listening and start getting fearful or angry yourself. We all react this way when we feel attacked.

And that's only part of the communication. What about its *content*? People who get hostile or aggressive when angered are prone to distorting facts to highlight their perceived righteousness: "That's at least the tenth time you've forgotten to pay the phone bill!" "You are the *only* employee I've ever had who hasn't been able to master this system." They may indulge in name calling or cursing. They may even threaten to harm you in some way ("If you don't finish that yardwork in 30 minutes, you're fired!"). When added to a loud, forceful tone of voice and threatening body language, these verbal messages can make anyone see red. Worse, unpleasant words have a tendency to stick with us. I've found they often create long-lasting resentment or even a rift in relationships. So, if your wife seems to overreact when you're "making a point," could it be that she's remembering the way you made your last such point with her?

Recalling the way hostility and aggression directed at you have made you feel can make you more sensitive to their effects on others and, in turn, more inclined to want to avoid the reaction that we all have to these faces of anger. To help spot these tactics in yourself, try to pay attention to *how* you communicate whenever anger arises in you using the Daily Anger Log recommended in Chapter 2 or a modified version of the Anger Analysis in Chapter 7.

To pay attention to his wife's complaint that he was very intense when anything went wrong during vacation travel, Marshall decided to record any anger episodes in the daily organizer/calendar he always kept with him. When a hotel clerk "messed up" his reservation, he recorded: "I loudly interrupted the clerk and found myself glaring at him and name calling—'This is ridiculous and you're obviously incompetent'—shaking my head in disgust and breathing very hard. My wife got very embarrassed and told me I was making a scene. We later argued about what had happened, ruining part of the day."

By keeping written track of his words and actions when angry, he soon realized that his wife's conclusions were correct and became more aware of these anger actions before they escalated.

Indirect and Passive Anger

How does it feel when the significant others in your life refuse to discuss their anger but act indirectly to annoy or punish you?

You notice a spouse's *tone of voice* is tinged with sarcasm or has an "edge." Or a close friend talks less or freezes you out with sighs and silences, while thwarting your best efforts to discuss the issue openly.

Body language can signal that the other person is upset without using words. Lack of eye contact with you or expressions of annoyance, such as eye rolling or exasperated sighs, may be related to something you did, but you must interpret what's wrong if your partner denies a problem or ignores you.

Passive and indirect *actions* may withhold something you desire or withdraw affection. How do you react when shut out or denied a reasonable request? Or when a significant other communicates anger with sarcasm, hostile "joking," or innuendo, yet blames you for having a "thin skin" if you protest?

Rather than frankly discussing her anger with her "workaholic" husband, Jeanne often punished him by withdrawing emotionally and sexually. She would look away when he spoke, sigh, and avoid him when he tried to approach her. I encouraged her to identify a set of realistic expectations for her husband, based on the requirements of his job as a young attorney that he work 10- to 12-hour days, and then to sit down with him and try to problem-solve a solution agreeable to both. They worked out that he would leave home earlier on two mornings a week so he could be home for dinner on those days, a win–win solution for them both.

One of the biggest problems with passive forms of anger, of course, is that the goal is to avoid taking responsibility for being, and acting, angry. Therefore many of us become pretty practiced at denying that we're behaving in any out-of-the-ordinary way or that we're angry at all. When you review your log of anger episodes, ask yourself as you read through it, "Do I behave that way ordinarily?" or "Would I act that way if I were really happy with this person?" If your angry conflicts usually center around one particular person, you can customize these questions: "Is this the way I usually treat Jim?" or "Do I act this way when I'm happy to see Jim after a long day at work?" Also look at how long your passive anger seems to go on. Do you find that you "just don't feel like talking" to your husband for a couple of days sometimes, when earlier in your marriage you couldn't hold on to your "mood" for more than an hour or two? Also examine the thoughts that go through your head while you're being passively or indirectly angry. Sometimes we keep a running self-righteous script spooling through our mind just to keep up the ire and justify our behavior. Or we start coming up with euphemisms for our anger, to avoid owning not just our actions but also our feelings. Do you think of yourself as "just disappointed" or "kind of depressed" over whatever happened? Sometimes this is a smokescreen for anger—and a way to make the other person feel bad about the hurt that her actions have caused you—rather than owning up to being plain old angry. Passive anger is almost impossible to admit to when you're in the throes of the role, but later you may be able to look at your emotions and actions more honestly and also see how counterproductive they may have been.

Fortunately, there's another way to get your message across—to make sure the person you're angry at hears how you felt about the incident and what you would like to have change. While you can't control what the other person says or does when differences arise, you can influence how the communication turns out by adopting a rational communication strategy and inviting the other to join you: This strategy is assertive problem solving.

Productive Anger: Assertive Problem Solving

Assertive problem solving begins with discussion that is assertive while not being aggressive: The message is clear and direct while nonthreatening. You look at your friend or partner as you talk and listen, conveying interest and a caring and responsive attitude with your facial expression. Your gestures and body movements are not abrupt or distracting but smooth, and they calmly emphasize the points you're making. Your voice intensity is moderate, and your tone conveys interest and concern. If your partner gets louder or more forceful, you stay the course and continue at your calm level or use a "stop" phrase to end the discussion if things get too intense.

When negotiating differences of opinion, problem solving is the means to a win–win solution that both of you can live with.

But before you can communicate successfully, you must be clear as to what you want the other person to know. By taking a few minutes to assess your awareness on an issue, you prepare yourself to fully communicate your position.

Step 1. Awareness: Knowing What You Think, Feel, and Need

Just communicating that you're angry tells another person how you feel but doesn't provide much of the information needed to solve the problem. Just blurting something out can make the situation worse, as we all have learned. Once you've taken steps to dampen your anger, take a few minutes to consider your awareness of the triggering event, which can be divided into four parts: factual events, feelings, thoughts, and needs. Each part must be considered when you decide what you wish to communicate to the other person.

Out with friends at a restaurant, Serg was furious when Sophia interrupted his account of a trip to Europe to illustrate how disorganized he was, even forgetting the plane tickets. Serg "went along" with this "ribbing," even though he believed Sophia was publicly "putting him down." His hot face immediately signaled he was at a 50 or more on his anger scale, and he knew he had to derail his escalating anger. He began the STOP method (Chapter 7) by leaning back and taking a deep signal breath as he forcefully told himself to stop his train of thought (S). He decided that his self-talk—she was purposefully "putting him down"—was a distortion: "mind reading" and "personalizing" (T). He realized that the objective *facts* were that Sophia was an exuberant person who often made remarks or offered additions to others' comments (O). He decided the best plan was to assertively discuss his awareness with her once they arrived home and ask her to make some changes (P).

To implement this plan he began by reflecting on his awareness, considering the facts of what had happened, while also recognizing how he felt in reaction to Sophia's actions. Then he reflected on his thoughts/opinion about what had happened, which helped him decide what he needed from Sophia then and in the future.

Using the camera check (Chapter 7) as his guide, Serg recalled the *factual events*, just as a camera would have recorded them. He concluded that Sophia did interrupt him but did not say anything that was overtly a put-down. He could not "see" into her mind and could not factually conclude that she was trying intentionally to humiliate him. In fact, she was usually very supportive of him and often complimented him.

In addition to his anger, he concluded he *felt* humiliated by her comments.

His most significant *thought/opinion* about the situation was that he believed he had the right to conclude his statement without interruption and that private and personal events in their marriage should not be shared by either of them without permission.

Finally, Serg decided that he really *needed* Sophie's full attention when he communicated. He also needed to feel that she was not undermining him or revealing personal or embarrassing information to others without his consent. He felt these needs could be communicated to his wife in clear behavioral terms (e.g., "I would really appreciate it if you would not bring up embarrassing personal information about me unless I've agreed it can be shared"). Rather than expecting perfection, he realized it would take some time for her to change; it would not occur overnight. With these new, realistic expectations, he knew he would be less likely to anger himself.

Step 2. Planning: Communicating at the Right Time for Maximum Impact

Communicating when the listener is likely to be ready, willing, and able to listen—not distracted—goes a long way toward ensuring that you'll be heard. This means first finding the right setting: a time and place when distractions and discomfort won't prevent you from being heard. Be seated to decrease arousal and invite the other to be seated. Don't try to communicate with someone while you're driving a car, eating in a restaurant, or shopping, for example. These activities will likely distract the other person and make your attempts to be heard stressful for both of you. Also, don't choose family gatherings, parties, or other group settings as the time to express an important need to someone. The last thing you want when expressing important needs is to instigate defensiveness, which will surely block listening to you and perhaps fuel an argument.

Just as important as picking the right setting is being aware of the other person's physical, mental, and emotional state. You've been learning to recognize your own arousal level to head off unproductive anger expression, and you can also attune yourself to recognizing in others the external signs that strongly suggest the internal building of emotion. Your friend's or partner's arousal level—the degree to which he or she is physiologically prepared to "fight or flee," an automatic response described in Chapter 2—plays a tremendous role in how the person is likely to perceive and react to your heartfelt statement of your thoughts, feelings, and needs. Recall recent times when the person you want to communicate with was clearly angry and aroused. What did you notice in his or her facial expression, tone of voice, body position, and movements, as well as the content of his or her communications, right before and during the anger episode? Was the person's face flushed? Was she glaring at you or visibly turning away to avoid eye contact? Was she shaking her head in disagreement while you were talking? These are all facial expressions that say that anger may be building. Physical movements and body language can be revealing too. When people are angry, they may get right in your face, point at you, use choppy, forceful hand or arm motions, poke you, or block your path if you try to exit the area. Or they may do the opposite, turning away from you or leaving. Verbal signs of anger include not just the obvious—yelling or interrupting—but using an exaggeratedly low tone, laughing sarcastically or nastily, giving abrupt responses like "Whatever" and "Right," or just refusing to talk at all. In addition to how it is said, what is said can be a signal of building anger: cursing, severe criticism, name calling, blaming, defensiveness, and changing the subject. If the person you're trying to reach always seems to act in these ways when you attempt to talk, you need to employ one or more defusing strategies like those you will find in Chapter 9.

Finding another time to talk when you feel strongly about an issue may be frustrating for you, but pursuing a discussion with a person who is physiologically aroused to anger is generally fruitless and will likely lead to an argument or worse. At higher levels of arousal, your friend or relative's ability to focus and hear what you're saying is compromised. Even worse, arousal makes it harder to put on the brakes and inhibit expressions of anger.

Step 3. Assertive Communication

Imagine how Sophia would have felt if Serg had waited for her to get comfortable, then loudly bombarded her as they drove home: "Okay, you succeeded in making me look like an idiot in front of our friends. Don't ever interrupt or try to embarrass me again or you'll get the same from me."

What's wrong with this way of communicating? Serg's message came in the form of what psychologists call a "you" message: Focusing only on Sophia, he tells her what she did wrong in a blaming/threatening mode, characterizing her motives and cutting off any mutual discussion.

To make matters worse, Sophia can't see her husband's face or body language because they are in a car at night. All she has to go on are his words and his loud, sarcastic tone, so naturally she now feels attacked. Consequently, her options are limited and all negative.

Think about the last time you got angry at someone. Did you use a "you" message? Here are the main ingredients to avoid:

1. Not talking about your own awareness, but placing all responsibility for what went wrong on the other person.

2. Characterizing the other person's thoughts or feelings ("mind reading") or imputing a negative intent ("personalizing") with no data to support your allegation.

3. Using communication roadblocks such as those found in the sidebar on page 166, which derail mutual discussion and may threaten the other person. Look over the sidebar and consider which of these you find yourself using.

In fact, Serg's discussion with his wife went well because he used an "I" message, which focused totally on the four parts of his awareness without blaming and threatening Sophia. The "I" message is at the heart of assertive communication and is used to communicate your awareness on any issue in a way that fosters listening and resolution.

Keeping in mind the impact of your voice, facial expression, and body language, the form for the "I" message is as follows:

"*When* [fill in the factual event you observed] *happened* [fill in when it happened (e.g., last night at dinner, at our friends' house Sunday night)]."

"*I felt* [fill in your emotions (angry, sad, embarrassed, fearful, etc.)]."

"*My thoughts are that* [fill in your opinions, ideas, reactions, interpretations]."

Roadblocks to Effective Communication

"Roadblock"	Illustrations
"Kitchen-sinking"	➤ [Adding more new issues] "Well, what about the way you treated me at Christmas, and what about how you never pitch in around here?"
"You-tooing"	➤ "I may have interrupted you, but you interrupt me all the time." ➤ "Your temper is just as bad as mine ... admit it."
Past "historicizing"	➤ "What about last year when you ... ?" ➤ "You forget that you lost money in the market two years ago."
Overgeneralizations	➤ "You always forget something." ➤ "You never bring what you need."
Labeling	➤ "You are irrational." ➤ "You are a moron, completely misinformed."
Mind reading	➤ "I know you are angry with me." ➤ "You love to argue, don't you—just to ruin my day?"
Fortune telling	➤ "This will never work. You will blow it again." ➤ "We can't ever work things out ... it's useless."
All-or-none remarks	➤ "This whole discussion is a waste." ➤ "Your position is completely illogical and without merit."
"Exasperating"	➤ [Big sigh, eyes rolling] "It's just hopeless and exhausting trying to talk with you." ➤ "Will you ever get to the point?"

"What I'm requesting of you in the future is [fill in a "polite request" that fulfills what you need the other person to do in clear and specific (behavioral) language]."

Using the personal pronoun "I," Serg calmly tells Sophia about each part of his awareness, then invites her to comment or offer ideas:

> "Sophia, now that we're home I need to talk about something that happened this evening. When you broke into my story and told the others I was so disorganized [*factual event*], I felt pretty humiliated and angry [*feelings*]. I believe that you didn't say anything that was mean-spirited, but I think we both have a right to finish a story without interruption [*thoughts*]. I'm pretty private and need you to respect my privacy and not reveal personal things to others without asking me first [*polite request*]. What do you think?"

After describing the facts of the situation without embellishment, Serg shares each part of his awareness in any order he pleases (e.g., first share thoughts, then feelings, then needs). His tone of voice is level; he leans back and uses smooth gestures as he looks at Sophia with a serious but nonthreatening facial expression. Sophia reacts to what he has said by paying close attention, called "active listening." She is not threatened by Serg's statements and thus feels no need to defend herself or counterattack.

Carefully showing your partner your full-faced interest, as Sophia did for Serg, promotes calm and reflective discussion. The sidebar (page 168) "Active Listening: Putting Your Best Ear Forward" shows the important ingredients of active listening. Try out these listening ideas when someone else is upset and trying to make a point with you. The other person is more likely to remain calm and will then willingly listen to you because he or she has had a chance to express his or her full awareness without being interrupted or threatened.

In contrast, notice more carefully what happens when you interrupt, act impatient, or challenge others before they are finished talking.

When Differences Arise: Defusing Conflict with Assertive Problem Solving

When assertive communication leads to a mutual understanding, you may discover that you completely agree on a solution to fix the problem

Active Listening: Putting Your Best Ear Forward

Mode of communication	What to focus on
Voice	*What you say can invite calm discussion or stifle it. How you say it is important, too.*
Statements	➤ Avoid interrupting. The focus is on understanding the other person. ➤ If confused, ask for clarification of feelings or the other person's position. ➤ Paraphrase the other person's feelings, thoughts, and needs at appropriate times and always before you state your own position.
Tone and loudness	➤ Keep your voice even, showing interest. ➤ Avoid "stair stepping": Do not raise your voice even if the other person does.
Body language	*Remember, body language is a major communicator of your message to another person.*
Facial expression	➤ Look at the other and show interest. Avoid facial negatives like eye rolling or frowning.
Body position	➤ Position yourself to fully face the other, sit comfortably, and lean forward a bit to show involvement.
Movements and gestures	➤ Use smooth movements and gestures. Sit in a "receptive" position with arms uncrossed. ➤ Avoid nonverbal negatives like shaking your head "no" as the other person talks. ➤ Nod affirmation that you are listening or agree when appropriate.

and now must decide who will take responsibility for implementing it. For example, after much discussion you and your spouse find you completely agree that your "hyper" son should be in bed by 8:30 P.M., but now you must decide how to get him there and who will take the lead.

But often you'll discover that your expectations of how to resolve an important issue are different from the other person's. As you know by now, anger will continue to be fueled when your expectations are not met. When a difference leads to an unacceptable outcome today and the possibility that the issue will continue to be unresolved, the stage is set for resentment.

Resentment is a kind of chronic anger that reemerges every time you think about a triggering situation that was not resolved to your satisfaction. Resentment may be further intensified when the issue continues to arise and you still have not reached a resolution that feels acceptable to you. For example, you and your brother continue to disagree on how much money each of you should contribute to your elderly parents' care. Every time you write a check for an amount you feel is "unfair," your anger reemerges from resentment lying just below the surface. If you don't resolve a disagreement, you can count on continuing resentment. So try to solve your problems now, before they start to fester. More on preventing resentment from building is in Chapter 11.

Problem solving, a strategy by which two parties collaborate to reach a win–win solution, is the answer to disagreement at any level. To illustrate the steps of problem solving, which is preceded by assertive communication, consider the standoff that was created when Gio and Alana could not agree on where to take a vacation.

Alana felt angry and frustrated by Gio's insistence that they could not afford more than a brief local getaway. Gio was angry that Alana wanted to "squander" the money they had set aside for their retirement account on a trip to Europe.

After two days of outright bickering followed by the silent treatment, both were open to my suggestions about how to communicate their opinions in a way that kept things calm. Using assertive communication and active listening, they were amazed they could understand each other's position and actually disagree without raising their voices. A first!

Next, they needed to resolve their differences using the following steps to problem-solve. Reaching resolution would remove the fuel for future resentment on this issue. Think about how you could apply each step to problem-solve a recent difference you've had with another person. Keep in mind that merely discussing differences can trigger anger. At all times be aware of your level of anger arousal and be ready to use the STOP method as soon as your anger reaches a 40 on your anger scale. Remember to take a time-out using a "stop" phrase if your level climbs above 50. Nothing derails problem solving more quickly than angry words and actions.

Summarizing Positions: A Prelude to Problem Resolution

Once Alana and Gio completely understood each other's position, I encouraged them to summarize what they had learned, asking the initiating person (who placed the issue on the table to begin with) to take responsibility for the summary. The summary should be brief and balanced, considering the positions of each without adding personal interpretations.

In summarizing these different positions, it's important to focus on what you do agree on as a starting point, then point out important differences that need to be resolved.

> ALANA: "We both agree that we should go on vacation in August. Gio, you feel we can't afford to spend much money and suggest we vacation locally for no more than a week. I feel we need to travel to Europe for two weeks, because we won't be able to once we have kids. Is that your sense of where we stand?"

Gio immediately pointed out some "flaws" in her summary, and Alana felt her anger growing (her jaw felt tight) with the thought "Here we go again. Gio can't stop criticizing me long enough to try this." Recognizing that her thinking was fueling her anger, she countered with the thought "I won't be derailed. I'll listen and try to include his points when I resummarize." When she restated the summary, including Gio's points, he seemed satisfied and they moved on.

Setting Priorities

Next, both state their priorities so that critical needs are incorporated into a final resolution. They take turns, each considering and stating what is most important.

Alana's most important objective is spending intimate time with her husband away from the stress of their jobs. A second priority is that they travel in August, during nice weather. Finally, she would like to travel outside the United States. Contributing to retirement is a low priority for now. For Gio, funding their retirement comes first, but he is persuaded that they can afford a holiday if they can still save $500 a month. A second priority is spending time with his wife, but he doesn't care where they go, provided they can meet his savings goal.

They are now ready for the next step: generating lots of ideas so they can find one or two that work for both of them.

Meeting in the Middle

Once differences and priorities are identified, the focus should be on finding a mutually acceptable solution to reduce anger on both sides. Neither party should be pushed into agreeing to a solution that is unacceptable or perceived as aversive (thus setting the stage for resentment and further problems). There are two possible methods to achieve a win–win solution: *accommodation* and *compromise.*

Accommodation is a mutual agreement to support one person's position now, with the understanding that the other's agenda will be fulfilled at a later date (e.g., "Okay, I'll agree to postpone a vacation for now if you would agree that we holiday out of the country for at least one week next summer"). Accommodation may be the only resolution strategy possible when the two positions are so incompatible that compromise is impossible (e.g., going to Europe and staying home for a local holiday).

Accommodation should be avoided if one party is being asked to suffer a solution that really feels unacceptable, given personality and important values and beliefs (e.g., agreeing to attend a church that violates your spiritual beliefs to accommodate your spouse). This unfortunate outcome will only set the stage for more resentment in the future.

Compromising involves crafting a position that substantially fulfills the priorities and needs of both parties. For example, spending the morning of a holiday at your parents' home and the afternoon at your spouse's parents' home is a compromise position, fulfilling the needs of both. I like to think of compromising as a way of artfully capturing the priorities of both parties, while minimizing objections each might have. Compromising does not mean compromising your values, because you certainly should never do that in any negotiation. Sometimes a completely new solution is reached that neither person originally thought of.

Generating Solutions: Brainstorming

When resentment is present, a compromise solution may be hard to reach. Rather than staying stuck in a rigid position that continues to fuel anger, it can be useful to use a structured problem-solving approach, called "brainstorming," which you're undoubtedly familiar with. In brainstorming both parties try to come up with as many ideas for a solution as they can think of. Some of these ideas may turn out to be impractical, unacceptable, or just plain silly, but the assumption is that a good idea will emerge in the burst of collaborative creativity. Here are some guidelines for effective brainstorming.

> ➤ *Suspend judgment at first.* Even a poor idea may stimulate a good countersuggestion. Try not to let your anger stand in the way of listening. If you find yourself repeatedly saying "yes-but," coming up with objections that derail problem solving, try to refocus on reaching a solution.

> ➤ *Remember that quantity counts; quality comes later.* Try to generate as many new and creative possibilities as possible. You can later pare these down, using all or parts of certain ideas as building blocks for an ultimate solution.

> ➤ *Don't review the past; stay in the present.* Don't become focused on what did or did not work before. View all the ideas as being of value, if only to stimulate new thinking.

> ➤ *Let others share the wealth.* Invite others with special knowledge or awareness to participate in generating ideas. Some of us, for unknown reasons, seem to have an incredible ability to look at situations in a multidimensional manner.

I recommend writing these ideas down so that you can later review them with an eye toward picking the best or combining two or more proposed solutions into a new, even better idea.

Alana suggests, "Let's see how many ideas we can come up with that meet each of our priorities. I've always wanted to go on a cruise, and I understand there are some good discounted rates available. How about if I look into this and see what the prices are and what we could afford?"

Gio raises his voice to say, "Wait a minute, you know I get seasick. How can you be so selfish in suggesting this?" Again finding her anger rising, Alana asks Gio for other suggestions as a way of obtaining a few moments to "stop" her anger with a deep signal breath. As she leans back in her chair, focusing on keeping her voice at a calm level, she acknowledges his issue of seasickness while not picking up on his criticism to keep things moving.

After Gio suggests they travel by air "anywhere that is not too expensive," Alana says, "Gio, I'm sorry I forgot about your seasickness. Yes, air travel is fine, but I propose we look into some vacation packages to countries outside the United States. I understand you get a better deal on a package. Any ideas as to destinations outside the United States?"

Gio agrees to evaluate their budget and "see if I can thin things and find some more money, but I know that $4,000 is our limit." Alana agrees to call some travel agents, and the couple ends with a feeling of success.

By focusing on priorities while brainstorming some new ideas, Alana and Gio finally came to a compromise position. They found that they could cut back on expenses and afford a package vacation to the Bahamas. Both were happy with this outcome. Most important, the couple now had more faith in their ability to resolve differences before their discussion devolved into an argument.

Staying the Course

This chapter has suggested ways you can communicate successfully once your anger gets triggered. Whether it is your closest intimate partner or a colleague at work, these ideas will make it easier to communicate about issues and to resolve differences quickly.

But sometimes, as hard as you try to communicate effectively while managing your anger, the other person doesn't cooperate. You have to stay the course while others are using one or more threatening faces of anger against you. Chapter 9 will offer a short course in maintaining your cool when the weather around you is getting stormy.

When Anger Is Aimed at You

In Chapter 8 you learned what is probably the most important anger management skill of all: assertive problem solving. Keeping your anger under control, avoiding expressing it inappropriately, is only half the battle. You still have to deal with whatever triggered your anger in the first place, whether it's a true wrong that needs to be righted or an old, unrealistic expectation that should be put to bed once and for all. Assertive problem solving is the way to do that. It gives you something to do in place of the destructive faces of anger that got you nowhere in the past, and it allows you to resolve conflict in everyday life.

Chapter 8 showed you how to communicate in a way that expresses your feelings—you're angry—while stating your intention to solve a problem, not start a war. Then it showed you how to pursue and implement possible solutions. In many cases, the techniques described will defuse conflict and produce practical solutions that everyone involved can live with. But what if the other person (or people) involved in the conflict is so angry that nothing you do seems to work?

Go back to Chapter 8 and reread the opening quote. If Maria's husband, Ben, communicates appropriately and uses assertive problem solving skillfully, Maria might begin to hear him again, leading to a resolution acceptable to both of them. But even if he behaves like an expert in anger management, she might not respond as desired. Ultimately we are powerless over others. You may find yourself in a situation where you are sincerely trying to keep your cool, as Ben was, but the other person's face of anger keeps pushing you to the brink. How can you successfully use the anger management ideas we've discussed so far without being engulfed as the flame of another's anger is escalating out of control?

There are things you can say and do that are less likely to further aggravate the other person, while setting the stage for resolution of the conflict. An evaluation of hundreds of close personal relationships by the researcher Dr. John Gottman reveals that what you do *can* directly impact what the other person is likely to do next. And even when your behavior doesn't mitigate the angry behavior of the other person, you can learn to recognize when the situation is just too uncomfortable or threatening and it's time to make a graceful exit.

Your goals when someone else is so angry at you that assertive problem solving is ineffectual and you start losing control over your own anger are twofold:

1. Try to defuse the situation by attending to your own anger arousal first.

2. Provide no payoff for the face of anger directed at you.

Step 1. When Provoked by Someone's Anger, Dampen Your Own Arousal

Think back to the last time someone "attacked" you unfairly with words. Didn't you instinctively try to defend yourself or to get aggressive in return? Social psychologists tell us it is human nature to bring the interaction into this negative "balance." Your wife yells at you for forgetting to take the newspapers out to the garbage on recycling day—*"again!"*—and you shout back that you "just haven't had time!" Your 15-year-old sneers at you and calls you "totally out of touch," and before you can stop yourself you call him an "obnoxious little jerk." The guy who cuts you off on the highway gives you the finger as he drives by, and you find yourself rolling down the window to make some rude gesture back at him, even though he's long gone by the time you've gotten the window open.

Of course you don't *have* to respond in kind. Now that you have a lot of experience with awareness of your anger arousal, you can start to calm yourself the minute you recognize the physical signs that your anger has soared in response to the other person's ire. Take a signal breath, initiate your favorite relaxation technique, and quickly take stock of your thoughts. By dampening your own arousal and refusing to participate in any escalation of intensity, *you* set the terms of the exchange, and the other person has to come into balance with *you*.

James quickly noticed his chest tightening and his voice becoming loud as he and his wife tried to resolve how to handle their son's poor grades. They disagreed on tactics, and James decided to begin the STOP method to manage his rising anger, sitting down, taking a signal breath, and inviting his wife to be seated. When she refused and continued escalating the conflict by calling him "irresponsible" in a loud voice, he decided to take a time-out, using a "stop" phrase to let her know he needed to halt the discussion until they could sit calmly and use assertive problem solving together. He left the room and used dampening methods to calm himself, returning later to invite his wife to continue the discussion.

When you try to set the terms of the interaction by calming your own anger, but the other person doesn't respond in kind, you always have the option of ending the conversation with a "stop" phrase, still in control of how *you* decide to react.

Step 2. Deny the Other Person Any Payoff for an Angry Face

A person who gets aggressive or hostile toward you when angry may succeed in intimidating you, provoke an angry reaction, or get you to say and do something that will cost you in emotional upset or worse. Passive faces of anger may be intended to make you feel rejected or guilty ("What did I do wrong?" or "What will it take for you to talk to me?"). When you refuse to provide the desired payoff, however, the other person is faced with a dilemma: How can he or she get your attention now? Obviously this face of anger isn't working, so he or she will have to try something else. In some cases the person will choose to escalate the "attack" even further, and if the encounter gets too uncomfortable, you'll have to call a "stop." In the best-case scenario, the other person will realize that this negative face of anger was ineffective and will try something more positive. But even when that doesn't happen, you haven't failed. You have succeeded in remaining in control of yourself, reducing your own discomfort. Also, in your closest relationships, your friends or family will learn that provocative faces of anger don't work with you, which may influence the way they approach you in the future. So even if you don't succeed in defusing the conflict, it's important to stay the calm course and remain in control of yourself and your own anger.

This chapter offers ideas for defusing conflict and refusing to provide a payoff when provoked by each face of anger you may encounter in others. The most overtly threatening faces of anger are, of course, aggression and hostility.

Encountering and Overcoming Hostility and Aggression

Intense faces of anger are hard to ignore, whether they're directed at you or you're just a bystander. That couple arguing loudly outside the restaurant draws a lot of furtive glances, though everyone gives them a wide berth. It's painful to watch a parent angrily spanking a child in a store, but still we can't seem to ignore the scene. These faces of anger are intrusive and often demand some kind of response, if only provoking a desire to get away as fast as you can. When directed at you, they are even more unpleasant, and it's easy to end up contributing to the problem by going with the knee-jerk response to fight or flee. Instead, a thoughtful reaction is called for.

Sadly, these faces of anger occur all too often in our culture, and it may be because they can be effective in the short run. The "squeaky wheel," unfortunately, does often get the grease. The person who confronts you with an intense face of anger may have learned that yelling, glaring, and using forceful body gestures seem to get the job done.

How do you defuse these angry faces while not paying them off by becoming intimidated, defensive, or overtly angry yourself?

It's Not Just What You Say, But How You Say It

Defusing with your voice requires that you make a conscious effort to avoid "stair stepping"—raising your volume to meet or exceed the other person's. Inevitably, stair stepping leads to one person trying to outdo the other so that both end up shouting, with neither listening. While there is no guarantee that you can influence the other person by maintaining a level, calm tone of voice, you can certainly defuse the situation by refusing to escalate on your own. In my experience with clients, in fact, it's more likely that your partner will match your tone or be forced to give up in frustration. If not, it helps to set a verbal boundary for what you're willing to withstand: "I know you're very angry, but it's hard for me to listen unless we can talk calmly. If not, we better discuss this later, when we're both able to listen."

To reduce the tension in a discussion, sit down if possible and assume a relaxed posture as you invite the other person to be seated. Your body position not only reflects your emotions but also contributes to them.

When you maintain a calm voice and posture and invite others to join you, some people may conclude that you're trying to be superior or behaving pompously (e.g., "Who are *you* to tell me to calm down?"). Examine your demeanor to ensure you're not dictating from a haughty position by standing over or getting in the other person's face with demanding language. Instead, join *with* your partner in suggesting a different approach for both of you: "I'm really feeling intense. Could we both sit down and try to slow down the volume and pace of this discussion? I want to listen to your ideas. What do you think?"

Once seated, use the active listening strategies suggested in Chapter 8 for your voice, facial expression, and body language. Active listening is probably the best defusing technique available to you. If you permit others to let off steam by fully telling their version of events, they will feel understood and are more likely to calmly attend to what you have to say when you have the floor.

If the other person invades your personal space by stepping in too close, ask him or her to step back and ideally be seated. When you react, avoid getting in the other person's face since this is very threatening and is a sure way to escalate conflict or even trigger physical aggression.

Don't Touch!

Touch is often the ignition for physical violence, so it should be avoided when another person is angry with you. Consider these recommendations:

> Don't attempt to block or restrain someone who wishes to leave, regardless of how benign your intentions are to "work it out."

> Never use physical touch to emphasize a point or get the other

person's attention, like bracing his or her shoulders or using your finger to poke the other in the chest to "make a point."

> ➤ Avoid throwing even the most benign object (e.g., a newspaper or towel) at or toward another person when anger is flaring.

> ➤ Needless to say, any form of hitting or holding another person is clearly abusive and should be avoided unless you are defending yourself. If another person physically threatens or touches you in anger, you should immediately leave the situation to remain safe and consider calling the police.

Strategies for Defusing Aggression and Hostility

Sometimes carefully listening may not be enough to defuse the intensity of someone's anger. One or more of the following defusing strategies is worth considering. Notice how each person in the examples that follow uses the steps of anger management to keep his or her anger arousal in check so that calm communicating is possible.

Calm Clarifying

Ask for a clarification of the other person's thoughts, feelings, or needs as a way of getting him or her to reflect on and restate what was said. When forced to reconsider, the other person may realize that his or her statements were an overreaction or placed unrealistic demands on you. Also, answering a question forces the other person to pause and think, thus interrupting the escalation of anger. Asking for clarification also communicates that you're listening and interested. Also, it gives you time to begin the STOP method. As the other is clarifying, you are calmly exhaling your breath.

> CHRISTOPHER: "I've just had it with the way you try to take over meetings before I have a chance to talk. How do you think that makes me look in front of Melinda [their mutual supervisor]?" Chris's voice is rising in intensity, and he's beginning to pace around the room.

Feeling threatened by Chris's rising anger and physical pacing, Lee notices his early anger signal when his chest starts feeling tight and his breathing is constricted. He decides to sit down, lean back, and take a signal breath, then ask Chris to be seated before permitting the conversation to continue: "Chris, would you mind sitting down so I can focus on what you're telling me?"

When Chris grudgingly sits down, Lee says: "I'm a little confused about what I do to take over the meeting and what you would like me to do differently. Could you give me an example?"

> **An entire literature on family violence suggests that tolerating verbal or physical abuse only encourages these actions in the future, no matter how much remorse may be expressed after the fact. If you are in a verbally or physically abusive relationship, reading a self-help book is not sufficient. You should seek advice from a mental health counselor or program with expertise in resolving relationship abuse issues.**

Agreement in Fact or Principle

When others make accusations or statements that involve you, they are going to be correct, partially correct, or completely inaccurate based on your recollection of the situation. Immediately disagreeing sets the stage for further escalation. Instead, take a few moments to consider the facts of the situation. If the statements are essentially correct, by all means agree and acknowledge the person's stated feelings.

> "You're right. I did interrupt you in the middle of your story. I was wrong and can understand you feel hurt and angry."

If you agree with most of a statement, your reaction should emphasize the substantial agreement that exists, without quibbling over small discrepancies.

> MAYA: "I can't believe you never call Mom and Dad. There they sit, getting older and needing more contact from all of us. I just think it's pretty selfish that you're so busy you can't even pick up the phone."

At first Nathan feels his anger rising (hot face) as he hears Maya's labeling ("selfish") and categorical statement ("can't even pick up the phone"), reflecting these cognitive distortions on her part. He begins his STOP method as he listens further, leaning back, loosening his muscles (S). He recognizes his thoughts (T) are focused on "how unfair" she is, and his anger is rising rapidly. Quickly looking at the objective facts (O), Nathan has to acknowledge that he doesn't call often enough. Rather than picking up on Maya's inflammatory way of communicating, Nathan decides on a plan (P) to agree with the substance of what Maya is saying: "You know something, Maya? You're right. While I do call sometimes, I need to talk with them more often. I'll really make an effort." He notes that this takes the wind out of her sails, and she begins to lower her voice, and they get on with a calmer discussion.

In other cases you may substantially disagree with others' recollection or view of a situation but can agree with the principle raised.

> LIAM: "Why is it that you never support me with the kids? I'm their father, and I deserve their respect. For example, you completely undercut me when I told Alison to go directly to bed, undermining my authority as you always do."

> NANCY: "Although I don't agree that I 'always' undermine you, you're right that we should support each other in discipline. I'll really make an effort to support your parenting and will let you know in private if I have any disagreement. How does that work for you?"

Liam reacts with a much calmer voice: "Well, I think you do undermine me pretty often, but I'm glad that you see it's wrong. I'll let you know when I think you're stepping on my toes, and you do the same for me, okay?"

Refocusing on Process

While a conflict may arise over a substantial issue, it may be the process of how the two of you are talking that is undermining any resolution. In that case, use a "stop" phrase to redirect the discussion to *how* you are communicating and to establish ground rules to keep the discussion calm and on track.

While standing over his wife, Anne, Samuel points his finger and yells: "I can't believe that your credit card has reached its limit again.

Don't you care about our finances? You obviously are incapable of following the budget you agreed to."

Anne feels angry at Samuel's lording this foible over her. What can Anne do to defuse her husband's rising anger and refocus this communication? If she permits Samuel to continue his bullying tactics, you can bet this behavior will occur again in the future. Anne has both negative and positive options for redirecting this discussion.

Letting her anger escalate, Anne reaches a point of intensity that makes the following dysfunctional exchange almost inevitable: "Stop your yelling and inciting. You're acting like a bully and are too self-absorbed to even listen to why the credit card was used." Anne gets in Samuel's face: "Grow up or get away from me if you're going to act like this."

Samuel screams at his wife: "I'm not yelling. I have a right to be angry because you're the one who created this whole mess. It's hopeless to even try to talk to you." He leaves the living room, slamming the bedroom door, and the couple's interaction devolves into cold anger for the rest of the evening.

We can all understand why Anne might react this way to Samuel's intense tactics. She feels she has to take a firm stand but permits her anger to escalate to a point where she is less resilient and is unable to control her unfortunate reaction, meeting Samuel's intensity with the same behaviors she deplores. Did you notice how her use of "you" messages versus "I" messages made matters worse? As an alternative and desirable example, how does this assertive approach for shifting from content to process sound to you?

> ANNE: "Samuel, I'm sitting down, and I'm asking you to be seated so that we can talk about this calmly."

Samuel continues to stand. Anne restates: "Samuel, I need you to be seated so I can listen to you better." Samuel hesitates, mutters a bit, but sits down. (If Samuel refused, Anne would then walk away from the situation, after using a "stop" phrase.) Using the first phase of STOP, she is seated, leaning back and using her signal breathing to control her anger arousal. Her plan is to set ground rules: "Thank you. Samuel, this discussion is beginning to feel really intense, and I want to listen to you but can't when things get loud and accusatory. Let's think about some ground rules if we're going to talk about credit cards and spending."

SAMUEL: "What do you mean ground rules? I'm angry, and I have a right to be angry."

ANNE: "How about if we agree not to personally attack each other? I'll listen to all you have to say without interrupting. Could I expect the same consideration from you when you're finished? If either of us feels intense, let's agree to take a 10- or 15-minute break, maybe get some coffee, to keep things calm. What ideas do you have for how we can work this out?"

After some discussion, Samuel agrees to continue under these ground rules, given that he wants to resolve the couple's finances. At one point Anne uses a "stop" phrase to call a time-out when Samuel's voice begins to rise. She is surprised to find Samuel calling for a "stop" a bit later on, not realizing that she was raising her voice as well. She recognizes that she must stay on top of her anger by continuing to pay attention to her body (shoulders tight, face warm) as a signal to begin anger management. They finally manage to reach a consensus about future use of their cards.

The Broken Record

Consider the power of simply repeating your point or a request, not letting others derail you with their intensity. Like a "broken record," stuck on one lyric, you continue to calmly make your statement until it is heard or it is time to end the discussion.

KRISTEN: "Joseph, I really think we need to talk about Jayden's behavior at school and develop a plan."

JOSEPH: "If you were just more consistent in disciplining Jayden, we wouldn't be having these problems in the first place."

Kristen notices her head beginning to throb after a few more exchanges like this one. To "stop" her anger from escalating, she sits down and, after a signal breath, says: "Joseph, I really think we need to sit down and talk about Jayden's behavior at school. When would be a good time to do that?"

Joseph yells: "Can't you see that you're too weak with him? You can't ever seem to follow through with anything, and the kid gets away with murder."

Continuing to breathe deeply and hearing a calming phrase—"I'm cool, I'm in control"—in her self-talk, Kristen avoids stair stepping and softly says: "Joseph, give me a time when we can sit down and plan how we will react to Jayden's behavior."

> JOSEPH: "Okay, I guess we need to decide what we're going to do. I don't have time right now, so could we talk this evening, once the kids go to bed?"

> KRISTEN: "That will be fine. Thanks for agreeing on a time."

Because Kristen has kept her anger arousal under control, she refuses to "bite" when Joseph again attempts to hook her into defending herself with inciting remarks that reflect his frustration with their son. Because she ignores these unhelpful statements and restates her request, he finally relents and agrees to a time. The broken record is simple, yet extraordinarily effective.

Keeping Your Sanity: Tactics for Confronting Indirect and Passive Faces of Anger

When someone is overtly angry and provocative, at least you know what you're dealing with. You can attempt to defuse the situation or leave until things calm down. In contrast, it can be maddening to cope with anger that is expressed so indirectly that it isn't even acknowledged. How do you react to passive faces of anger like sarcasm and passive-aggression? What do you do when someone completely turns you off in cold anger?

While you're powerless over another person's choice to use one of these frustrating faces of anger, you're in complete control of how you react. As with hostility and aggression, your goals are to defuse the conflict and provide no reward that may encourage this face of anger in the future.

Bring Your Feelings to the Surface, Even If the Other Person Doesn't

Even though others may be unwilling to discuss their anger or needs openly, you can't just ignore repeated destructive actions. Communicate with an "I" message the impact their passive actions have on you, clearly conveying the difference between the purported intent and the impact of these actions. Let the other person know that even though his or her stated intention may be benign—to make a joke, to be silent to give you both time to think, for example—the impact on you was unpleasant and unacceptable. This communication is firm and assertive.

"Preview" How You Will React Differently in the Future

Let the other person know that, regardless of the stated reason for a passive face of anger, you will react in a way that gets your needs met while providing no positive outcome for his or her actions. This lets the person know the consequences of these actions in time to make a change. If a passive face recurs, follow through with what you previewed.

Now let's apply these goals to each passive face of anger.

Responding to Sarcasm

People who use sarcasm frequently justify this behavior as "humor" or "just making a joke." If another person is sarcastic and you feel hurt by these remarks, it may feel unfair to be blamed for not having a sense of humor or being too "thin-skinned."

First, use your "I" message to make clear that the other person's actions are not pleasant or perceived by you as a "joke."

"I really felt embarrassed and humiliated last night when you kept referring to how much I was eating," Angel said to Isabella. "You know that I'm concerned about my weight."

Isabella retorted: "I didn't mean anything by it. Why are you so sensitive? Everybody knew I was just joking."

Angel noticed his face getting hot as he thought: "Isabella couldn't care less about me!" Using his STOP method, he leaned back in his chair, took a signal breath, and tried to focus on the objective facts: "She uses sarcasm with everyone, but I know she loves me. Maybe she's just unaware of how much it hurts." He decided (his "plan") to share his reaction, telling her: "You may have intended it as a joke, but it hurt. What's important is how I feel in response to what you said. If you truly don't mean to embarrass me, then please avoid any references to my weight with others."

The next time sarcasm creeps into the other person's statements, you can ask for a restatement that focuses on the underlying feelings and needs and not the surface sarcasm: "Isabella, how about telling me how you are feeling about me or what you need right now rather than trying to be humorous?"

If the behavior continues, preview your future reaction if you again feel sarcastically put down. Angel previewed the following with Isabella prior to going out with the same couples: "I'm letting you know that I'm going to tell you one time, in a calm, private way, to stop any sarcasm. If you continue, I intend to let you know, right at that moment, exactly how I feel about it."

Isabella was taken aback: "You mean you would embarrass us in front of other people just to make your point?"

Angel replied: "If you're embarrassed, you will have brought it on yourself. I'm no longer going to feel like a captive of your attempts at humor. It's up to you."

Ideally, Isabella will begin to think before she talks and reappraise the difference between a true joke and sarcasm at Angel's expense. Regardless, Angel now feels empowered to handle this behavior.

Responding to Passive–Aggression

Withholding a desired response, passive–aggression is an indirect way of expressing anger, while denying doing anything wrong or purposeful. Kayla's approach to Ethan's withholding is a good example of how to empower yourself when faced with this indirect and frustrating behavior.

When angry, Ethan would withdraw and respond minimally when Kayla tried to comfort him. He often would "forget" to do things that Kayla asked of him and in general withheld whatever she wanted when he was peeved. When confronted, Ethan denied he was angry, and Kayla was at her wit's end when she came into counseling. We reviewed the following ideas that focused on what *she* could do to influence Ethan and preserve her own dignity.

As you calmly identify your personal thoughts, feelings, and needs in response to withholding, avoid blaming or getting into fruitless discussions as to *why* the other person failed to respond as you asked. Instead, calmly use your "I" message to share your reactions, regardless of the supposed reason for your partner's response.

"Ethan," Kayla said, "last evening at dinner you avoided looking at me and barely said a word during the entire meal. You denied any-thing was bothering you. This makes me feel detached and very iso-lated from you. If you wish to go out with me, I expect you to make an effort to participate in the evening and to be clear about how you're feeling."

Ethan retorted: "Kayla, you've got it all wrong. I guess I just wasn't feeling very 'up' last night. Why are you making such a big deal of the evening? It wasn't so bad."

Kayla immediately felt her throat tightening, a first signal of anger arousal. She sat down and invited her husband to be seated as she took a deep signal breath, focusing on the thought "I will not let him push my buttons," tied to each moderately full regular breath. Once her anger was in check, she said, "I'm not going to challenge you on that anymore, Ethan. If you're feeling down or wish to withdraw from me, just simply state that."

When Ethan persists in denying his actions, Kayla simply previews how she will react the next time Ethan withdraws: "If I feel you're with-drawing, I will tell you, and you can change or I'll leave. I'd rather be by myself than with somebody who is ignoring me."

Notice that Kayla does not accuse Ethan of purposely ruining the evening, "mind reading" his underlying feelings. Instead, she clearly and simply states her needs for the future and gives herself a plan to stay in control and get her needs met if the behavior persists.

It's also important to separate your own behavior from the passive-aggressive actions of the other. Regardless of what that person fails to do, you are going to continue behaving in a way that you consider fair and effective in getting your needs met. For example, Kayla might say, "Ethan, because you failed to follow through with painting the outside of the house as you agreed, I've decided to hire a painter who can start on May 3. If you can begin the project by that time, I won't call the painter. If not, I intend to have him start painting. You decide what you want to do." Even though the financial costs are greater, Kayla is not stuck because of Ethan's passive–aggressive response.

Responding to Cold Anger

When another person turns off or withdraws from interacting with you, what are your options for reacting to this cold anger? Will you try to console or placate the other or make heroic gestures of contrition to get a response? It might work, but you will surely perpetuate cold anger in the future. Or will you "freeze" the other out as a punishment, using the same behaviors you deplore?

Instead of meeting cold anger with either of these ineffective responses, consider using your "I" message to simply identify the behavior that you've observed, while expressing curiosity, puzzlement, or surprise at these actions. Then let your partner know what you need.

Noah would get furious when his wife, Melanie, refused to talk with him, sometimes for days at a time. His outward expression of anger only served to fuel more cold anger in response. Noah decided to try out some of the strategies discussed in this chapter to break this endless cycle. In the following exchange in my office, Noah directly confronted Melanie's cold anger:

"I noticed that you didn't speak or look at me this morning," Noah said to Melanie. "Later, when I asked you about your day at work, you barely responded and made a grunting sound. I felt confused. I don't have to be much of a mind reader to know when something is wrong. I'm willing to listen when you're ready to tell me how you're feeling and what you need of me."

Noah includes a preview of his future reaction: "In the meantime, you have a right to withdraw, avoid speaking, or anything else. I'm going to continue speaking to you when I need to. If you choose to respond, that would be really nice. But I'm going to move ahead with my day."

In not responding to Noah, Melanie will experience some natural consequences in losing the fun and enjoyable activities they are capable of sharing together, while not receiving any of the "gains" she was used to (Noah reacting, pleading with her to respond, becoming furious). As Noah keeps the situation as normal as possible and calmly invites Melanie to participate, there is little reason for her to continue her cold anger; it just doesn't accomplish anything for her anymore.

Remaining on Track

In the previous chapters you've learned each of the important steps in regulating your anger. From an awareness of what triggers you through how to communicate your thoughts, feelings, and needs, each chapter has offered ideas and examples that must now be practiced to become "automatic," taking the place of your old face(s) of anger.

Self-help books often provide this kind of information, but just reading about it is not enough. Chapter 10 will offer ideas for making what you've learned a new "habit," permanently available to influence your reaction to challenging events as the unforeseeable future unfolds.

Often you will encounter roadblocks along the way. It is hard to sustain these new behaviors when life stresses escalate or you encounter another person's particularly toxic face of anger. Chapter 12 will provide some guidance and reassurance as to how to proceed when the seas get really rough.

Just for Practice

In your journey to being a better communicator when anger arises, whether your own or another's, the place to start is practicing how to be a good listener. Based on the concepts presented in the sidebar on active listening in Chapter 8, start looking for opportunities to give your full attention to others, at work, with friends, and at home. No other act is more powerful in preventing conflict than giving an important other your undivided attention, sincerely trying to understand that person's inner world. Remember that anger usually escalates when you or others feel misunderstood or disregarded.

Next, begin practicing using "I" messages in every aspect of your life. It might be easiest to begin by expressing appreciation or offering other forms of positive feedback to others. For example, after your spouse prepared a special meal for you: "You really worked hard on this meal. I feel so satisfied and happy right now and hope I can think of some special things to do for you, too. Thanks so much." Find opportunities to practice expressing negative feelings when it's easier and the stakes don't seem as high, like returning an unacceptable meal in a restaurant ("I'm dissatisfied with how this steak was cooked. I need you to bring one prepared medium-rare, please. Thank you."). Or, in a low-level meeting at work you can practice disagreeing with others and asking for consideration of your ideas: "I'm confused [puzzled, surprised, concerned] that you seem to have ignored my proposal. I would appreciate it if we could discuss it right now." As you practice expressing approval and calm dissatisfaction in places like retail stores, restaurants, with colleagues at work and with your family at home, your ability to quickly formulate an "I" message will be greatly enhanced and available to you when needed.

Based on what you learned in this chapter, think about the last few times you were in conflict with someone. Using your imagination, close your eyes and vividly picture where you were and what triggered the conflict. Imagine what you and the other person said, how you said it, and what you did with your actions and nonverbal behaviors. You may not remember exactly, but your best is fine. Now replay the encounter using the ideas you learned in Chapters 8 and 9.

1. First, as you listen and observe the other, give your complete attention, speaking only to clarify what is said. Take a few minutes and paraphrase what the other person has said before you talk.

2. Now think about your awareness: what was *factually said and done*, your *feelings, thoughts*, and what you *need* from the other person.

3. Practice assertive problem solving. First, formulate an "I" message to communicate this awareness to the other. As you imagine yourself talking, look directly at the other person and make sure your facial expression, gestures, and body language all communicate a calm and caring attitude. Be aware of your voice, keeping your volume at a low to moderate level and your tone commensurate with the message you are sending. Use this form: "*When* [describe the other's actions or the situation], *I felt* [tell the other how you feel/felt]. Then let the other person know your ideas and opinions about what happened: "*In my opinion* . . . ," followed by stating what you need in the future—"In the future, *I would appreciate it if you would. . . .* "

4. Imagine what conflict has arisen between your stated position and the other's. Imagine yourself implementing the steps of problem solving, first taking the floor and *summarizing positions*, the other's and then yours, as objectively as possible. Ask the other person if this summary is accurate and, if not, amend and restate the other person's position. Now you have a clear and agreed-on summary of positions. Then focus on *prioritizing* what is most important to each party. Then try to *meet in the middle* with an accommodation or compromise position, followed by *generating a solution* using the steps of brainstorming.

5. Practice using the defusing strategies in this chapter for past experiences you've had with direct faces of anger.

> ➤ Imagine using *calm clarifying* to ask for more information as to the other person's thoughts, feelings, and needs. This buys you time to think.

> ➤ Imagine *agreeing in fact or in principle* to what the other person says.

> ➤ Imagine that your discussion is degenerating into angry expression. Imagine calling for a *refocusing on process* and an agreement on new ground rules for the discussion.

> ➤ Practice in imagery the use of the *broken record* to repeatedly state what you want from the other person, without escalating the intensity of the discussion.

Whenever possible, practice using these communication strategies in real-life encounters. To gradually build your skills, you might begin by noticing when your anger is at a low level or a triggering situation seems less daunting for initial practice. Try to use all of the skills you've learned.

For example, you might notice irritation (your shoulders are tight and your self-talk is filled with thoughts like "I can't hear myself think") with the level of noise coming from your friend's office, next to yours. Pausing to reflect on your awareness, you note the noise level is objectively loud, you're irritated, and you think this behavior is discourteous. Because he is a friend and fairly easy to talk with, you decide to practice using an "I" message and then trying to problem-solve a solution with him (e.g., closing his door when he talks on the phone, letting you know when he's going to have a large meeting in his office that is bound to be noisy). When he first objects that he doesn't think the noise level is "all that bad," you practice using the "broken record," politely restating that it's disrupting your concentration. He gets the message, and you feel good about how you handled the situation and a bit more confident in yourself.

You have a good relationship with your brother but find you often disagree on political issues, getting irritated with each other. To practice the skills of active listening, using "I" messages, and defusing conflict while trying to dampen your own anger arousal, you engage your brother and really try to keep in mind and use these newfound skills. You find that when you really listen and paraphrase what he's said, without interrupting, his voice remains calm and he's more likely to listen to your points. When he says your position is "ludicrous" at one point, you notice your anger rising as your throat feels tight and your breathing is more rapid. You use your STOP method, leaning back and signal-breathing, then using calm clarifying to defuse the tension. It works and you stay on track. By practicing with him, you've had the opportunity to test yourself when the risk of serious consequences is low. After all, you and your brother have been disagreeing about politics for years, and he still loves you.

Practicing when the stakes are not as high makes your skills more readily available when a truly challenging situation arises. The more you practice, the better.

For an extended review of the many ways you can defuse and derail another's anger, consider reading my book *Overcoming Anger in Your Relationship: How to Break the Cycle of Arguments, Put-Downs, and Stony Silences* (see Suggested Resources).

Step Six

Staying the Course
Sustaining New Behavior and Coping with Roadblocks

NOW THAT YOU HAVE MASTERED THE BASICS OF RATIONAL anger expression, you have to integrate these ideas into a busy daily life and cope with the setbacks and roadblocks that will surely occur. How do you ensure that you'll remember to use these new ideas? What happens when you blow it and feel discouraged? Chapter 10 reviews ideas for successfully building these steps of anger management into your life so they're more automatic and available to you. One major impediment to progress is the continuation of unresolved anger—resentments that smolder beneath the surface of your life and can suddenly and unexpectedly erupt in flames. Chapter 11 discusses the costs of holding on to resentments and offers ideas for resolution and even forgiveness when the situation warrants it. Chapter 12 describes the setbacks you might experience, how to diagnose the "problem," and ideas for quickly getting back on track.

10

Establishing New Anger Habits

Referred to me for losing his temper at work, Stan seemed to learn the steps of anger management quickly and easily. He had no trouble learning to notice his shoulders tightening, his signal that he was getting angry. Most of the time when this early warning appeared, he was able to turn down the heat and halt his anger before he got into trouble at the office again. But then one day his boss asked him to work over the weekend so they could meet a major deadline on time—just when it was finally Stan's turn to use the company skybox for the Redskins game. He'd called his wife and told her to line up family and friends, and they had planned to use the opportunity to celebrate the 60th birthday of her father, a lifelong fan. Now his boss was asking him—no, *telling* him, Stan seethed—to give that all up " ... with about two minutes' notice." Stan recognized his growing muscle tension, but only in passing as he lost himself in a cacophony of self-talk about his boss's "outrageous demands" and "total lack of consideration" and "unbelievable arrogance." Before he knew what was happening, he had stomped across the office, flung open his boss's door, and let all that vituperation spew out.

This time Stan's blowup had been aimed directly at his superior, and the powers that be had made it painfully clear that the only reason he wasn't fired on the spot was that he had seemed to gain such self-control in recent weeks that they'd decided to give him one more chance. Stan was dejected and frustrated when he came to see me. He just couldn't seem to catch and halt his old thinking quickly enough, he told me, let alone replace it with rational self-talk. What could he do?

Stan is finding that change isn't as easy as reading a self-help book or briefly attending therapy and just trying to remember what you've learned. Realistically, rational thinking, emotional self-control, and assertive communication and problem solving must be repeated numerous times if they are to become ingrained habits. Clearly, Stan just hasn't practiced new ways of thinking often enough.

What Stan needs—what we all need—is to develop anger management skills so strong that they will override old ways of expressing anger, even in the most challenging circumstances. Exercises in the preceding chapters have provided opportunities for you to begin to make the individual skills your own. But it wasn't until Chapter 9 that I asked you to practice in the way I mean it here: both in your imagination, as a kind of rehearsal, and out there on the stage in the performances we call daily life. Your goal in this chapter is to put all the individual skills together and conduct both practice and rehearsal of the entire anger management process. The longer and more frequently you do this, the more deeply ingrained your new anger habits will become. Until they become your automatic reaction to triggering circumstances, your old faces of anger will continue to repeat themselves, at least occasionally.

In addition, even when you feel you've learned how to react to anger triggers more effectively, you may find yourself backsliding from time to time. When this happens, many people feel discouraged, sometimes to the point of futility, as if all their effort has been for naught. Please know that this is not true. There are many reasons for relapsing into old faces of anger, and virtually everyone falls prey to them at some point. To help you respond effectively when the inevitable relapse occurs, read Chapter 12, which will help you diagnose the cause of your setback and institute remedies to help you stay the course.

Planned Practice

Like the grooves a wagon makes in an old trail over many years or the path worn in a carpet between the front door and the living room, old habits run deep and strong. Rather than spending time agonizing about your mistakes, you must now find opportunities to apply your new anger skills often enough to blaze a different trail to guide your actions automatically in the future. One strategy is to plan opportunities to practice in real situations, rather than just waiting for them to occur naturally. The problem with waiting is that you may not get in enough repetitions to build a new habit before you're in the middle of a tough situation and find yourself unprepared.

Madeline's young children have tested her patience to the point where she often finds herself yelling in anger. Having grown up with "screaming" parents, Madeline feels guilty every time she sees her children reacting with the same fear she experienced as a child. In addition to learning anger management with me, I suggested that she take a class to improve her parenting skills.

When her "hair-trigger" temper confounds her efforts at calm parenting, she decides she needs more practice. Rather than merely waiting for her kids to act up, she decides to practice in more manageable situations, like taking them to restaurants and stores during less busy times of the day. Recalling the "Five S's," she knows she will be more likely to stay in control in a less stressful setting.

Along these lines, Madeline decides to practice in the morning at first, when the kids are rested, making it easier to manage her anger as she improves her parenting skills. She also starts taking them to the movies alone, knowing she'll feel less tense about potential misbehavior if she isn't worrying about what her friends and their kids will think of her at the same time. Practicing in these lower-pressure situations gives her plenty of chances to strengthen her skills in preparation for the "meltdowns" her kids often have when they're tired and cranky. Of course she can't predict exactly when her children will challenge her to the limit, but she is stacking the odds in her favor by practicing as much as possible in advance.

How could you find opportunities to practice particular anger skills that need more polishing? First you need to identify where your weaknesses lie. Use the Anger Analysis process that you learned in Chapter 7 to figure out where in the sequence of events you're having trouble.

Deng, for example, has had trouble using newly learned assertive communication, particularly at work. His old style was to raise his voice and interrupt others often to make his point forcefully known. When a coworker tells him to "lighten up," Deng realizes his old habits have resurfaced without his awareness. He decides he needs a lot more practice to unlearn his old habits and to work on using active listening and "I" messages more comfortably and automatically, even when his irritation is minimal. Whether returning unacceptable food in a restaurant, requesting that his secretary make changes in a typed report, or asking his wife to refrain from leaving newspapers on the living room floor, Deng looks for opportunities to use calm, assertive communication. Paying close attention to tension in his chest as his anger signal, he practices using the STOP method to calm down and address the situation with an "I" message. He soon finds that he is better able to access his newfound skills when he is really upset and needs to let the other person know why without becoming insulting and harsh, as in the past.

Barbara has been accused of being impatient and hostile, interrupting others, and showing nonverbal disdain in the form of gestures like rolling her eyes, sighing heavily, and grimacing. Rather than waiting for the next triggering situation, she decides to practice active listening by seeking conversation with others who are slow talkers. She soon finds that by sitting down and paying attention to her breathing rate and tension in her shoulders, she is able to remain more relaxed and patient while listening. The positive reaction she gets from others for this new "calm" reinforces her efforts.

Cueing: Reminders That Work

Many of us write down reminders in a daily organizer, BlackBerry, or iPad as a prompt to do something at a particular time. Similarly, you can use many existing events or objects to cue you to practice your new anger skills.

To remind himself to lean back, loosen his muscles, and take frequent signal breaths to keep his tension level low, Jeff decides to link these new actions to each time he checks the time by glancing at his watch. To further help him remember to link the two, he decides to wear his watch on his right wrist over the next two weeks so that glancing at his empty left wrist cues him to lean back and take his signal breath. Jeff finds he checks the time at least five times every hour, which means he is aware of and taking steps to relax much more often than ever before. He soon notices that his neck is less tight and he is less irritable with his customers.

Nathan often gets angry when other drivers fail to meet his expectations for "courtesy." While he has found that the STOP method works when he remembers to notice his anger signal (tightness in the shoulders and flushing in his face), he often forgets and goes into automatic "yelling" mode. To cue himself to remember his anger skills, he decides to put a cue card in a visible place. Every time he goes to fiddle with the car radio he is likely to look at a card he has placed right above it (which has *STOP* written on it in red ink), reminding him of the STOP method. He soon finds that he is approaching his drive with anger management in the forefront of his thinking and is able to derail his aggressive face of anger early on.

Think of the many activities in your own life you could now use to remind you of your new anger skills. Consider these activities that my clients have used as cues. For example, link a new anger skill (e.g., taking a signal breath, making a calming self-statement, scanning your body for signs of tension) to one of the following:

> ➤ Every time you end a telephone call

> ➤ Whenever you take a sip of the water bottle you keep on your desk

> ➤ Every time you check your e-mail

> ➤ Whenever you brush your hair off your face

> ➤ Each time you pick up one of your children's toys from the floor

> ➤ Whenever you pause at a stoplight if you spend a lot of time in your car

> ➤ Whenever you hit the "save" button on your computer

> ➤ At the beginning of any transition from one activity to the next

You're limited only by your creativity! Think about the actions you take often in your day. Anything you do two or more times each hour could be used to strengthen a new anger skill.

Before the Storm: Rehearsing New Anger Skills

Finding opportunities to practice in real situations still limits you to times when you can make a combination of situation and other people come together. An alternative is to rehearse in situations that simulate the real thing, like rehearsing a talk in front of an imagined audience or in front of a mirror. Anyone who has been in a school play or participated on a sports team has "rehearsed" new actions in simulated situations to get ready for the "real" thing.

Research indicates that two kinds of rehearsals are likely to greatly strengthen new anger skills so you can count on them when needed. While each offers you the opportunity to practice as often as you wish, they have unique strengths and some limitations. Knowing what those are will help you decide which works best in a particular situation you face.

Practicing in Your Imagination

Chapter 6 discussed the ways that imagery can fuel anger in the present and sustain resentment each time you imagine an upsetting past event. By changing the way you imagine a triggering event, you can readily change how you feel about it.

Using imagery to create a scene in your mind and rehearse new ways of reacting, before you actually have to use them with others, can be a powerful way to build new anger habits. Your imagination is limited only by your creativity and ability to vividly picture the scene.

Sy became so irritated and defensive during his last job review that his supervisor suggested he seek professional help for his anger. He knew he had to get it right at a repeat review in three weeks' time or face serious consequences. The only option we had for practice was rehearsal. After he had learned the steps of anger management, I suggested that Sy practice his new skills in his imagination, playing out each reasonably possible scenario with his supervisor (getting a poor rating, being asked to improve, or being frankly criticized).

Sy pictured each scene vividly, imagining what his boss might say to him, noticing his anger building (his face getting hot or his voice getting louder), and then using his STOP method to let go of his rising tension and rethink the situation. Also, using imagery permitted him to pause the scene and practice his new anger actions repeatedly. He decided to practice for about 15 minutes each evening until his review the next Thursday.

When the meeting finally took place, Sy was surprised that even receiving criticism from his boss did not inflame his emotions. After all, he had already practiced the most difficult scenarios he could think of, so the actual meeting seemed tame by comparison. He felt prepared and in control, making him more relaxed during the meeting. Further, Sy was reinforced for his efforts by his boss's compliment for the "new leaf" he had turned over in managing his emotions.

Oksana often avoided speaking to her husband for days at a time after he had spent big chunks of the weekend away from the family with his male friends around some sports activity. Uncomfortable with confrontations since childhood, she would nurse her inner rage, telling herself that her only power was in withholding the intimacy that he desired. Now she had begun to realize that her face of anger actually robbed her of any power to get her needs met. Her passive–aggressive tactics only aggravated her husband, if anything making him more steadfast in not giving in to Oksana's requests. Her behavior was actually making things worse.

To change this pattern, Oksana decided to work on being more assertive and direct whenever her husband informed her of his plans to go out. Imagery permitted her to rehearse her new anger actions so they would be strong and available when she needed them next.

Oksana thought about times when her husband had "abandoned" her and the children for entire weekends to attend sports events. She often thought of him as "selfish" and "uncaring." Rather than using those provocative labels with him or just turning off as she had always done, she decided to practice using a firm "I" message to let him know how she felt. She imagined reacting in this new, direct way to a series of difficult scenarios (e.g., her husband calling at the last minute to inform her he would be home late, announcing he would be gone for a weekend golf tournament without discussing family plans with her).

After numerous practice runs in her imagination, she tried out her new communication methods when he told her he was extending a business trip to fly to Las Vegas with a friend. She was really gratified to find she could get his attention by being assertive and telling him clearly that she expected him to be more directly involved with her and the children. To her surprise, he expressed appreciation that she was being direct with him and canceled the extra travel.

The advantage of practicing in your imagination is that you can include any scene, person, or situation your mind is capable of picturing vividly. You can quickly go anywhere and control the degree to which the other person antagonizes you or pushes you to your limits, thus practicing for extreme or really threatening situations in advance, before they just hit you in the face unexpectedly. As you look over these brief examples, think of really aggravating, tough situations you've faced or are facing right now that could be practiced using your imagination.

Jon has real difficulty using assertive problem solving with anyone in authority. Growing up with a father who was aggressive and condescending, Jon has always felt very threatened by teachers, supervisors, or others he thinks are trying to tell him what to do, particularly when they glare at him, get too close physically, or touch him in any way. He recently blew up at his boss for "unfairly" pulling him off an assignment. His anger seemed to build before he even had time to think how to use an "I" message or try to problem-solve a win–win solution with his boss. Because he couldn't practice directly with his boss or other authority figures, Jon decided to use his imagination to replay what had happened, this time practicing assertive problem solving. I suggested that he get in touch with his boss's verbal and nonverbal mannerisms that he found particularly provocative and incorporate them into the scene he pictured.

Picturing himself in his boss's office, Jon vividly imagined the scene unfolding. He conjured up a series of situations that had been the toughest for him to cope with in the past: his boss becoming sarcastic about Jon's ability, his boss glaring at him while telling Jon he just didn't "have what it takes" to do the job, his boss acting condescending. Jon practiced using his STOP method, taking a signal breath and leaning back as he imagined himself objectifying his self-talk as his boss continued talking (repeated self-talk: "This isn't personal. I need to stay in control and make my point"). He pictured himself listening without interrupting and using some defusing techniques (such as asking for more clarification about his boss's reasons for this decision) as he continued to imagine himself regaining control of his initial anger while he listened. Then he imagined using a clear "I" message to express his confusion and surprise at this decision and to suggest they discuss it further, attempting to problem-solve to best use Jon's talents: "I feel really surprised that you don't see a continued role for me on this project, particularly since my reviews have been well above average. I'm confused about what you have in mind. I need to discuss this decision with you further so we can figure out how I can make the best contribution. Could we discuss this some more?"

Each time Jon practices in his imagination, he further refines how he will approach his boss until he feels he has it "just right" and is ready to confront him directly. Also, his boss's power to infuriate Jon with his "superior attitude" or with sarcastic or critical remarks dissipates each time Jon replays each tough scene. Through repeated exposure to each scene, Jon feels more in control, and his boss's words and manner make less of an impact because they become "old hat," expected and manageable.

You could use your imagination to practice thorny situations like the following:

> Imagining using assertive problem solving when your mother gets very loud and argumentative in offering unwanted parenting advice. You imagine her interrupting you with a loud voice and your anger escalating and then using your STOP method to sit and begin to dampen arousal as you invite her to be seated so discussion can continue. Because your mother is unlikely to comply with your request for calm discussion, you imagine using a "time out" to end the discussion until rational discussion can take place.

> Telling a coworker that his off-color jokes and sexual remarks are offensive, without losing it or just turning him off with cold anger (which so far hasn't worked). You picture how you will use your anger skills in response to his worst possible reactions (e.g., he tells you that you are a "prude" and belittles your feelings).

> Dealing with your best friend's monopoly of the conversation when the two of you are with others, interrupting you to change the topic. What's worse is that she minimized your feelings when you tried to tell her about it—"You're just too sensitive; grow up"—making your blood boil. You have avoided talking with her further because you fear a confrontation. In your imagination you decide to practice assertively telling her exactly how you feel and how you will calmly react to aggravating things she might say.

When is practice in imagination less likely to work? Consider how well you can vividly reproduce a scene in your mind. If you have a hard time "seeing" your supervisor's face or "hearing" your sister's voice as she scolds you, imagery may not work well for you. In addition to being able to clearly imagine, how do you feel when you imagine an upsetting event? If your imaginings seem so "wooden" or artificial that you can't feel anything when trying to portray a triggering scene, you may not gain as much benefit from this kind of practice. You will be missing the opportunity to experience the scene emotionally and to begin

to overcome your felt anger before the fact through repeated expo-
sures, as Jon experienced in the previous example. You may be among
those who should practice only in real-life situations or who should use
behavioral rehearsal, which follows.

Practicing "Out Loud": Behavioral Rehearsal

Using new anger skills in actual situations that simulate reality is called
behavioral rehearsal, another way of establishing your new habits. Actual
practice gives you an opportunity to get the feel of new actions before
you have to use them when it counts. You must actually perform a new
behavior to know you can carry it off and how it feels when you do. For
example, you could learn the rules and what clubs to use by practicing
golf in your imagination, but it is doubtful you could learn to hit a golf
ball without actual practice. I think behavioral rehearsal is a must if
you want to ensure you can "pull off" your new anger skills, particularly when "under fire."

Sometimes called *role playing* or *behavioral practice*, behavioral
rehearsal is used to prepare people for many different events. Standing
up and giving a speech out loud before presenting it to an audience,
practicing tennis strokes with a ball machine prior to an actual tennis
match, and taking your child for a dry run of her walk to school are all
life examples of behavioral rehearsal.

While you can rehearse by practicing out loud alone—to an imagi-
nary audience or by talking into a tape recorder for immediate feedback—the practice becomes more authentic when you have a partner
stand in for the other person in the encounter you're anticipating. With
a little forethought, I bet you can find a willing partner—a very good
friend, a spouse, or someone with special talent or interest in your
issue—to practice with, whether it's to stand in as your supervisor at
work, the sister you have repeated conflicts with, or the professor you
believe is treating you unfairly.

Maddy was in the habit of expressing her anger with intense
aggression when her husband questioned her competence or criticized
her, often slamming doors or screaming at him "so he will shut up."
While she had now learned all the steps of anger management, she
found she couldn't remember what to do when her husband got in her
face, as she put it. Frustrated that she was having trouble applying what
she'd learned, she decided to try behavioral rehearsal and asked her
sister, Nell, if she'd help.

Before rehearsals could begin, Maddy had to decide how she wished to react differently during the confrontations with her husband. She decided that she needed to be more aware of jaw tension and her throat constricting, her first signals of anger arousal. Her plan was to practice using the "broken record," to ask John to sit down with her and to work on really listening to each other. Once seated, Maddy decided to practice beginning her STOP method, leaning back and taking a deep signal breath as John expressed himself, while she actively listened. She also decided to use a calming instructional phrase in her self-talk, tied to slow breaths if John began firing questions at her: "This is just his opinion, not an attack on me; I can handle it." Finally, she decided to practice asking John for a time-out when the situation got intense (she reached a 50 to 60 on her anger scale).

Nell had heard Maddy describe her confrontations with her husband many times, but because behavioral rehearsal produces its greatest effect when the scene is as realistic as possible, Maddy started out by instructing Nell in how John (the "antagonist," the person who has provoked the anger) talks and acts so she could play his part realistically. Maddy, as John, stood up and got within 8 inches of Nell's face, pointing a finger, talking very loud and fast: "Maddy, I just can't believe that you can't control your spending. Look at this charge at Nordstrom. What is this for? We're never going to get ahead with you having a credit card. You just can't handle it." "I get the picture, Maddy," Nell said. "I think I can play John."

Now Maddy set up a scene (a place and circumstance) for the rehearsal. In this case, Maddy decided she and Nell would pretend that Maddy had just gotten in from work and John was approaching her about an unexplained credit card statement. As they played out the scene, the two occasionally paused to discuss how Maddy was doing. During those breaks, Maddy would ask Nell how she was feeling as Maddy tried out her new anger actions. At one point Nell said, for example, "Maddy, you're doing fine at sitting and not raising your voice, but your face seems intense and threatening." They would then continue the action—or start over for a new rehearsal if they had been approaching the end of the scene—with Maddy making adjustments in response to Nell's comments. The two rehearsed several times, until Nell felt that Maddy was responding to "John" rationally and calmly, in a way that would lead to constructive problem solving. They agreed to rehearse a couple more times until Maddy felt that she was playing out the scene in real life with John in the same way.

You can use behavioral rehearsal to practice your own responses to a variety of triggering situations, including the following:

> ➤ You often lose your cool when your five-year-old son refuses to cooperate with your requests. Another parent who took a parenting class with you offers to role-play (as your "son") as you practice making firm, direct requests while keeping your voice calm and managing your anger when "he" doesn't immediately comply. After each rehearsal, the two of you talk about how the role play went and further refine your use of positive discipline.

> ➤ You have decided to ask your supervisor for a raise. Other new hires are being paid more than you, and your anger about the "unfairness" of how you've been treated makes it hard to even discuss the issue without getting furious. You decide to practice staying in control as you make an assertive request with a colleague playing your boss. During the rehearsal, you focus on leaning back in your chair, keeping your muscles loose, and taking some occasional signal breaths. After each rehearsal, the two of you discuss how it went, and your friend offers to show you how he would approach the situation by playing you. You get some good ideas from his portrayal. When you actually discuss the raise with your boss, it seems less aggravating because you've already done it numerous times in rehearsal.

Whenever possible, behavioral rehearsal should be used in addition to practicing in your imagination. Because it is one step closer to the "real thing," it is the only way to ensure you can actually recall and put into action your new anger skills. Whether they will readily come to mind in a real anger situation depends on how often you practice.

Practice Makes Perfect?

If you look for opportunities to practice your newfound anger skills, you can begin to say good-bye to your old face(s) of anger. Each repetition increases the likelihood that you'll recall and use these skills with proficiency when the next triggering situation arises. Most of the time, anger is provoked when you least expect it, and you have a fleeting opportunity to influence whether a situation goes well or deteriorates quickly. Firmly instilling your new anger management skills through practice is the best way to ensure that you'll get your anger under control and turn it into a constructive emotion.

Notice, however, that I said "begin" to say good-bye to your old anger patterns. Human behavior does not usually change abruptly, as if controlled by a switch. You already know that change takes a concerted effort, and even when you are trying hard you will sometimes blow it. What's important is that you understand and learn from these setbacks.

Chapter 12 stresses the importance of forgiving yourself when setbacks occur. Ideas for diagnosing and learning from a setback should help you quickly get back on course. In the meantime, as in the real estate mantra about location, the important thing to remember is practice, practice ... well, you get it by now.

11

Resolving Resentment and Considering When to Forgive When You Can't Forget

Rihanna won't come to Christmas dinner at her mother's this year. She would love to be a part of this tradition, but her sister, Carol, will be there, and Rihanna can't bring herself to forgive her for drinking too much and blurting out a confidence that Rihanna had shared with her. Rihanna tells herself that Carol's actions cannot be condoned, and so another holiday event goes by without the sisters talking.

Rob was "unfairly" passed over for a promotion at work. His boss used to be his friend, and now Rob can barely look at the man and feels angry whenever he has to interact with him—which is all too often. Rob has considered quitting but needs the job in this tight economy. His resentment boils over at times with other staff and colleagues, and he has trouble sleeping and managing the constant headaches brought on by his brooding about how he was mistreated. He knows his anger is killing his future chances for promotion and is lowering the quality of his day, but he can't seem to let it go.

Rihanna and Rob have in common anger toward another person that has never been resolved. The events that triggered their anger are well in the past, but their angry feelings are as intense as if they had been triggered yesterday. Their lives continue to be impacted in negative ways, and there is no end in sight as long as this anger rages on silently, beneath the surface of their lives. The preceding chapters have addressed anger as a reaction to unmet expectations fueled by how we think about what just happened. Sometimes we're unable or unwilling to resolve an anger-provoking situation. When we are exposed to the object of this resentment, we experience angry emotions that may be hard for us and others to understand.

Ideally, this resentment dissipates on its own, but as is true for Rihanna and Rob, it can actually become more intense over time. For example, you may be "filtering" in the most upsetting parts of the event in your self-talk or imagery, making it seem even worse than it was to begin with. Holding on to resentments that are unseen, lying just below your awareness when you interact with others, can make resolving your anger a daunting task as you are not directly identifying and confronting the real cause of your irritation—an issue you have never resolved.

This unresolved anger, bubbling beneath the surface of everyday events, may emerge suddenly when you're confronted with the object of your anger. If the person is unaware that you harbor resentment because you've never aired your feelings, he may be completely mystified by the way you act around him. If the person is aware of your resentment, she may feel threatened by it and quickly aroused to an angry comeback when confronted unexpectedly by your ire. Even more baffling to others is when a new situation that merely *reminds* you of what you've come to resent triggers a reaction beyond reason.

James had been making great progress in managing his anger until a new friend was late for a luncheon date. His anger quickly escalated as the minutes ticked by. When she arrived, he immediately confronted her in a loud voice about her "rude and inconsiderate" behavior. Stunned by this reaction, she walked out after telling James to "get a grip." Feeling remorseful about his tirade, James realized this setback was fueled by unresolved resentment related to his former girlfriend, who often took advantage of him, standing him up numerous times at theaters and restaurants. The current situation "rhymed" with his past and thus brought his unresolved resentment to the surface. The problem is that his new friend had nothing to do with his old anger, and the fact that she is now bearing the brunt of it is definitely straining the relationship.

More complicated and certainly more intense are situations in which you have been injured emotionally or physically by another's actions, as happens when you or a loved one is the victim of a crime such as physical or sexual assault. Your resentment may be worsened if the perpetrator was never brought to justice or if you feel the punishment was too lenient.

Janet's father raped her numerous times during her preteen years, and she was too frightened to tell her mother, feeling she would not be believed. These assaults affected every aspect of her life—how she did at school, her relationships with boys, and her self-confidence—for the three years that the abuse went on, until she finally threatened her father with the police and he left her alone. Now she has only horrible memories of these times and is filled with hatred for her father, who has died of cancer, while continuing to resent her mother for not see-ing what was happening and stopping it: "How could my mother live in the same house and not see how poorly I was doing in school and not take steps to protect me?" While she cannot confront her dead father directly, she has refused to have anything to do with her mother and keeps her two sons away from their grandmother. She just "cannot" forget what happened and can't conceive of forgiving her mother. "If I begin inviting her into our home, it will be like condoning what she did. It will be like I am forgetting and letting her off the hook. I can't do that!" Holidays are hard, and Janet hates being in this situation, but she feels stuck in her resentment and the impact it has on her whole family. She loses sleep and serenity agonizing over what she can do that will feel right for her.

Resentment seems to feed on itself. Past anger becomes current anger and thus affects future anger—such as when others get angry in response to your resentment. My greatest problem with resentment is that it continues to victimize the resenter more than the object of the resentment. Every time you re-anger yourself by rehashing an upset-ting event of yesterday, your arousal rises to create the negative face of anger you show to others today. You feel upset and agitated, and the other person now has to make sense of your actions, perhaps reacting with more anger, which only fuels conflict. What if the person you are harboring resentment toward has no idea you are so upset and suffused with agitating anger or even rage? When this person's head hits the pil-low at night, he gets a good night's rest. But what about you? How are you feeling, and what impact is this resentment having on your life?

How Anger Becomes Resentment and Why It Matters

This book has focused mostly on resolving anger that arises immedi-ately when expectations are not met. You have learned to halt your inner reactions as quickly as possible so that you can rethink the situation with fact-based, calming thoughts and a plan for resolution. Resentment, on the other hand, occurs when anger toward a person is not resolved and continues on. This can happen for a number of reasons. Even when you habitually use the anger expression and resolution skills in this book, events and circumstances can conspire to prevent true closure. Maybe you bit your tongue the last time your grandmother asked you if you'd put on a little weight, out of the lifelong habit of respecting your elders. Or you let a nasty "joke" slide because you were in a meeting and knew it wasn't the right time to sidetrack the agenda; you figured you could address it later, in private, but those opportunities never seemed to arise. Sometimes we let certain people get away with obnoxious behavior because we think they can't help it, they don't mean it, or we owe them something. Unfortunately, none of these rationales protect us from resenting them later.

Anger occurs when an important need, expressed by an expectation for ourselves or others, is not satisfied. When we identify what we expect (e.g., an apology, a new behavior, a specific request) and use our cognitive tools to ensure it is realistic, we can immediately resolve this anger by taking steps to communicate what we want and collaborate with the other person to reach resolution (e.g., the other person apologizes, you both agree to handle the situation differently) using the ideas found in Chapter 8. Once the need is fulfilled, the anger stops. But when we do not or cannot communicate our feelings and needs to the other person, the issue remains unresolved and the anger transforms into its chronic form: resentment. I have found that the longer resentment is permitted to continue, with your repeated thoughts and actions reinforcing its strength, the more entrenched it becomes as a source of negative energy that influences your actions. Resentment can gradually transform from an unwanted event you were angry about to a forceful belief that impacts you and those you love (e.g., "I can NEVER forget what he did to me," "Dad hates his brother, so don't invite them over at the same time."). The trouble with resentment is that it feeds on itself. Even if you'd characterize some resentment you feel as minor or intermittent or nothing you can't ignore, you might find at some point that the untreated wound has festered and spread resentment like an infection throughout your system, where it will pop up at all kinds of unexpected times and places.

Chris is having a nice moment with his wife, selecting home furnishings, when he begins thinking about her objections to his purchasing a new car. Suddenly, he feels angry that she is willing to spend money for "what *she* wants" while ignoring *his* feelings. Chris's voice tone immediately changes, and he begins responding minimally to her comments and then criticizes her taste in decorating. She wonders where this anger came from and says, "There you go, angry and ruining our day again. I've had it with your mood." Chris wonders how things went south so fast. He thought he had put his resentment at being denied a new car behind him, seeing that it made sense to put off such a big expense till next year, as his wife had said.

Annie resents her boyfriend's children from his first marriage coming over on weekends and never expressing appreciation for all that she does to make them happy. Things didn't start out that way. At first she thought she and the kids just needed time to get used to each other's style. But when she started feeling like they were taking advantage of her goodwill and expressed these feelings to her boyfriend, he told her she was just "overreacting," heightening her resentment further since there was no "valve" to release her suppressed anger. Now she finds herself responding curtly and going to bed early, this "cold anger" emerging from the resentment that has never been discussed or resolved successfully. In turn, her boyfriend is angry with Annie for "rejecting" him and his kids, and the cycle of anger escalates, fueled by the hidden agenda of resentment Annie feels unable to resolve.

Try not to ignore "little" resentments, even if bringing them to the surface of your mind instead of shoving them back underground makes you feel petty. Resentment left to fester has all kinds of ill effects. Dr. Robert Enright, who has studied the effects of resentment on our health and wellness, defines resentment as "remembering the injury and re-feeling the emotions surrounding the hurt. Anger is like a flame; resentment is like a hot coal." Many researchers have studied the ill effects of unresolved resentments that may linger for months or even years. Persons unwilling to let go of this anger are reported to have:

> Higher blood pressure.

> More depression.

> More stress-related health issues.

> Higher rates of heart disease.

> Lower immune functioning.

Unresolved anger may lead to marital dysfunction and is a predictor of divorce. It also impacts children, who don't learn to express and resolve their anger when these skills are not modeled by their parents.

When Is Resentment Worth Banishing?

Clearly, holding on to resentment is not good for you. It is like the "gift" that keeps on giving—except in this case it is not a gift at all and may even endanger your health. If it seems rational to let go of resentment, why is it so hard to do so? Can you identify with any of the following indications that resentment may be affecting you?

You avoid certain situations because a particular person will likely be present, even when to do so negatively impacts others. For example, you avoid going to a wedding rehearsal dinner because your brother is likely to be there. This greatly disappoints your wife and children, who decide to go without you.

You find yourself painfully reviewing a past situation when you got really angry at another person. You start to catch yourself doing this often, and the feelings are not resolving—in fact, they may even be intensifying.

You have passed up an opportunity at work or in your personal life because it would force you to interact with a person you are uncomfortable around. For example, an opportunity to work on an exciting new project at work comes up, and you turn it down because you find a certain coworker will also be on the team.

Others have urged you to forgive a person who did something that you have decided up until now was unforgivable. You see no options other than to hold on to your ire and avoid any contact with this individual. This situation is affecting a person you love. For example, Torie could "not forgive" her sister for spanking her son when he was acting defiant at a family event. Torie's mother has begged the two sisters to reconcile, but Torie holds on to her demand for an abject apology from a sister she was close to for years prior to the discipline incident. Holidays at Mother's house must now occur in "shifts"—one sister coming first and leaving before the other shows up—to everyone else's dismay.

"It's No Big Deal"

Sometimes people react to their own feelings of resentment with shame or guilt. They identify resentment with being petty or "sweating the small stuff" or just not being very nice (that is, forgiving). If you were raised to believe that anger, even righteous anger, was inappropriate in some way, you may find lingering anger, in the form of resentment, just as unacceptable. You may repress the feeling enough that you're not always aware it's pulling the strings of your behavior. Take a look at the following situations. Are any of them familiar to you?

> You are at a rock concert with your family and friends but find yourself moody and irritable. You seem to be looking for something to complain about.

> You find yourself intense and punishing your children for something that, let's face it, is not that big a deal. Your spouse wonders what's wrong.

> You are in a situation that anyone else would envy. You're on a tour visiting chateaus in France, and the biggest objective concern you have is to avoid eating too much good food. Yet you're irritable and your anger quickly flares for "no good reason."

In all these cases you either end up apologizing for your mood or just feel guilty afterward, but you're confused about why you lost it. To illuminate your reactions, try to figure out what you might resent that hasn't been resolved by surfacing thoughts that focus on disbelief or *should*s:

> "I can't believe Grace and the kids are just enjoying this show without any thought of what it's costing us or how much trouble it was for me to get these tickets."

> "I never got to do half of what these kids just take for granted. I had to pay for everything I got, and my kids get too much and don't appreciate any of it!"

> "Steve should be making it easier for me to avoid gaining weight by not sitting there eating foie gras and chocolate mousse right in front of me, but he never thinks of me first."

Now try to fill in the following blank:

"The thing that really irritates me about what Grace/the kids/Steve did is:_____."

Or ask yourself this question:

"Grace's/the kids'/Steve's behavior reminds me of what upsetting thing she/they/he or someone else did in the past?

You might be surprised by your answer. For example:

"She never should have gone behind my back and revealed what I told her in confidence. I'm finished with her."

"I never forget when someone lies to me, like my first wife did. That's it. I want nothing to do with that person."

"Every time I'm with Bob I get angry all over again, but I won't give him the satisfaction of letting him know why I'm so distant."

These positions are typical of the kind of thinking that sustains resentment. Someone has done something that violated important expectations you held about issues like fairness, courtesy, or morality, and you became angry. Perhaps you tried to resolve the issue at the time by speaking out and letting your feelings and needs be known and the other person refused to resolve the matter in a way that was satisfactory to you. Or you may have held your feelings inside, perhaps expressing them with cold anger or passive–aggression, refusing to reveal your reaction to the other person.

Once you've identified your underlying resentments you may ask yourself, "What can I do to resolve it?" It may not be as easy as "Okay, I know this is hurting me, so I'll just let it go." When you've rehearsed past hurts numerous times, your resentment becomes like any other habit, strengthened each time you experience it.

"I Was Wronged! Why Should I Do the Work to Resolve the Situation?"

Is it always necessary to resolve resentment? After all, you're justified in holding on to your angry feelings sometimes, aren't you? You were the one who was wronged—at least to your way of thinking. Right? You certainly have every right to hold on to your inner anger and can probably justify it with a litany of reasons. Perhaps the person or situation you resent is no longer a part of your current life. In other words, your resentment is not causing problems for you. For example, you cannot forgive the way your previous boss fired you without "good cause." You have moved to a new position and never have occasion to meet your old boss. You don't think about him often, and when you do your anger doesn't last long or affect your current life in any negative way. In this case there is no reason to invest the time and energy to resolve this resentment.

In contrast, even if the original person is no longer in your daily life, when your resentment emerges with others and in ways that cause discomfort or create problems in your current life and relationships or affects your health and wellness in the ways discussed earlier, it may be time to put it to rest. Consider these common examples.

> ➤ The person you resent is a family member, friend, or coworker you must continue to interact with. Containing your resentment while attempting to interact with this person would require extraordinary self-control.

> ➤ You have already found yourself "backsliding" into an angry face that created problems for you in the past or strained other important relationships (e.g., your continued resentment of your brother creates anguish for your parents at family gatherings).

> ➤ You find yourself dreading certain situations where the object of your anger will be present. You foresee a future of forced painful interactions with this person.

> ➤ You find yourself suddenly shifting into a dark mood, getting irritable, or overreacting without having any idea why, as described above. In those cases there's probably some resentment operating behind the scenes, and it's worth ferreting it out and sending it on its way so that it doesn't ruin the good times in your life.

So how can you let go of resentment? You may have decided that certain events must occur before you'll be ready to let go of this anger. If only the other person would:

> ➤ Pay you back the money you think is owed you.

> ➤ Admit she was wrong.

> ➤ Agree with your plan.

> ➤ Apologize to you in front of others.

The problem is that others may not be aware of these prerequisites for resolution that you are setting for them. Even if they're aware, you are powerless over whether they will agree to them. *You are thus making your relief from the ill effects of resentment dependent on what someone else does.* If others are unable or unwilling to comply with your conditions, you are stuck with your resentment, which may be hurting you much more than it's hurting them. If you are happy with this situation, then it's easy to continue with the status quo—and many people do.

But if you've decided that enough is enough and it is time to move on, there are numerous ways to resolve your resentment by directly discussing your feelings with the object of your ire or, when this is not possible or desirable, to employ your imagination and other symbolic strategies for attaining closure on the issue—to put your resentment to rest. One or more of these strategies may work for you as they have for my clients over the years.

I'm sure you're wondering whether forgiveness has to be a part of any strategy you choose for getting over resentment. Be assured it does not. Forgiveness has been found to produce clear benefits to the "forgiver," and we will consider the issues and methods for reaching a lasting inner sense of peace that forgiveness can provide to you. However, you don't have to forgive the person you feel wronged you. You may not have been willing to consider forgiveness in the past, because you think forgiving would mean condoning the other person's actions or minimizing the hurt those actions caused. That's not necessarily the case either. Later in the chapter we'll consider myths about what forgiveness is and is not so you can make a more informed decision about its merits.

Strategies for Resolution

But first, let's talk about how to reach resolution based on whether you can or cannot talk to the person who triggered your anger.

Confronting the Other Person Directly

If the other person is still accessible to you, you might be able to use assertive problem solving (see Chapter 8) to resolve your resentment.

You identify your thoughts, your feelings, and what you need from the other person and communicate this calmly and directly, engaging in a dialogue to reach resolution. When differences surface, you try to problem-solve a solution acceptable to both of you.

Whether assertive problem solving will be effective depends on a lot of factors, however, such as how much time has passed, how open the other person is to talking to you about this (or anything), and whether you'll feel comfortable with this approach. Ask yourself what you can realistically achieve by opening up an old topic at this point. If in fact there is any possibility of a dialogue that might result in resolution, it is worth giving assertive problem solving a chance.

Begin by deciding what you want for resolution to occur. I call this your *conditions for resolution*. To avoid setting yourself up for disappointment that may further fuel resentment, make sure each of your conditions is reasonable and attainable.

> ➤ Is your condition within the other's power to grant? For example, this person may not be able to alter an outcome that has been in place for a long time or is under the control of others (e.g., getting you your old job back, paying back money the other person no longer has).

> ➤ Is this person likely to be motivated to give you what you want? If so, why now, when it wasn't given willingly up to the present time? What has changed?

> ➤ Are your expectations one-sided in demanding a lot from the other person but giving nothing in return? If so, ask yourself why this person would accede to your conditions. Has he or she, to your knowledge, ever been able to see things from this perspective or act in the ways you wish?

Alan hasn't spoken to his father for almost five years. He resents his father divorcing his mother and treating her "poorly." Even though his father has often expressed an interest in making things right, Alan has refused to talk with him because "that would be giving in. He would assume that what he did was okay with me and it isn't." When he determines his conditions for resolution, Alan realizes that he wants his father to "make things right" with his mother, yet recognizes his mother has moved beyond her anger and is happily remarried. He also recognizes that he wants his father to suffer because "of the suffering

Mom and I went through." When he looks at the situation factually, he sees he cannot control his father's emotions and, in fact, his father has been happy since meeting and marrying another woman. Alan concludes his conditions are unrealistic and will only set him up for more disappointment since they are unattainable.

So how does Alan proceed if he wishes to confront his father? After thoughtful consideration, he decides on the following conditions.

He wants his father to meet with him and to just listen until he "gets out" all his thoughts and feelings about the divorce. Alan recognizes that he must in turn listen to his father's view of the situation. Based on his father's willingness to engage in this process, Alan concludes he can decide after they meet and he sees how it goes whether to meet again to try to put the relationship back on track.

Note that Alan is not expecting anything that is unrealistic, as defined above. There is no guarantee that things will be better after Alan confronts his father with these feelings, but it's a start. Alan now has put aside conditions that were roadblocks to ever setting things right. He can decide whether to forgive his father once he has opened a dialogue and the issues are on the table.

But what about his old desire to punish his father? Alan recognizes that his continuing resentment was only hurting him and ruining any possibility for his children to have a relationship with their grandfather. In addition, it often made him moody and irritable around his family whenever other siblings spoke of their continuing relationship with the father.

What If Your Meeting Doesn't Go as You Envisioned?

Sometimes your efforts at meeting with the person you resent don't turn out as you would hope and expect. For example, what if Alan meets with his father but can't communicate his feelings because his father spends the entire time lecturing Alan and defending himself? What is Alan to do? What if the father won't even agree to meet with Alan? I would reiterate that you need to evaluate your expectations before you confront the other person. Based on past experiences (the factual reality of your past interactions with this person), you can preview possible likely scenarios that might include the *worst expected,* *expected,* and *best expected outcomes* when the meeting occurs and then think about a plan to cope with each in advance. You might practice how you could respond to each possible outcome using your imagination, vividly picturing what you might say and do. This previewing and planning first discussed in Chapter 3 increases your sense of control and preparedness—likely to lower your discomfort and increase your feelings of confidence as the meeting approaches.

Confronting an Unavailable Other

But what if the person you resent is unwilling or unavailable to discuss your issues? I have often worked with clients who resent a partner who ended a relationship and is now unwilling to have any contact. My client feels stuck with resentment that is now a roadblock to new relationships and a continuing source of pain. What of a spouse or parent who dies before you have a chance to confront him or her with your resentment? You may feel angry about how this person treated you but guilty at having these feelings for someone who is now deceased. What do you do to resolve these feelings?

1. *Write it out.* I have found that writing out your full awareness of an issue of resentment can be helpful as a first step toward resolution. By exhaustively expressing your thoughts, feelings, and needs about what happened, you uncover information that has been stored away, coming up in bits and pieces to make you miserable each time. By looking at your awareness in the light of day (and then perhaps sharing it with another) you begin to habituate to the pain of what originally triggered your anger.

Habituation means that by continuing to look at, think about, and reconsider what happened, you gradually reduce the emotional reaction this information elicits. Think of any fear you've overcome in the past. You did it by continuing to do the thing you feared (e.g., giving a talk in front of classmates, swimming farther out into the lake). Through repeated exposure, what you feared loses its power to evoke intense emotions. The same is true with anger and resentment. So consider writing about what you resent again and again until it begins to lose its power to make you upset. It works.

2. *Talk it out with someone who can relate to what you feel.* Those who have been laid off, have already cared for aging parents, have survived divorce, or coped with cancer may be able to relate to your similar issue with experience-based ideas and empathy that comes from having walked in your shoes.

3. *Express your feelings in writing.* Since the object of your resentment is unavailable, write a letter, construct a poem or song, or make a drawing that somehow represents your feelings. This may seem far out, but have you ever found that just by fully expressing your feelings in a letter you felt differently and didn't really need to send it (whether you did so or not)? By writing the letter, you accomplished your goal (and habituation was at work as well).

Leticia could not let go of her anger toward her ex-fiancé, who abruptly called off their wedding. She felt embarrassed and confused, yet her ex-fiancé would not speak with her so she could confront him with these feelings. She found herself easily angered when men she now dated acted "distant," and she recently lost a friendship when her anger got the best of her. Her friends told her to seek help for her anger and hurt, and she finally made an appointment for counseling. At my suggestion Leticia wrote a letter to her "ex" and then decided whether to send it. She could say everything she wished in the letter without being interrupted, which "felt really good" to Leticia. Over several weeks she refined the letter until it felt "just right." After sharing the letter with two close friends who supported her position and encouraged her to let go of her resentment (e.g., "He isn't worth any more of your anguish"), Leticia decided her "ex" wasn't worth the time to send it to him. Instead, she decided to have a ceremony to "burn" the letter as she and her friends shared a glass of wine. As the letter burned, she felt her resentment turn to ashes, which blew up the chimney and away from her.

Any symbolic act of letting go of resentment may be helpful, like Leticia's ceremony, where she in effect turned her resentment to ashes. Reading or writing a poem that captures your resentment toward others may facilitate letting go of it once and for all. Tearing up and flushing away a drawing or playing/singing a song that captures how you feel may give you a sense of closure.

4. *Confront the other person in your imagination.* As you know from previous chapters, imagery is an effective way to practice new behaviors, often creating the same feelings as a real-life situation. You can use your imagination to transport yourself into a situation where you can at last confront the person you resent in any way you wish. Unlike the past, where you may have felt powerless, imagery lets you control the setting, the action, and the outcome.

Sam's father died before Sam had a chance to express his resentment about the way he'd been punished and berated by his father over the years. Sam found himself resenting his two brothers, who played sports and seemed to be favored by their father, leading to cold anger and frequent sarcasm that Sam directed at them. A recent blowup over a minor issue caused Sam to examine his underlying resentment, which seemed to spring forth around his brothers at the most minor provocation. Sam wanted to focus on the good his father had done but had a hard time letting go of his anger about these childhood events. Unable to discuss these feelings with his father directly, Sam decided to imagine himself in a sailboat (Sam's favorite sport, which his father never participated in) with his father. He "told" his father about a series of hurtful events as he pictured his father listening to him without interrupting. He imagined himself getting out everything he could think of that had hurt him during childhood. He chose to ask his father to forgive him for being so angry and distant from him during the later years of his life. After playing out the scene a few times, Sam felt purged of his resentment. His relationship with his brothers greatly improved as he now realized his anger toward them had been misdirected. He spoke with each of them individually to discuss these feelings and apologize for his actions over the years. Sam truly felt "done" with his resentment.

Some resentment is deep seated and may be related to traumatic past life experiences (e.g., childhood physical or sexual abuse), which can make it hard to resolve on your own. If the ideas already mentioned don't work for you, consider getting professional help to put your old anger to rest. When resentment is tied up in posttraumatic stress, professional help is definitely warranted.

Forgiveness: The Ultimate Resolution for You?

The methods in the preceding section are designed to help you craft rational, realistic conditions for resolution so that your resentment can be put to rest and free you up to resume your life and relationships with others of significance. Research has shown that there are many benefits to taking the further step of forgiving the person you believe has wronged or hurt you. Have you considered or actually tried to forgive this person in your mind? When the harm done to you or someone you love is severe, it can be very hard to forgive. Yet the great benefit of forgiving is a truly transformed relationship with the other—not just getting the anger out and off your chest, but transforming your deepest emotions toward that individual, who may continue to be a part of your life—a brother, a child, a parent. Forgiveness can provide an intangible benefit, letting you be truly more at peace with this person. According to Dr. Robert Enright, you forgive to "quiet your angry feelings," to alter destructive thoughts, to act more civilly to this person, thus improving your communication and improving this relationship, which may be important not only to your own life but to your spouse and children. For example, you can now have holidays with your brother and his family so that your own children can relate to an uncle and cousins they have not gotten to know—roadblocked by your unresolved anger. For others, forgiveness can have a spiritual dimension, putting them more at peace with God and their spiritual beliefs. On the other hand, let's look at what forgiveness is not by reviewing common myths about it. According to Dr. Fred Luskin, director of the well-regarded Stanford Forgiveness Project:

> Forgiveness is not condoning—when you forgive, you are not saying that what the other did is okay with you.

> When you forgive, you cannot be expected to forget what happened. The old adage "forgive and forget" is usually impossible for us to achieve. Our brains are hard-wired to remember painful events. But we do not have to forget to forgive.

> Forgiveness does not require that you be religious or have an "otherworldly" experience.

> When you forgive, you are not expected to immediately let go of all painful feelings. That will come with time, and at the end you may always feel some degree of pain when you think about what happened.

> Forgiveness is not reconciliation—the act of reestablishing a relationship with the object of your anger. In most cases it may be in your best interest to reconcile for the good of all parties who are affected by what happened. But it is not essential, as in cases where you decided to forgive someone who is now incarcerated for harming you or someone you love.

What Are the Steps to Forgiving?

If you have decided to forgive this person, much research and clinical practice offers guidelines for how to proceed. I will synthesize the many ideas into a series of steps that should work well for you. While experts in forgiveness may disagree as to the ordering of these steps, each is present in most of their schemes for forgiveness.

First, *let yourself fully feel and accept the anger* you have felt for this person. Try to recall the events that led up to resentment and permit yourself to describe, perhaps in a journal, exactly how you feel. The Daily Anger Log found in Appendix 2 could be used to surface how you feel when resentment toward this person arises. Get in touch with the pain these feelings arouse and think about how your anger is affecting you now:

> ➤ How often does this anger rear its head as you go about your life?

> ➤ Is the level of pain decreasing over time, staying pretty much the same, or is it even worsening as time goes on?

> ➤ How does remaining angry with this person affect your health and the quality of your life?

> ➤ How is your anger altering the ways you interact with this person, your family, or others you must relate to?

> ➤ Are others whom you love affected by your resentment, like your spouse or children or extended family? How do you feel about this impact?

> ➤ Has anyone expressed his or her own pain about the continuation of your resentment?

Ask yourself if the pain of continuing to hold on to this resentment is worth it to you. What are you getting out of it that is good versus the cost to you and to others you love?

Second, try to *reframe* the events that led to your resentment by looking at what happened from a different perspective—a kind of new "lens." Enright (see Bibliography) offers the following questions to help you look at this person differently, which may alter your current feelings and assist you in forgiving.

1. What was life like for him or her when growing up? Henry has not spoken to his mother since his dad died. He blames her for being cold and unfeeling. "She never had a kind word for my dad—always complaining about not enough money or his 'failure' at being a good provider." Henry decides to ask her sister and others about his mother's childhood and her parents. He learns that his grandfather was an alcoholic who never provided for the family, and they often went without enough food or other necessities. Often the power was turned off, even in winter months. Her mother had to work and was gone most of the time, and Henry's mother had to care for the younger children. He begins to realize why she felt so victimized by her own life and so critical and unforgiving about money. He decides that she never had much of a childhood herself and was probably bitter, which led to Henry's experience of her as critical and unforgiving of his father.

2. At the time of the offense, what was life like for this person? Henry begins to recall the months prior to his dad's death when his mother had to stop working to care for him as he fought lung cancer. He recalls that she spent hours by his side and was his nurse as they could not afford home health care. He begins to realize how she could not forgive him for continuing to smoke when she kept begging him to quit and may have felt abandoned by his death, which she could not prevent. He begins to get some idea of how lonely and bitter she is with meager social security to live on and no hope of a change in her limited and lonely life.

3. Are you able to tell the story of your relationship with this person in a broader sense than the offense itself? Henry begins to empathize with his mom's plight for the first time since his dad died and starts to understand that her negative attitude and criticisms of his dad emerge from a pretty painful and unhappy early life and an adult life filled with unmet dreams and scraping to get by. As bitter as she was, she always kept her children fed, clean, and pushed them to do well in school—sometimes with a lot of criticism—so they could have what she had never had. He acknowledges the times when she sat up with him late into the evening, helping him with his homework to ensure he would get a good grade. He recalls how she went without new clothes or a new washing machine so her children could have the latest clothes and thereby have the chance to fit in that she did not have.

Has he judged his mom too harshly? What was behind her actions that he "hated" at the time? Answering these questions forces Henry to consider a new perspective or window through which to view his mom's negativity and critical words and actions. He begins to see that his dad was not a saint as he had thought and that his mother worked hard to keep the family afloat and functioning through hard times. Instead of focusing only on the negative things she did, he is now seeing the world through her eyes. This more empathic framing of the journey that was her life immediately begins to arouse more understanding of why she may have become so bitter and negative.

Third, *commitment* to forgive must precede whatever you decide to say or do directly with the other person. Consider the pain your resentment continues to kindle in your present life for you and your loved ones. Are you willing to let this pain continue and for how long? Can you begin to see the other's perspective, and does this help you better understand why the other person did what he or she did even though you may never condone or forget it? Remember that forgiveness is a choice that only you can make. Are you ready to let your anger go and try to forgive, or would you rather postpone this until a later time? You must decide. The other person did something you may be powerless over. But now you have the power to decide whether or not to forgive. That can feel truly powerful and compelling.

Fourth, take some *concrete steps to forgive* the object of your resentment. Experts on forgiveness have mixed opinions about whether you must actually tell the other that you forgive. In some cases that person may not be available or even has died, so that direct communication is impossible. The important thing is to forgive in your mind and heart: "I choose to forgive you." This can be done in imagination using the strategies in the preceding section. Find a comfortable time and place to imagine yourself sitting down with this person and letting him know your thoughts and feelings about how what the person said or did affected your life. "Hear" yourself saying that you forgive and imagine how that feels. Or you could write a letter of forgiveness and either send it or not. The important thing is that you have taken the inner step of letting go of this anger and forgiven, without expecting anything in return (e.g., an apology).

When the other person is a part of your everyday life and you want to resume some kind of relationship, forgiving in person can be done in a private meeting you call. You do not have conditions for resolution—you have made a choice to forgive, and it is in your exclusive power to do so, regardless of what the other says or does. At that time you can either ask for reconciliation—a renewal of the relationship—or not. Again this is within your power. Rather than being a continuing victim of the inner pain of hatred and unresolved anger, you are now freed up to begin to pursue your life without the burden of resentment. While it would be nice to think that you will feel great and free of all pain once you decide to forgive, this is not a realistic expectation. Forgiveness is the beginning of a journey of letting go that may take some time, but you may decide it is worth it to you.

If you decide to forgive, there is good reason to believe that you will feel much better in the long run. It is in your hands and no one else's—that may be the real power of forgiveness.

12

So You've Had a Setback
Getting Back on Track

You've learned the steps of anger management. You pretty much know what to do, and your efforts have been paying off. You're spending less time on damage control following outbursts. Your relationships seem to be on a more even keel. You've gained a sense of well-being that just wasn't possible when you were under constant stress and carrying around a load of shame and self-recrimination. Perhaps you have successfully resolved a resentment that was harming an important relationship. Life feels pretty good.

But then you find yourself backsliding. Faces of anger that you thought you had thrown off for good start popping up again. You're confused and dismayed. Is your anger going to take over your life again? If you suddenly find your anger is getting the best of you as it did before, you may feel disgusted with yourself and discouraged that you've gone "back to square one." You're not alone. Everyone has setbacks. There's no such thing as never losing your temper, never letting your guard down, never relinquishing control.

Colin suddenly blows up while discussing a difference of opinion with his wife: "I still don't know what happened. I had planned on having a calm discussion, and it just got out of control like it used to." Colin has been under a lot of stress at work and hasn't been sleeping well.

When Mara unexpectedly asks Lesley for a favor at the office, Lesley is shocked to find herself losing it, blowing up with screaming so loud that other employees report her to a supervisor. She can't believe what she just did. Sure, she lost respect for Mara when Mara took credit for her marketing survey six months ago, but she thought her intense anger was a thing of the past.

Dwayne expects more sexual intimacy from Tanya, who often complains that she's just too exhausted from working full-time and trying to parent two young sons. Still dissatisfied and disgruntled, Dwayne finds himself returning to an old pattern of withdrawing into cold anger, responding to his wife's questions with grunts and looking through her when she tries to talk. When Tanya accuses him of falling back into complaining and pulling away from her, he walks off in a huff. He knows he should talk to her calmly and collaboratively about their sex life, but he feels like he just hasn't had time to practice his new anger skills. It just seems easier to go off by himself. He's tired too, after all. Sitting alone in the den, pretending to read the paper, he feels completely stuck—frustrated, powerless, and lonely.

At times like these, you might feel like all your work has been for nothing, that your anger is a monkey on your back that you're never going to get rid of. This conviction may very well be reinforced by the disappointment, anger, or disdain of important people in your life. Hearing someone you respect and care about say something like "I thought you were making progress—you really fooled me there for a while, but you haven't changed at all" can really cement despair.

If you find yourself stuck like Colin, Lesley, or Dwayne, turn to the tools you've worked so hard to acquire. They can help you fight despair just like they help you exert control over anger. Telling yourself that you have to start all over, that your efforts have been futile, that you'll never conquer your ire is negative self-talk that will undermine all your progress so far. Interpreting one setback as a sign that you've gotten nowhere in anger management is self-defeating and simply false.

In the wake of a setback, go right back to the methods that have worked for you so far. Instead of immersing yourself in negative thoughts, analyze the episode. Diagnose what happened. Why did you blow up when you're aware it is so counterproductive? How did you come to withdraw in cold anger when past experience tells you that it only frustrates your spouse and creates resentment?

Making Mistakes and Moving Forward

When you blow it, there is always an explanation. Learn from it and you'll be able to apply your new insight to the next anger trigger that comes along. Recall the stages of an anger episode from Chapter 4. Before any anger action there is a prelude that influences how you end up acting. By thinking back to the minutes and hours before your unfortunate face of anger, you can uncover the reasons for your slip.

Also, consider what happened during the episode as well as your reflections after the fact. The brief quiz on pages 231–232 may shed some light on why this setback occurred so you can do something about it.

Which of the preceding reasons for your setback has the highest score? Did you have a score for more than one reason? Now that you have some ideas as to why this setback occurred, think about ways you can make changes in your life to insulate yourself from further backsliding. In the following pages I'll describe each of these possible reasons for a setback and offer some solutions you should consider.

Just Not Enough Practice

The simplest explanation for a setback is that you haven't fully learned your new anger skills so that they're automatic. Chapter 10 spoke forcefully about the importance of repetition in grooving in new habits so they occur almost without thinking. Before you're too hard on yourself, think realistically about the number of years you had to "practice" being aggressive or sarcastic. Your old faces of anger have a life of their own and are the default behaviors most likely to occur unless you're paying close attention to how you're reacting. They must now be replaced with your new anger skills through repeated practice.

I suggest you renew your efforts at practice. It might be a good idea to reread Chapter 10 as a place to start. To focus on specifically what you need to practice, review this setback in your mind, while your memory is still fresh. Focus in detail on what happened so you can decide how you will handle the situation differently next time. Then look for opportunities to use planned practice or behavioral rehearsal. Behavioral practice is a must if you know what to do but feel awkward at actually doing it.

Often your review of the situation will reveal that the other person really pushed your buttons. You may not have had time to carefully consider which anger skills to use. If it happened once, it may occur again unless you've learned to stay the course no matter what he or she does. For this reason it's important to make your practice as realistic as possible, simulating likely conditions of provocation and stress.

Diagnosing My Setback

Carefully imagine the situation in which you lost control of your anger, using each of your senses to replay the scene vividly in your mind. As you do, keep in mind the steps of anger management you've learned in this book.

Which of the following statements are true about my setback?

1. Things happened so fast it just didn't occur   T   F   [A]
   to me to use my new anger skills.

2. I'm having a hard time forgiving this person   T   F   [D]
   for something that happened in the past.

3. I was feeling pressured and under a lot of   T   F   [B]
   stress just prior to this setback.

4. I am not sure how I would handle the   T   F   [A]
   situation differently if it happened again
   today.

5. As usual, this person just didn't consider my   T   F   [C]
   feelings and needs.

6. It's hard to find time to even think about   T   F   [A]
   handling my anger differently.

7. I haven't been sleeping well lately—easily   T   F   [B]
   feel exhausted and overwhelmed.

8. It's rare that this person does what I want   T   F   [C]
   him/her to do.

9. Now that I think about it, I was drinking an   T   F   [B]
   alcoholic beverage (or had a lot of caffeine)
   just prior to this setback.

10. I just don't have the time to practice my new   T   F   [A]
    anger skills.

11. I couldn't just calmly listen to this person,   T   F   [D]
    given how I've been treated in the past.

12. This person often disappoints me.   T   F   [C]

13. I was feeling pretty rushed, with too much to   T   F   [B]
    do, when this incident occurred.

14. Until I get an apology, I don't care how this   T   F   [D]
    person feels.

15. I feel this person will never change in ways   T   F   [C]
    that I want.

16. You can't expect me to treat this person as if   T   F   [D]
    everything is okay when it isn't.

Add up the number of items you marked "T" for "true" for each bracketed letter—A, B, C, or D—which define possible reasons for your setback. As you fill in the number of "true" responses for each, consider the content of the items you endorsed and how they relate to what you've learned in the previous chapters.

"A" items: _____. You haven't practiced enough using planned practice or rehearsals. You were unclear as to what to do or just didn't feel comfortable with your new anger skills.

"B" items: _____. You were under too much stress, were not eating or sleeping well, or made other choices that compromised your resilience in coping with the triggering situation (recall the "Five S's").

"C" items: _____. Your unrealistic expectations for this person or situation set you up for this setback.

"D" items: _____. Unresolved resentment of this person contributed to your unwelcome face of anger.

Dr. Mervyn Wagner developed the idea of "barbing," behavioral rehearsal with a twist: Your role-playing partner tries to push your buttons by challenging you in every way you would find most difficult while you practice your new anger skills. After thinking about what verbal and physical actions seem hardest to endure, you simulate one or more of these scenarios in your behavioral practice. As you try to recall and use your new anger skills, your partner repeatedly barbs you until you can keep your cool. This makes you more immune to setbacks in the future. Some examples may give you a better idea as to how to use barbing.

Kristian can't stand it when his wife raises her voice and loudly interrupts him when they're arguing. He "can't think" and recently experienced a setback by blowing up with actions like cursing and name calling to "get her to be quiet." His reaction only inflamed the situation.

Kristian decided to role-play trying to use the steps of the STOP method as a friend, playing his wife, barbed Kristian repeatedly by yelling and interrupting. Practicing this scene numerous times, he began to tune out the loudness. He practiced using the broken record to repeatedly and calmly ask his wife to join him as he sat down while signal breathing: "I want to listen. Please sit with me and calmly tell me how you feel." He also practiced taking a time-out to calm down when his "wife" ignored his request: "This feels too intense. We need to stop and take this up later." Kristian practiced walking away as his "wife" followed him. He did not react once he had used his "stop" phrase and went to a neutral part of the house to dampen his anger and problem-solve how to best approach her next time.

Recently, Jennifer couldn't remember how to use an "I" message when her husband, Miguel, got sarcastic and started "peppering" her with repeated questions. It made her feel so off balance that she gave in to what he wanted and retreated into cold anger the rest of the evening. As usual, she was angry with herself afterward for "wimping out."

Jennifer asked a best friend to practice with her, barbing her repeatedly with questions and comments as Miguel did while she tried to stay the course in asserting herself. She practiced using the "broken record" and setting ground rules with "Miguel"—only one person would talk at a time while both were seated, neither would put down the other, and they would focus exclusively on behaviors, with constructive feedback. She practiced how she would react if "Miguel" belittled her attempts at setting ground rules and taking a time-out to emphasize how important this was to her. After multiple practice scenes, she found the confidence to set boundaries for her "husband" (e.g., she refused to continue talking when "Miguel" repeatedly interrupted with questions). She felt much more in control as she approached Miguel that evening with a newfound strength to assert herself without losing it or giving up.

If you don't have a partner to practice with or you have a few minutes to spare, practice in your imagination can be accomplished anytime and anywhere that you can close your eyes and vividly rehearse your new anger skills. It all adds up, no matter what form your practice takes.

Regression: Old Habits Die Hard, and Stress Revives Them

If you've ever witnessed an eight-year-old child having a temper tantrum more suited to a toddler, you know what regression looks like. When we're taxed to our limits of resilience, it's not uncommon to retrieve old, well-learned habits. Drivers who scream at "morons" who "can't drive" and spouses who give each other the silent treatment for days remind us of narcissistic children who often cry out, refuse to do what they're told, and even hold their breath to get their parents' attention.

We sometimes engage in versions of these infantile behaviors as adults, regressing to self-talk and behaviors we learned as children, when others could be blamed for what goes wrong. Temper tantrums, petulance, withholding affection, or refusing to do what the object of our anger wants us to do are all examples of regression.

While we know intellectually that these are childlike and ineffective behaviors, we are all susceptible to these reversals at times of high stress, and they can contribute to a setback.

Rick has been burning the midnight oil at work. He's been missing meals and eating more junk food from the vending machines at work. Forced to get up early, he finds himself exhausted, and his wife has accused him of being more irritable and distant from the family. As suggested in Chapter 4, Rick's resilience is compromised as his life stress escalates. When he blows up at the children's "noise" during a sleepover, embarrassing his daughter and causing his wife to reprimand him, he storms out of the house to assuage his anger with more than a few beers at a local tavern.

Rick's behavior is uncharacteristic for him since he began taking anger management to heart some months ago. But this regression is almost predictable given that many of the "Five S's" (from Chapter 4) have been permitted to occur without Rick's awareness. His reversal is a blip on an otherwise positive chart of his progress in anger management. What's important is how Rick readjusts his life to remove those factors that contributed to this regression.

He decides to set a firm time to leave the office, to take at least a half hour for a nutritious lunch, and to get more sleep. He soon finds that his anger is under his control. He's back on track.

Another cause for regression is stress that is recurrent and becomes the norm. If you were coping with a spouse's long-term illness, constant financial stress because you were laid off, or the toll of caring for an elderly parent while trying to do everything else, your risk of a setback would be much greater. For example, you may find yourself feeling angry and then guilty for losing patience with your autistic young son or your spouse who is recovering from a chronic illness. While there is no "good" and compelling reason that you lost your temper (e.g., you can't point to one event that stands out), you may decide that this long-term stress has affected your ability to cope.

In either case, regression is an inevitable event in our lives. We can all relate to times when we said or did something we later regret or even "lost it" under times of stress. I would urge you to review Chapters 4 and 5, which discuss numerous ideas for identifying and managing stress that may be the cause of a regression.

For stress that has become long-term, taking steps to dampen arousal and to get enough rest and proper nutrition becomes even more important but will not resolve the underlying problem. Consider getting some help from knowledgeable friends or professionals to approach your stressful life differently. For example, you might look into getting other family members or community resources to help you care for a sick child or elderly parent. What resources are available in your community that can offer help or support? Sometimes psychologists and other mental health counselors can help you cope with the unyielding stress of being a caretaker or in resolving issues that might arise from a loss (e.g., loss of a job, death of a loved one). The risk of further regressions may be much less when you approach these unfortunate life challenges differently.

Are you depressed? Finally, you should examine your mood. If you haven't been sleeping well for no good reason (e.g., staying up too late, a recent loss), if you feel sad or your mood shifts from highs to lows without warning, if you are not enjoying things you used to like or feel hopeless about the future, these may be symptoms of depression that should be explored with your physician or a mental health professional. Has anyone who knows you well suggested that "you just don't seem like your old self" or that you seem depressed lately? Depressed mood can be a significant factor in a setback because it robs you of your resilience and tends to magnify the impact of problems and conflicts in your life. Explore the Suggested Resources on mood to learn more about how depression may be affecting your life.

Expectations Revisited

Like old habits, old expectations die hard. You may be finding it difficult to let go of expectations that are derived from core beliefs you've held on to for so long that change takes a concerted effort. For example, your beliefs about "proper" parenting, what constitutes "good" manners, or how a spouse "should" express feelings may create continual irritation in important relationships when others fail to conform. The fact is, you don't have to give up on these important standards as a yardstick for your own behavior, but you may wish to examine the expectations they create for others over whom you're powerless. How can you assess whether your expectations are setting the stage for setbacks and should be revised?

Shara is often irritated when her husband, Frank, "spends too much time" with lifelong male friends, whether it be sports outings or wanting to invite them over for dinner. She grew up in a family where her parents were so focused on family that they rarely socialized with others, forming Shara's belief that "family comes first." While she has to admit that Frank is loving and a good father to their children, she continues to expect that weekends will be focused exclusively on the family. She has had numerous arguments and spent hours and days withholding and withdrawing from Frank to punish him for his "selfish" behavior. So far he hasn't been willing to give up this time with his friends, and the problem seems "hopeless" to Shara.

What's wrong with this picture? It appears that Frank's beliefs about the importance of his friends are very different from his wife's. This has become a chronic problem and will likely lead to future setbacks unless resulting expectations are reconsidered. This would be a wonderful time for the couple to use assertive problem solving, each listening to the other's expectations so that a compromise can be worked out.

For example, Shara should perhaps learn to expect that on two weekends each month Frank will be spending an afternoon with his pals and the rest of the time with his family. When expected, these outings are no longer fuel for her anger. Frank agrees to let her know in advance so they can plan for these times—a win–win solution. Of course, there is an infinite number of possible compromises and accommodations that assertive problem solving can unturn. Not all of them will be as simple as this one or as easy to arrive at. For expectations that spring from those deeply held core beliefs that we all have, trial and error may be required. And if you find yourselves at a stalemate, consider enlisting the aid of a counselor or therapist, who may be able to supply the objectivity that will lead to new perspectives and solutions that neither of you have thought of before.

We often cling to our expectations because they're such an important part of the framework by which we define ourselves and make sense of the rest of the world. If I stop expecting my father to take my investment advice, will I have to relinquish my self-image as a competent adult with considerable financial acumen? If you stop expecting your sister to take the initiative in solving family problems, will it mean giving up your vision of family as a stable, cooperative system in which everyone supports one another individually and benefits collectively from family unity? Does sacrificing the expectations that are rarely met mean letting our whole world crumble around us, like a house of cards? No. A chink or two rarely threatens a whole foundation. Replacing parts of a foundation over time, in fact, can strengthen the whole structure.

So, if an issue in an important relationship or recurring situation continues to be a thorn in your side, don't avoid examining your expectations. Have you continued to expect something that rarely or never occurs? A "continuing argument" or ongoing conflict in any relationship is a clear signal that expectations should be assessed. Revisit Chapter 3 for ideas on putting unrealistic expectations to rest, once and for all. If you don't, your anger may simmer below the surface, developing into resentment, a form of anger that lasts well beyond the original triggering situation and often leads to setbacks.

Resentment: The Anger Trigger beneath the Surface

Sometimes we're unable or unwilling to resolve an anger-provoking situation. Each time we reconsider what happened to us or are exposed to the object of this resentment, our anger is retriggered. We experience a setback that may be hard for us and others to understand. Chapter 11 described the ways resentments develop and the real human and even health costs of holding on to them. If you have failed to resolve a resentment within an important relationship—particularly an ongoing one like a relationship with a family member, a close personal friend, or a colleague at work, who is likely to show up tomorrow and the next day—you should recognize that this is fertile ground for a setback. Under the right circumstances, like one or more of the "Five S's" impacting your resilience or a sudden triggering event that immediately reminds you of the unresolved feelings between you, the likelihood of a setback is great and must be addressed. Be sure to read through the many ideas for resolving resentment in Chapter 11 and challenge yourself to forgive this person if you can find it in your heart to do so. The benefits to you are likely to be greater than whatever satisfaction the other receives from your efforts. And the risk of future meltdowns melts away.

Some resentment is deep seated and may be related to past life experiences (e.g., childhood physical or sexual abuse), which can make it hard to resolve on your own. If the ideas in Chapter 11 don't work for you, consider getting professional help to put your old anger to rest.

Warning Signs of a Setback

Resolving the problems that have led to setbacks is one way of staying on course with anger management. Another is to see a setback coming and head it off. How can you be aware enough of your emotions and actions to use your new anger skills to derail a setback that is looming? Pay attention to these signs as an early alert system.

You find yourself *avoiding people or situations* because they seem too overwhelming or stressful. Do any of these examples ring a bell?

> ➤ Have you been calling with regrets at the last minute to get out of family gatherings or begging off when friends invite you to dinner because you just don't feel up to the stress of it? What is the impact on your spouse and children of missing out on these events?

> ➤ Are you making excuses to get out of weekly staff meetings that always seem to make you feel defensive because you're not doing enough?

➤ Have you asked your husband to attend your son's weekly soccer game because you're afraid you will lose it with that other mother who is always finding fault with your son's teammates?

➤ Have you been avoiding driving on the highway or found yourself taking a longer route when traffic is halted, even though it may end up costing you more time? You just can't stand waiting in traffic?

When forced to confront "problems," *you get exasperated quickly.* You find yourself reacting with sighs, rolling of your eyes, interrupting others, and in general showing that you have reached the end of your patience. Your ability to "roll with it" has been greatly compromised, and you end up losing it with others, who seem puzzled by your intensity.

You notice more *physical symptoms of discomfort.* You will recall from Chapter 2 the areas of your body that are affected by fight-or-flight arousal. For each, a variety of physical symptoms are likely to pop up as stress is unresolved. In particular, pay attention to sore muscles, headaches, stomach upset, chest heaviness, or difficulty catching your breath as signs that you are not managing life situations well.

Your *self-talk and/or imagery are becoming more negative.* Recalling the cognitive distortions we discussed in Chapter 6, have you noticed your thinking digressing to more pessimistic or catastrophic levels, like these example thoughts?

➤ You find yourself cursing or muttering about how bad things are, inflaming your anger or making a tough situation seem more upsetting.

➤ You are seeing more of the bleak side of things lately, less hopeful that you can work problems out.

➤ You notice that you often feel put down, personally criticized, or even attacked by others.

➤ You feel more thin-skinned as you easily feel hurt or being taken advantage of.

➤ You find yourself "thresholding," which you will recall involves setting inner limits to what it feels like you can withstand (e.g., "If I have to drive through another traffic jam, I know I'll lose it"; "One more thing goes wrong and I'm giving up on the whole thing!").

It may be hard to recall accurately how you've been thinking over the last few weeks. It may help to ask a trusted other person like a spouse or close friend what he or she has heard you say and how you've been acting. As your thinking regresses to old, irrational habits, an unwanted face of anger will follow close behind. If it appears that your self-talk has been contributing to your irritation, review Chapters 6 and 7 to regain a handle on your thinking.

Your *voice and manner are more intense*. If you've become a good self-observer, you may be aware that you've been interrupting others or acting impatient more frequently. You may find yourself talking louder and gesturing more dramatically or failing to listen to others. Have important others been accusing you of being more "irritable" or "crabby" lately? While you may have initially discounted these remarks, can you honestly look at whether you've been getting more of these comments recently?

If no one has confronted you directly, consider asking others you trust for their observations of how you've been coming across to them. If your communication has deteriorated, a rereading of Chapters 8 and 9 would be useful to refocus your efforts toward assertive problem solving.

Preventing Setbacks: Taking Your Future into Your Hands Right Now

In addition to making changes in your life to address each of the preceding reasons for a setback, it is worth reemphasizing the "Five S's," so often a factor in your progress. Think of how each of these events has affected your life and how you can change.

➤ *How were you sleeping in the days before you lost it?* Have you been up late for any reason or having interrupted or poor sleep? I have been teaching anger management for over 25 years and still find myself losing it at times, usually when I'm exhausted. If you aren't sleeping well or sleeping at least seven hours as an adult, it is unreasonable to assume you will have the resilience to calmly handle provocative and emotionally challenging situations. Implement regular times for going to bed and awakening, making sure your bedroom is free of light, is quiet, and is at a comfortable temperature. Check out the materials on sleep in the Resources section at the end of this book and apply some of the ideas offered. If this doesn't work in four to six weeks, consider a medical evaluation to determine the cause of your sleep disturbance.

➤ *How many changes and adaptations have been occurring in your life in the last few weeks?* Is it hard to keep up with your workload? Do you find yourself dreading having to do "one more thing"? Is the noise level of your life getting to you? Have you been experiencing one or more of the physical symptoms that indicate a high level of fight-or-flight arousal? If one or more of these questions is answered affirmatively, how are you taking steps to manage your stress? Consider changing the amount of work, the time you spend, and the number of different things (changes/adaptation) you encounter each day as a place to start. You will not be able to consistently use anger management if stress is robbing you of the energy and resilience you need to think straight and recall the new things you've learned.

➤ *When your face of anger got the best of you, had you been drinking?* Alcohol is probably the most frequent reason for "backsliding." I often hear, "But Dr. Nay, clearly I'm not an alcoholic—so why is alcohol responsible for my losing it?" I believe that alcohol's impact on resilience is huge. As you drink socially, you become more disinhibited in good and bad ways. On the plus side, you may feel more relaxed, better able to converse fluidly with others and less inhibited. On the negative side, if you do become irritated with someone, the same disinhibition will likely make your reaction more impulsive and less thoughtful. Ask yourself how often alcohol has been present when you lost control of your anger. If alcohol is part of the problem, then you have an alcohol problem even if you're not alcoholic. You should consider curtailing your drinking by establishing strict self-imposed rules (e.g., never more than two glasses of wine, no provocative topics or discussions when drinking, no drinking when you are upset). If alcohol continues to be a problem, consider abstaining completely and finding a professional to evaluate your drinking.

➤ *Had you eaten breakfast or lunch?* Were you wolfing down your food or eating junk food prior to your anger incident? Without proper nutrition, you're likely to be irritable and less resilient. You must maintain proper blood sugar level to function at optimum performance.

Now is the time to recommit yourself to eating breakfast every day and taking at least 30 minutes for a nutritious lunch break that is free of work.

➤ *Were you ill or experiencing discomfort prior to the anger incident?* Even a headache or stomach acid can increase irritability and reduce your resilience when the next trigger arises. When you're ill or in pain, consider reducing your schedule or taking time off to recover. Placing yourself in stressful situations when you don't feel good sets you up for anger loss. Take appropriate medication and reconsider the demands you are placing on yourself.

Managing Your Anger Is a Journey

Learning to express this most human emotion of anger is indeed a long-term journey that is likely to have its ups and downs. Because anger is associated with survival as your fight-or-flight nervous system is aroused, whether for rational reasons or not, it seems to take precedence over other emotions as you quickly find yourself mobilized in a defensive or aggressive posture. It is a fact of life we all have to contend with as others and situations rarely meet our expectations for long.

I have offered numerous ideas in the steps of anger management to help you better attend to this powerful emotion so you can control it and steer its expression. By now you should be aware of your particular faces of anger and also more aware of anger developing in others. This awareness, as well as the tools for dampening your anger arousal and challenging the thinking that evokes and directs your face of anger, should serve you well as you move through a day of unpredictable happenings. When necessary, you now have communication strategies to quickly defuse another's anger as well as your own and to move the discussion to resolution.

A few final words of caution and advice: Keep in mind that we are all creatures of habit. Think of the desirable as well as the undesirable habitual behaviors you engage in automatically in your life. To create lasting change, consider that your new anger responses are in their infancy while your old faces of anger are fully mature "adults." You must actively work at practicing your new anger skills or they will disappear quickly ... and guess what behaviors will remain? Your greatest nemesis is finding yourself too busy or preoccupied to take the time to practice when you don't have to. Getting motivated to recall and use anger management only when faced with conflict or discomfort will surely lead to a less than stellar effort.

Another roadblock to lasting change is concluding after a setback a version of "This stuff is not working. My anger is part of my personality. I guess I just can't change it." This is a copout. Instead, give yourself permission to be human and make some mistakes. It is not always easy to stay the course, but consider the alternative. Do you really want your anger to continue to rule you, or do you want control over it? You wouldn't have read this book if your current expression of anger was a "walk in the park." It has created some form of pain for you or others who you care about.

So take a deep signal breath and consider how to use a setback constructively. Confront rationalizations in your self-talk that blame your setbacks on others or tell you you're not capable of changing. It won't always be easy, but continuing in your old ways isn't easy either and can cost you in human terms more than you're willing to pay.

I wish you great success and useful setbacks on this journey. Visit my website at *www.wrobertnay.com* for support along the way. Hope to hear from you.

APPENDIX 1

Self-Assessment of Anger Questionnaire (SAQ)

First, check the box in front of any of the following descriptions that apply to you (or the person you are completing this for).

How Big a Part Does Anger Play in Your Life?

Reflect on the past six months: what you recall about your own experiences and what others have said to you about your anger. Add up the scores for the items you checked off. [Note: If you are completing the SAQ to describe the likely anger responses of another person who has asked you to fill it out, follow these directions: Based on your experience with this person over the past six months, check the box that describes how he/she would likely answer, given factual events you've observed or learned about this person.]

- ❏ You handled an aggravating situation poorly. (score 1)

- ❏ You feel/felt embarrassed or guilty about the way you handled your anger. (score 2)

- ❏ Another person has told you that your way of expressing anger was a problem. (score 2)

- ❏ An important relationship at home, at work, or among friends or family has been strained by your expression of anger. (score 3)

- ❏ Someone you care about has urged you to get help for managing your anger. (score 3)

- ❏ You have gotten into serious trouble because of the way you

From *Taking Charge of Anger, Second Edition.* Copyright 2012 by The Guilford Press.

expressed your anger. Examples might include a reprimand at work, a legal problem or arrest for "road rage" or assault, being hurt or hurting another, a separation or divorce. (score 4)

Scoring. Add up your total score. If you scored 3 *or more,* you likely have a problem with anger that should be addressed. A score of 6 *or more* indicates you may have a serious problem with the way you express your anger. If you checked off the last item, you should consider seeking the help of a mental health professional who specializes in treating anger issues.

How Do You Express Your Anger?

Next, consider the following ten challenging situations. As you read each of them, think how you might react if this or a similar situation occurred in your own life now or in the recent past (within the last 30 days). Because you may express your anger in various ways, perhaps depending on how you felt at a given time, be sure to circle as many of the possible reactions as apply to you for each item. *For each situation described, circle one or more of the reactions you could see yourself having to this or a similar situation. If none of the specific descriptions applies, circle "Other."* [Note: Again, if you are filling this out for another person, answer as you think this person would respond, based on your experience with him/her, to each of the hypothetical situations].

1. Your partner does something you've repeatedly said you dislike. Your reactions might include:

   ➤ Withdrawing from your partner, just wanting to be alone and not to discuss it. [C]

   ➤ Thinking of something to say that will make your partner squirm or feel uncomfortable. [B]

   ➤ Acting very forceful in getting your point across. It's important that your partner hear how upset you are whether he/she wants to hear it or not. [E]

   ➤ Feeling very intense and irritable, which could lead you to do things like talk louder, slam a door, or drive faster. [D]

> Thinking to yourself, "Just wait until he/she wants something from me." [A]
> Other. It's unlikely I would react in any of these ways.

2. On your way to work in the morning with some friends, another driver suddenly pulls in front of you, forcing you to slam on your brakes. The reactions you might have include:

   > Feeling so intense and angry it's hard to shake it off as you begin your day at work. [D]
   > Trying to pull next to the other driver to tell him/her off or make a rude gesture. [E]
   > Trying to pull ahead of the other driver, then slowing down, holding him/her up as a payback. [A]
   > Trying to think of put-downs or cutting remarks that describe his/her lousy driving skills. [B]
   > Getting so upset you stop talking with others in the car with you, holding your anger in. [C]
   > Other. It's unlikely I would react in any of these ways.

3. A close friend keeps you waiting at a restaurant for 30 minutes. When he/she arrives unapologetic, acting as if nothing happened, your reactions might include:

   > Immediately accusing him/her of acting inconsiderately, raising your voice to let him/her know just how irritated you are with this rude behavior. [E]
   > Feeling so upset that you eat fast, get impatient with the waiter, and in general feel tense and grumpy during the entire meal. Hard to shake it off. [D]
   > Minimally responding to his/her comments. Making him/her do most of the talking because you just can't act like everything is fine—it isn't. [A]
   > Telling the other person you cannot remain any longer and leave him/her sitting there. Now maybe the other person will realize just how rude he/she was. [C]
   > Making a biting remark like "I'm really glad you value our friendship so much that it's at the top of your priorities." [B]
   > Other. It's unlikely I would react in any of these ways.

4. You are waiting in a long line in a convenience store. The check-out clerk is "gabbing" with a coworker and not paying attention to her job. Your reactions might include:

   ➤ Muttering under your breath and to other customers something like "This person is clearly incompetent" and/or "The store should never have hired him/her." [D]

   ➤ Getting so upset you end up leaving your items in the store and walking out and/or deciding never to do business there again. [C]

   ➤ When you finally get to the counter, acting like you are praising the clerk with a remark like "Keep up the good work. You have a real future here." [B]

   ➤ Deciding to tell the clerk just how angry you are and how incompetent and inconsiderate the store is for hiring him/her with a remark like "If you can't do this job properly, you should care enough about the customers to quit." [E]

   ➤ Slowly placing your items on the counter with the computer codes turned away so the clerk has to work harder to scan them. [A]

   ➤ Other. It's unlikely I would react in any of these ways.

5. You are furious with your spouse/partner for making plans for you both to go out with friends without asking you. As he/she is telling a story to these friends at the restaurant, you might react by:

   ➤ Walking away on some pretext (e.g., going to the rest room) as soon as he/she begins telling the story. You are not going to sit there and be an audience. [C]

   ➤ Making a wry remark to your friends that kind of puts down his/her story with humor, like "What an interesting story. Are you plumbing the depths of *Reader's Digest* again, dear?" [B]

   ➤ Avoiding eye contact with your spouse/partner, not reacting in any way to his/her story and quickly changing the topic. [A]

   ➤ Putting down what he/she says by forcefully questioning his/her facts or criticizing. You are angry and he/she needs to know it. [E]

   ➤ Feeling impatient for him/her to finish the story. After a brief time interrupting him/her to ask someone else a question. [D]

   ➤ Other. It's unlikely I would react in any of these ways.

6. You feel hurt and angry because your partner seems to be neglecting you/is not affectionate enough and won't talk about it. You might react by:

> ➤ Deciding that the next time he/she wants something from you, "Forget it." You will show him/her how it feels. [A]
> ➤ Giving the other a dose of his/her own medicine by withdrawing from conversation and going to bed early. [C]
> ➤ Making a remark with an edge, like "It's really great that you're so loving—I can always count on you to be there for me." [B]
> ➤ Letting your anger out by forcefully telling the other that he/she is cold and acting like a [fill in an uncomplimentary name]. You are not standing for this. [E]
> ➤ Feeling so upset and tense about his/her letting you down, you find yourself irritated with others (e.g., your children, a friend, your fellow drivers). [D]
> ➤ Other. It's unlikely I would react in any of these ways.

7. You have just been told that your supervisor is giving another employee a perk or position you think you should have been given and never even discussed it with you. Ways you might handle this include:

> ➤ Going to your supervisor and letting him/her have it. You are not going to take this unfair mistreatment, and he/she is going to know it. [E]
> ➤ Running thoughts through your mind about just quitting and getting out of there. If they don't appreciate you, why stick around? [C]
> ➤ Deciding you will be too busy to help your supervisor out by staying late or taking on additional work. [A]
> ➤ The next time you see your supervisor, making a remark like "I really appreciate the fair way you treat your employees. It's great working for you." [B]
> ➤ Noticing more muscle tension and inner tightness and more impatience with others and things (e.g., slow elevators, busy signals). [D]
> ➤ Other. It's unlikely I would react in any of these ways.

8. You are ready to leave for an important occasion, and your partner is already 20 minutes late after you have specifically told him/her how important this is to you. Your reactions might include:

   ➤ Finding yourself increasingly tense, pacing and/or muttering under your breath, "I can't believe how long this is taking." It is hard to relax and accept this lateness. [D]

   ➤ When he/she is finally ready to leave, telling him/her off by saying something like "I can't believe anyone could be so rude [*or* hopeless *or* just plain irresponsible]." [E]

   ➤ Making a remark like "I can see you really listened to my feelings about getting there on time. You are a wizard of efficiency and organization." [B]

   ➤ Not speaking as you usher him/her to the car. You avoid him/her for the rest of the day. [C]

   ➤ Even though the other did something special or well, refusing to compliment him/her for the rest of the day. Why should you? [A]

   ➤ Other. It's unlikely I would react in any of these ways.

9. After putting in a lot of effort on a community project, the committee chairperson acknowledges everyone else but you at an awards banquet. You feel angry at the slight, and your reactions might include:

   ➤ Refusing to speak or responding minimally to the chairperson later in the evening when he/she tries to talk with you. [C]

   ➤ When the chairperson acknowledges the omission, not acknowledging his/her statement and changing the topic. You will not let him/her off the hook that easily. [A]

   ➤ Finding yourself telling an embarrassing story about the chairperson to other committee members and kind of enjoying seeing his/her discomfort when others laugh. [B]

   ➤ Telling him/her off for being so inconsiderate of your feelings and noticing that he/she is kind of intimidated by your intense voice. This feels good given what he/she put you through. [E]

   ➤ Being so upset that on your way home you find yourself driving faster and being more likely to yell at other drivers' behavior. Feeling tense and noticing that you are easily irritated for the rest of the evening. [D]

> Other. It's unlikely I would react in any of these ways.

10. Your neighbor fails to return something he/she borrowed from you even though you've mentioned it numerous times. You see this neighbor using your item in the yard and might handle your irritation by:

> Ignoring the person when he/she tries to start up a friendly conversation. How can you talk to so inconsiderate a person? [C]
> Deciding to park your minivan in front of the neighbor's house when you know it infuriates him/her. [A]
> Telling your neighbor you really appreciate living next door to someone who is so considerate. [B]
> Deciding to do yard work later and going inside because just looking at your neighbor causes you stress. You find it difficult to quickly "let go" of your tension. [D]
> Forcefully demanding your item back, telling him/her to forget borrowing in the future and to stay away from you. Why be around someone with no morals? [E]
> Other. It's unlikely I would react in any of these ways.

Scoring the SAQ

How you express your anger is indicated by your score on each of five scales. Each scale represents a mode of expression, a "face" of anger that is unhelpful and likely to lead to further problems for you or others who interact with you.

To obtain your scores, add up how many "A," "B," "C," "D," and "E" items you circled. Now fill in your totals on the corresponding scales below.

SCALE A: PASSIVE-AGGRESSION _____. You tend to withhold from others when you are angry by failing to do what they want, being late, or otherwise holding back. You minimize or deny that you are angry when others express frustration or question your actions.

SCALE B: SARCASM _____. You use sarcasm, biting wit, or "humorous" put-downs as a way of expressing your anger indirectly. Your facial expression/tone of voice may convey disgust or criticism, which you deny. When others find your comments or actions hurtful or complain, you may accuse them of being too sensitive or minimize their feedback.

SCALE C: COLD ANGER _____. When angry you refuse to talk things out and may withdraw from others, with minimal or no contact for hours or days at a time. You may secretly enjoy punishing others by making them work hard to get you to respond, but would not admit it.

SCALE D: HOSTILITY _____. You handle stress poorly, often feeling very intense and acting it out with a loud, forceful voice and disgust and disapproval when others or situations do not meet your expectations. You may sigh, roll your eyes, and in general make nasty comments that others often find stressful and intrusive. You hate to wait and suffer "fools" poorly.

SCALE E: AGGRESSION _____. You act in a manner that may intimidate or harm another person, either emotionally or physically, whether you intend to or not. Yelling, name calling, and put-downs may threaten or intimidate your spouse, friend, or coworker. While not directly assessed by the SAQ, physical aggression includes physically blocking, holding, pushing, hitting, or restraining another person without express permission to touch. This face of anger is the most serious and often requires professional help, especially when levels of verbal and/or physical abuse are harming others.

Did you score highest on one particular scale? This mode of anger expression should be a focus for your efforts at making changes as you apply what you learn about anger management. Are you surprised at scoring highest on this scale?

Did you score on multiple scales? If so, you need to reflect on the "mix" of behaviors you reveal to others and decide which to target for change first as you set priorities.

How do your scores compare with how others have completed the SAQ? Remember that you asked someone who knows you well to fill out the SAQ as he/she thinks you would have completed it, based on what he/she knows about you and how anger affects your life. In what ways do your responses vary from this person's? Reflect on why the other person may have responded this way. Perhaps you could discuss this with that person in a nondefensive way to learn what actions on your part led to his/her responses on the SAQ.

Based on the above, do you believe that your expression of anger should be explored further? If so, Chapters 2–11 will help you diagnose your anger in more depth, offering six steps of anger management to help you make those changes that seem in order.

APPENDIX 2
Daily Anger Log

TRIGGER/SITUATION (Where were you and what did others say or do?):

THOUGHTS (self-talk about your other, yourself, and why this happened):

FEELINGS (Are you anxious, guilty, angry, fearful? Be sure to record your physical sensations as well—e.g., stomach tight, face hot, shoulders tense—and place a number [1–100] on the intensity of your feelings):

ACTIONS (what you did or said in response):

OUTCOME (What personal or external outcomes occurred? How do you now feel about these outcomes?):

YOUR PLAN IF THIS HAPPENS AGAIN?

Adapted with permission from *Overcoming Anger in Your Relationship* by W. Robert Nay. Copyright 2010 by The Guilford Press.

APPENDIX 3

Personal Anger Scale

Ratings	Physical sensations	Desired behaviors
0–20		Awareness of self
21–40		Be aware of body—"signal breathing" as needed—use a self-instructional phrase to stay focused, like:
41–60		Begin "STOP" method: STOP (sit, signal breath, count down anger), THINK, OBJECTIFY, PLAN. Take time out if cannot reduce tension below "60."
61–80		Should be gone before you reach this level. If not, leave immediately. Continue STOP sequence.
81–100		Should be gone well before this. If not, use a STOP phrase and leave situation immediately—continue to signal breath and STOP method until ready to return to the triggering situation.

From *Taking Charge of Anger, Second Edition*. Copyright 2012 by The Guilford Press.

APPENDIX 4

Anger Analysis

What happened	What you would like
Situation (who, where, what happened):	Camera check:
Implicit expectation:	Realistic expectation:

From *Taking Charge of Anger, Second Edition*. Copyright 2012 by The Guilford Press.

Thoughts/self-talk:	Rational self-talk (think, objectify, plan):
1.	1.
2.	2.
3.	3.
4.	4.

Angry feelings/body sensations:	How I would like to feel:
Rate feelings (0–100): _____	
Behavior/face of anger:	Desired behavior/face:
Outcome:	Desired outcome:

APPENDIX 5

The Relationship Anger Profile (RAP)

Write in the name of the angry person for whom you are describing your feelings and actions: _____. Think about the last few times this person got angry and how you felt in response.

Which of the four core feelings do you experience when this person acts in an angry way toward you, whether he/she withholds what you want or withdraws in cold anger or acts sarcastic, intense, hostile, or loud/aggressive? Once you've circled Y (yes) for **one or more** emotions—anxious/tense, irritated/angry, responsible/guilty, or afraid/fearful—answer the questions that follow the ones for which you circled Y.

I feel ANXIOUS (e.g., apprehensive, worried) when this person gets mad:
Y   N.   If YES, then carefully consider and answer yes or no (circle Y or N) to the following questions:

1. When I think this person might get angry, I carefully   Y   N   [a]
   consider exactly what I am about to say before
   expressing it.

2. I often find myself avoiding saying how I really feel so   Y   N   [a]
   the other person won't get mad at me.

3. There are certain topics I avoid if this person seems   Y   N   [a]
   upset.

4. Sometimes I try to change the topic or keep things from   Y   N   [b]
   upsetting this individual (e.g., keep our children away,
   reduce noise, make sure everything is perfect) to avoid
   this person's anger.

5. I have given in and changed my own plans or avoided   Y   N   [b]
   going places with this person when I was concerned
   about an escalation of anger.

6. I find I will avoid certain people or couples this person   Y   N   [b]
   dislikes to avoid any possibility of anger becoming an
   issue.

Reprinted with permission from *Overcoming Anger in Your Relationship* by W. Robert Nay. Copyright 2010 by The Guilford Press.

I feel GUILTY (e.g., responsible, sorry, apologetic) when this person gets mad:
Y   N.   If YES, then carefully consider and answer yes or no (circle Y or N) to
the following questions:

1. At times I find myself trying to make excuses for this   **Y**   **N**   **[g]**
    person's anger—to somehow justify it to myself or
    others.

2. This person can't help how angry he/she gets—it's just   **Y**   **N**   **[g]**
    a personality trait that can't be changed, so I must live
    with it and adjust to it.

3. When this person gets mad, it must be my fault also. It   **Y**   **N**   **[g]**
    takes two to start any argument or conflict.

4. Giving in to this person is the easiest way to get the   **Y**   **N**   **[h]**
    anger to stop or avoid it in the first place. Life is too
    short to make a big deal out of things, so I just do it his/
    her way to avoid the hassle of it all.

5. I try to make up for conflicts with this person by doing   **Y**   **N**   **[h]**
    something nice to make him/her forget about it.

6. I know this person will get his/her way eventually, so I   **Y**   **N**   **[h]**
    just don't fight it anymore. It's easier just to give in and
    get over my feelings.

I feel ANGRY (e.g., irritated, annoyed, enraged) when this person gets mad:
Y   N.   If YES, then carefully consider and answer yes or no (circle Y or N) to
the following questions:

1. I spend a lot of time defending myself around this   **Y**   **N**   **[c]**
    person.

2. I cannot let something this person says go if it's wrong   **Y**   **N**   **[c]**
    or unfair—I feel I have to defend or justify my position.

3. I find that I am very alert to this person's negative   **Y**   **N**   **[c]**
    comments about me and react to them immediately.

4. When I get mad, I sometimes do just the opposite of   **Y**   **N**   **[d]**
    what this person wants, just to let him/her know that I
    matter too.

5. I find myself withholding what he/she wants as a kind of payback.   Y   N   [d]

6. I get so mad that I sometimes stop talking or withdraw physically (e.g., leave the house, go to another room) and refuse to have anything to do with this person for hours or even days at a time.   Y   N   [d]

7. When this person criticizes me, I get so annoyed I often criticize something he/she said or did in return.   Y   N   [e]

8. I get very impatient and act angry myself when I am treated unfairly by this person.   Y   N   [e]

9. Sometimes I raise my voice in response to what this person says.   Y   N   [e]

10. At times I have been known to yell back at this person.   Y   N   [f]

11. When pushed to the wall, I have gotten physical with this person by (one or more) blocking, pushing, holding, using my hands in anger, or throwing.   Y   N   [f]

12. Sometimes I have said things to this person when I'm angry that I would never want repeated to others I care about—it would embarrass me.   Y   N   [f]

I feel AFRAID (e.g., fearful, terrorized) when this person gets mad: Y   N.   If YES, then carefully consider and answer yes or no (circle Y or N) to the following questions:

1. When this person gets angry, I sometimes feel so fearful that I am kind of paralyzed and just go along with it so it will stop.   Y   N   [i]

2. I imagine this person will do something, whether intentional or not, that results in me or someone I love (e.g., a child, other family member) getting hurt emotionally or physically. This causes me to give in.   Y   N   [i]

3. I sometimes feel I cannot act or speak out for fear that the situation will just get worse.   Y   N   [i]

4. Sometimes I just don't know where to turn to cope with this person's anger—it is so overwhelming.   Y   N   [j]

5. I have thought of ending this relationship because of   Y   N   [j]
   the anger, but still care and want it to work. I feel stuck
   between the two.

6. I feel so powerless and overwhelmed at times I just shut   Y   N   [j]
   down.

Now look over your answers: Which of the core emotions did you report having? Being able to identify this emotional reaction gives you a chance to
react differently, instead of immediately responding with one or more of the
feelings, thoughts, or actions described below each core emotion. Look at the
letter in brackets after each feeling, thought, or action for which you circled
Y. Each represents an unhelpful response to the other person's anger. Write
in the number of "yes" answers for each letter.

a—EDITING: _____

b—REDIRECTING/RESCHEDULING: _____

c—JUSTIFYING: _____

d—PASSIVE–AGGRESSION/WITHDRAWAL: _____

e—HOSTILITY/CRITICISM: _____

f—AGGRESSING: _____

g—RATIONALIZING: _____

h—APOLOGIZING/ATONING: _____

i—SUBJUGATING/SURRENDERING: _____

j—SHUTTING DOWN: _____

Looking at your responses, for which actions did you score at least a 1? Even
a score of 1 is important as it represents an action on your part that may
significantly affect how you continue to feel. To help you understand the
meaning of your score on the RAP, first look at the table below, which shows
unhelpful reactions you just identified from the RAP to each of the core emotions when another is acting angry.

Core Emotions, Goals, and Unhelpful Reactions in Response to Your Partner's Anger

Core Emotion	Goal	Unhelpful Reactions
Anxiety	Avoiding	Editing
		Redirecting
		Rescheduling
Guilt	Atoning	Rationalizing
		Apologizing/Atoning
Anger	Defending	Justifying
	Punishing	Passive–Aggression
		Withdrawal
		Hostility/Criticism
		Aggressing
Fear	Staying Safe	Subjugating/Surrendering
		Shutting Down

Suggested Resources

Managing Anger in Your Life and Relationships

Books

Nay, W. R. (2010). *Overcoming anger in your relationship: How to break the cycle of arguments, put-downs, and stony silences.* New York: Guilford Press.

  This book is for readers who are in a relationship with an angry partner and want to know how to set boundaries and defuse anger before it has a chance to ignite.

Nay, W. R. (2009). *Managing anger and aggression: A compendium of resources, handouts and forms.* McLean, VA: Author. Available at *www.wrobertnay. com.*

  Contains numerous handouts, logs, sidebars, and learning materials to help you implement the ideas in this book.

Blog

Nay, W. R. *Overcoming anger.*

  The author's regular blog on anger in relationships for *Psychology Today.* Go to *www.psychologytoday.com/blog/overcoming-anger.*

Website

For more information on managing anger in your life or to order the author's newsletter, books, and other materials, go to *www.wrobertnay.com.*

Communicating Your Anger More Effectively

Books

Gottman, J. M., & DeClaire, J. (2007). *Ten lessons to transform your marriage: America's love lab experts share their strategies to transform your marriage.* New York: Three Rivers Press–Random House.

    Based on John Gottman's years of studying what makes relationships succeed or fail.

Patterson, R. (2000). *The assertiveness workbook: How to express your ideas and stand up for yourself at work and in relationships.* Oakland, CA: New Harbinger.

    Practical strategies for becoming more assertive and effective in communicating your ideas and needs.

Stone, D., Patton, B., Heen, S., & Fisher, R. (2010). *Difficult conversations: How to discuss what matters most.* New York: Penguin Books.

    Based on the Harvard Negotiation Project, the authors help you prepare yourself for communicating with difficult people on difficult subjects, while defusing conflict and achieving resolution.

Tannen, D. (2001). *You just don't understand: Women and men in conversation.* New York: Quill.

    A noted linguist reviews research on how men and women communicate very differently and how to improve effective communication with your partner.

Websites

Couple Communication Program
www.couplecommunication.com
    Since 1972 Dr. Sherrod Miller and colleagues have offered a wonderful program, first developed at the University of Minnesota, to reduce conflict and improve communication in relationships.

Anger and Health

Books

Burns, D. (1999). *Feeling good: The new mood therapy.* New York: Avon Books.

    Many who have problems with anger also experience a mood disorder, which sometimes must be addressed with medication and/or treatment. This comprehensive book helps you assess whether you have a problem with depression and how to use cognitive-behavioral therapy to manage your mood. It also reviews the most common antidepressant medications.

Gilbert, P. (2008). *Overcoming depression: A self-help guide using cognitive-behavioral techniques.* New York: Basic Books.

How to use CBT, the most researched and effective depression management strategy.

Nezu, A., Nezu, C., & Jain, D. (2005). *The emotional wellness way to cardiac health.* Oakland, CA: New Harbinger.

Wehrenberg, M. (2011). *The ten best-ever depression management techniques: Understanding how your brain makes you depressed and what you can do to change it.* New York: Norton.

Excellent review of effective techniques to manage your mood by an outstanding teacher.

Williams, R., & Williams, V. (1998). *Anger kills: Seventeen strategies for controlling the hostility that can harm your health.* New York: Harper.

An excellent review of how anger impacts your health by a leading researcher. Includes strategies for controlling hostility.

Website

For information on the role of anger in health or any other question related to mental health, go to:

Psych Central
www.psychcentral.com

Managing the "Five S's"

Sleep

If you are finding it difficult to get required amounts of sleep, these books may help you assess whether you have a sleep problem that can be helped by medical treatment. Regardless, numerous well-researched ideas for changing your sleep schedule are offered.

Books

Cohen, G. J. (Ed.). (2002). *American Academy of Pediatrics guide to your child's sleep.* New York: Villard Books.

If your child's sleep problems are affecting your own night's sleep, this book offers the latest ideas from pediatricians for getting your child to settle down and sleep.

Dement, W. C. (2000). *The promise of sleep: A pioneer in sleep medicine explores the vital connection between health, happiness and a good night's sleep.* New York: Dell Books.

A well-regarded sleep researcher describes sleep problems you may be experiencing, teaches you to assess your own sleep habits, and then offers a "sleep-smart" lifestyle and tips for getting a good night's sleep.

Edlund, M. (2011). *The power of rest: Why sleep alone is not enough: A 30-day plan to reset your body*. New York: Harper One.

Epstein, L., & Marder, S. (2006). *The Harvard Medical School guide to a good night's sleep*. New York: McGraw-Hill.

Jacobs, G. D. (2009). *Say goodnight to insomnia*. New York: Holt Books.

Based on the insomnia treatment program developed at Harvard Medical School, a six-week program found to dramatically reduce insomnia.

Websites

Both of these websites provide an extraordinary amount of information about fostering good sleep and assessing and treating sleep disorders.

Sleepnet
www.sleepnet.com

American Academy of Sleep Medicine
2510 North Frontage Road
Darien, IL 60561
(630) 737-9700
www.aasmnet.org
Offers sleep information for both professional and public consumers.

Stress

It is imperative to manage daily anxiety and stress that lowers your resilience, making you vulnerable when the next trigger comes along. These resources can help you set some new goals for how you manage your day.

Books

Bourne, E. (2011). *The anxiety and phobia workbook*. Oakland, CA: New Harbinger.

An outstanding treatment manual offering numerous ideas for managing all forms of anxiety—all of which can make you more susceptible to an anger episode.

Davis, M., Eschelman, E., McKay, M., & Fanning, P. (2008). *The relaxation and stress reduction workbook*. Oakland, CA: New Harbinger.

An award-winning presentation of effective techniques to promote relaxation and stress management. Written in clear language and easy to read. Highly recommended.

Luskin, F., & Pelletier, K. R. (2005). *Stress free for good*. New York: HarperOne.

Website

American Institute of Stress
124 Park Avenue
Yonkers, NY 10703
(914) 963-1200
www.stress.org

This nonprofit provides comprehensive information and resources on identifying and managing stress at home and at work.

Substances

Overuse or addiction to alcohol or substances greatly increases the likelihood of losing control of your anger. Each of these references may be helpful in assessing and altering your own use of substances or give you ideas to encourage someone you care about to seek help.

Books

Anderson, K. A., Marlatt, G. A., & Denning, P. (2010). *How to change your drinking: A harm reduction guide to alcohol* (2nd ed.). Seattle, WA: Create Space Books.

Fletcher, A. (2002). *Sober for good: New solutions for drinking problems–advice from those who have succeeded*. New York: Houghton Mifflin.

Ketcham, K., & Asbury, W. F., with Schulstad, M., & Ciaramicoli, A. (2000). *Beyond the influence: Understanding and defeating alcoholism*. New York: Bantam Doubleday.

Updating the seminal book *Under the Influence*, chapters review the impact of alcohol use on health, stages of an alcohol problem, and ideas for sustaining abstinence. A good book to read if you wonder if you have a problem.

Prentiss, C. (2007). *The alcoholism and addiction cure*. New York: Power Press.

Websites

Join Together
www.jointogether.org

A thorough listing of alcohol and substance abuse information.

SAMHSA's National Clearinghouse for Alcohol and Drug Information
ncadi.samhsa.gov
    A wealth of fact sheets, the latest in research, and many online resources are
provided, along with a great search engine to satisfy your specific questions.

Sustenance

Books

Balch, P. A. (2006). *Prescription for nutritional healing* (4th ed.). New York:
    Avery.
        An excellent and comprehensive review of foods, vitamins, and miner-
    als necessary for optimum health and emotional management. Written
    by a nutritionist, each medical or emotional condition is listed separately
    with specific nutritional recommendations.
Nurtman, J. (1999). *Managing mind and mood through food.* New York: Harper-
    Collins.
        An MIT research scientist reviews how what you eat affects how you
    feel and cope with life stressors and makes recommendations for the
    basis of a new nutritional plan.
Rosenthal, J. (2007). *Integrative nutrition.* New York: Integrative Nutrition Pub-
    lishers.

Sickness

Caudill, M. A. (2009). *Managing pain before it manages you* (3rd ed.). New York:
    Guilford Press.
        Chronic headache, musculoskeletal disorders, and other chronic pain
    conditions can greatly increase irritability and make it harder to cope
    with triggering events. Pain management solutions are offered that you
    can begin to use immediately.
Schneider, J. (2004). *Living with chronic pain: The complete health guide to the
    causes and cures for chronic pain.* New York: Healthy Living Books.

Website

National Library of Medicine
8600 Rockville Pike
Bethesda, MD 20894
(888) 346-3656
www.nlm.nih.gov
    A wonderful resource for information on any illness that might be affect-

ing mood or anger. A search engine "Health Information" asks you to list the topic of interest.

Resolving Resentment

Books

Enright, R. D. (2001). *Forgiveness is a choice: A step-by-step process for resolving anger and restoring hope*. Washington, DC: American Psychological Association.

    An excellent stepwise approach to identifying resentments and strategies for resolution. Based on the author's research.

Luskin, F. (2001). *Forgive for good: A proven prescription for health and happiness*. San Francisco: Harper.

    How a grievance is created, the health value of forgiveness, and four stages of "Becoming a Forgiving Person."

Luskin, F. (2007). *Forgive for love: The missing ingredient for a healthy and lasting relationship*. New York: Harper-Collins.

Websites

Stanford Forgiveness Project—Dr. Fred Luskin
www.learningtoforgive.com

Serious Problems of Aggression in Relationships

Immediate Crisis

Phone the National Domestic Violence Hotline: 800-799-7233

Websites

While this may not apply to most readers, sometimes anger in a relationship has reached the boiling point and someone may be hurt. These websites alert you to help you can find locally and what to do.

Futures without Violence
www.futureswithoutviolence.org

The National Coalition Against Domestic Violence
www.ncadv.org

Associations and Organizations You Might Find Useful

There are no well-respected associations or organizations specific to anger, but in addition to the organizations and websites already mentioned, each of these provide useful information, readings, treatment recommendations, and other valuable data. Each has a search engine for locating specific topics (e.g., anger management, stress disorders). Websites to get you quickly to the public information they offer are listed for each.

American Association for Marriage and Family Therapy
112 South Alfred Street
Alexandria, VA 22314-3061
(703) 838-9805
www.aamft.org/index_nm.asp

American Psychiatric Association
1000 Wilson Boulevard, Suite 1825
Arlington, VA 22209-3901
(888) 35-PSYCH
www.psych.org

American Psychological Association
750 First Street, NE
Washington, DC 20002-4242
(800) 374-2721
www.apa.org

Mental Health America (*formerly* National Mental Health Association)
2000 N. Beauregard Street, 6th floor
Alexandria, VA 22311
(703) 684-7722
Toll-free: (800) 969-6642
www.nmha.org

National Alliance on Mental Illness
3803 N. Fairfax Drive, Suite 100
Arlington, VA 22203
(800) 950-6264
www.nami.org

National Institute of Mental Health
6001 Executive Boulevard, Room 8184
Bethesda, MD 20892-9663
(301) 443-4513
www.nimh.nih.gov/publicat/index.cfm

References

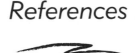

Alberti, R. E., & Emmons, M. L. (2001). *Your perfect right: Assertiveness and equality in your life and relationships* (8th ed.). New York: Impact.

Benson, H., & Stuart, E. M. (1993). *The wellness book: The comprehensive guide to maintaining health and treating stress-related illness*. New York: Fireside Books.

Branson, R. (1988). *Coping with difficult people*. New York: Anchor Press/Doubleday.

Burns, D. (1999). *Feeling good: The new mood therapy*. New York: Avon Books.

Cassidy, J., & Shaver, P. R. (Eds.). (2009). *Handbook of attachment* (2nd ed.). New York: Guilford Press.

DiGiuseppe, R., & Tafrate, R. C. (2004). *The Anger Disorder Scale (ADS)*. Toronto: Multi-Health Systems.

Dodge, K. A. (1985). Attributional bias in aggressive children. In P. C. Kendall (Ed.), *Advances in cognitive-behavioral research and therapy*. New York: Academic Press.

Dutton, D. G. (2008). *The abusive personality* (2nd ed.). New York: Guilford Press.

Enright, R. D. (2001). *Forgiveness Is a Choice: A Step-by-Step Process for Resolving Anger and Restoring Hope*. Washington, DC: American Psychological Association.

Feindler, E. L., Rathus, J., & Silver, B. (2003). *Assessment of family violence*. Washington, DC: American Psychological Association.

Goldstein, A. S., & Glick, B. (1999). *Aggression replacement training*. Champaign, IL: Research Press.

Gottman, J. M. (1979). *A couple's guide to communication*. Champaign–Urbana, IL: Research Press.

Gottman, J. M. (1985). *Why marriages succeed and fail*. New York: Fireside Books.

Holloway, J. D. (2003). Advances in anger management. *APA Monitor, 34*(3), 54.

Jacobson, N. S., & Gottman, J. M. (1998). *When men batter women.* New York: Simon & Schuster.

Kassinove, H., & Tafrate, R. C. (2002). *Anger management: The complete treatment guidebook for practitioners.* New York: Impact Press.

Lerner, H. G. (1985). *The dance of anger.* New York: Harper & Row.

Luskin, F. (2009). *Forgive for Love: The Missing Ingredient for a Healthy and Lasting Relationship.* New York: Harper-Collins.

McCullough, J. P., Huntsinger, G. M., & Nay, W. R. (1977). Self-control treatment of aggression in a sixteen-year-old male: A case study. *Journal of Consulting and Clinical Psychology, 45,* 322–331.

McKay, M., Rogers, P. D., & McKay, J. (1989). *When anger hurts.* Oakland, CA: New Harbinger.

Meichenbaum, D. (1977). *Cognitive-behavior modification: An integrative approach.* New York: Plenum Press.

Meichenbaum, D. (1985). *Stress inoculation training.* New York: Allyn & Bacon.

Murphy, T., & Oberlin, L. H. (2005). *Overcoming passive–aggression: How to stop hidden anger from spoiling your relationships, career and happiness.* Philadelphia, PA: DeCapo Press.

National Coalition against Domestic Violence. (2009). *Domestic violence facts.* Washington, DC: NCADV Public Policy Office.

National Women's Health information Center. (2008). *Safety planning list.* Washington, DC: U.S. Department of Health and Human Services.

Nay, W. R. (1986). Analogue measures. In A. R. Ciminero, H. E. Adams, & K. Calhoun (Eds.), *Handbook of behavioral assessment* (2nd ed.). New York: Wiley.

Nay, W. R. (1995). Anger and aggression: Cognitive-behavioral and short-term interventions. In L. Vandercreek, S. Knap, & T. Jackson (Eds.), *Innovations in clinical practice.* Sarasota, FL: Professional Resource Press.

Nay, W. R. (2009). *Managing anger and aggression: A compendium of resources, handouts and forms.* McLean, VA: Self-Published.

Nay, W. R. (2010). *Overcoming anger in your relationship: How to break the cycle of arguments, put-downs, and stony silences.* New York: Guilford Press.

Neidig, P. H., & Friedman, D. H. (1984). *Spouse abuse: A treatment program for couples.* Champaign, IL: Research Press.

Novaco, R. (1986). Anger as a clinical and social problem. In R. Blanchard & D. C. Blanchard (eds.), *Advances in the study of aggression* (Vol. 2). New York: Academic Press.

O'Leary, K. D., Barling, J., Arias, I., Rosenbaum, A., Malone, J., & Tyree, A. (1989). Prevalence and stability of physical aggression between spouses: A longitudinal analysis. *Journal of Consulting and Clinical Psychology, 57,* 263–268.

O'Leary, K. D., & Woodin, E. M. (2009). *Psychological and physical aggression in couples: Causes and interventions.* Washington, DC: American Psychological Association.

Patterson, G. R. (1982). *Coercive family process.* Eugene, OR: Castalia.

Scott, G. G. (1990) *Resolving conflict.* Oakland, CA: New Harbinger.

Tannen, D. (1990). *You just don't understand: Women and men in conversation.* New York: Ballantine Books.

Tannen, D. (1999). *The argument culture: Stopping America's war of words.* New York: Ballantine Books.

Tavris, C. (1989). *Anger: The misunderstood emotion.* New York: Touchstone Books.

Thomas, S. P. (1993). *Women and anger.* New York: Springer.

Weisz, A. N., Tolman, R. M., & Saunders, D. G. (2000). Assessing the risk of severe domestic violence: The importance of survivor's predictions. *Journal of Interpersonal Violence, 15,* 75–90.

Wetzler, S. (1993). *Living with the passive–aggressive man.* New York: Fireside Books.

Whitaker, D. J., & Lutzker, J. R. (2009). *Preventing partner violence: Research and evidence-based intervention strategies.* Washington, DC: American Psychological Association.

Index

About the Author

W. Robert Nay, PhD, is a clinical psychologist in private practice in McLean, Virginia, and Annapolis, Maryland, and Clinical Associate Professor at Georgetown University School of Medicine. He has trained thousands of mental health professionals nationwide to work on anger management and relationship issues with their clients. The author of the *Overcoming Anger* blog for *Psychology Today*, Dr. Nay lives in Annapolis with his wife. His website is *www.wrobertnay.com*.